Wild Things

The Joy of Reading Children's Literature as an Adult

Bruce Handy

Simon & Schuster

New York London Toronto Sydney New Delhi

Simon & Schuster
1230 Avenue of the Americas
New York, NY 10020

Copyright © 2017 by Bruce Handy

Portions of Chapter 3 were adapted from "Where the Wild Things Weren't," an essay published in *The New York Times Book Review*.

First Simon & Schuster hardcover edition August 2017

SIMON & SCHUSTER and colophon are registered trademarks of Simon & Schuster, Inc.

For information about special discounts for bulk purchases, please contact Simon & Schuster Special Sales at 1-866-506-1949 or business@simonandschuster.com.

The Simon & Schuster Speakers Bureau can bring authors to your live event. For more information or to book an event contact the Simon & Schuster Speakers Bureau at 1-866-248-3049 or visit our website at www.simonspeakers.com.

Illustrations © 2017 by Seo Kim

Jacket design and illustration by Thomas Colligan.

Endpaper design and illustration by Thomas Colligan.

Manufactured in the United States of America

1   2   3   4   5   6   7   8   9   10

Library of Congress Cataloging-in-Publication Data is available.

ISBN 978-1-4516-0995-0
ISBN 978-1-5011-5042-5 (ebook)

For Helen, who dreamt it

Contents

9

Going on Seventeen (Or Not): *Little Women,*

Little Houses, and Peter Pans

205

10

The End: Dead Pets, Dead Grandparents,

and the Glory of Everything

239

Afterword

263

Acknowledgments

267

Appendix

271

Bibliography

279

Index

289

"Remember always that the parents *buy* the books, and that the children never read them."

—Samuel Johnson, quoted by Hester Lynch Piozzi, *Anecdotes of the Late Samuel Johnson, LL.D., During the Last Twenty Years of His Life*

"SOME PIG"

—E. B. White, *Charlotte's Web*

Introduction

The New England Primer, thought to be the first American children's book, was published in Boston circa 1690. Through numerous editions it remained popular into the nineteenth century, though I can't imagine that any actual child, no matter how pious or masochistic or dull-witted, read it with much relish. Here, for instance, is one of the lessons from a 1777 edition (you will have to imagine the grim little woodcuts that accompanied it):

> Love God.
> Use no ill words.
> Fear God.
> Tell no Lies.
> Serve God.
> Hate Lies.

The *Primer* offered secular commandments as well:

> Cheat not in your play.
> Strive to learn.
> Play not with bad boys.
> Be not a Dunce.

If any children are reading *this*, that is actually not bad advice, to be not a dunce. Nevertheless, I quote it both to make easy sport of the past and to underline the fact that, while the painting, music, drama, and political philosophies of the eighteenth century have much to recommend them, no one would say that children's literature was one of the era's glories. Or, to put it another way: anglophone readers living in the twenty-first century should be very grateful for Dr. Seuss.

And for Beverly Cleary.

And for Margaret Wise Brown, Louisa May Alcott, Mark Twain, Beatrix Potter, L. Frank Baum, A. A. Milne, Laura Ingalls Wilder, C. S. Lewis, E. B. White, Maurice Sendak, Ezra Jack Keats, Russell Hoban, Eric Carle, Judy Blume, Mildred D. Taylor, Kevin Henkes, and Ian Falconer.

It should go without saying that the best children's literature is every bit as rich and rewarding in its concerns, as honest and stylish in execution, as the best adult literature—and also as complicated, stubborn, conflicted, and mysterious. Like any worthwhile art, great children's books are capable of speaking in many different ways to many different readers. You and I might each take something very different away from *Goodnight Moon* or *The Wonderful Wizard of Oz*, just as we might from *Invisible Man* or *La Dolce Vita*. And what we take away may well surprise or upset us. As the novelist and critic Alison Lurie writes in *Don't Tell the Grown-Ups: The Subversive Power of Children's Literature*, the most perceptive kids' authors "have had the ability to look at the world from below and note its less respectable aspects, just as little children playing on the floor can see the chewing gum stuck to the underside of polished mahogany tables and the hems of silk dresses held up with safety pins." Raise the perspective a few feet, to see the soup stains on ties and the sour expressions on faces that think they aren't being watched, and you have a pretty good description of what the better adult novelists do as well.

Lurie is one of a number of astute and lively writers on children's literature who have emerged in recent decades. Two more favorites of mine are Leonard S. Marcus, the critic, biographer, and historian; and the late Maurice Sendak, who was not only the creator of what will surely be some of the most enduring picture books of the twentieth and twenty-first centuries, but also a knowing, entertaining, and always generous critic. (It is almost unfair how good a critic Sendak was, though it is nice to have him in your pocket as a rejoinder whenever anyone insists that only people who can't make art bother with criticism.) *The New Yorker* has a long history of taking kids' books seriously and in recent years has published terrific essays on the subject by Joan Acocella, Adam Gopnik, Louis Menand, and John Updike. You will see their names cited throughout this book, and I am grateful to them for their insights and inspiration. I am equally indebted to the biographers listed at the back of this book; happily, someone has written at least one good life of nearly every major nonliving figure in children's literature. I hope an ambitious author gets cracking soon on Sendak.

But just as children's books are cordoned off in cozy kiddie sections at libraries and bookstores, and in isolated (though profitable) imprints in publishing houses, so too when it comes to criticism. It's a shame, for instance, that *The Horn Book Magazine*, which has been covering children's literature since 1924, isn't more widely read; it's full of smart, graceful writing. Elsewhere, however, kids' books are often written about in one of two limiting ways: either tightly swaddled in academicese, with all the spirit sweated out of them—"Seuss's books share with many others of the 1950s and 1960s an argument for the aesthetic life amid the everyday," *sigh*—or reviewed in strictly utilitarian terms as if books were cars or blenders being tested by *Consumer Reports*: Is this the sort of story that will engage a child? Does it lend itself to reading aloud? Can I give it as a gift without fear of embarrassment? Will it get the kids to go to sleep before the Game Six tip-off?

Not that those aren't legitimate questions. Here is another: Why haven't picture books earned the same pop culture cachet that comics and graphic novels have? Picture books are like poetry to comics' prose, a form every bit as sophisticated if not more so, and no less worthy of adults' attention and enjoyment. In a fairer world, Ferdinand the bull, Olivia the pig and Sam-I-Am the whatever-he-is, would be mentioned right alongside Krazy Kat, Superman, Popeye, Charlie Brown, and Lucy when discussing archetypal American characters. They might even deserve a seat at the table with Huck and Gatsby.

But this book is not an argument—or maybe it is, but only implicitly. One thing I hope to convey is the sheer pleasure of reading children's books, not just to whatever children you have on hand but also for your own enjoyment and enlightenment. As Ursula K. Le Guin has written, "Revisiting a book loved in childhood may be principally an act of nostalgia; I knew a woman who read *The Wizard of Oz* every few years because it 'made her remember being a child.' But returning after a decade or two or three to The Snow Queen or Kim, you may well discover a book far less simple and unambiguous than the one you remembered. That shift and deepening of meaning can be a revelation both about the book and yourself."

I can second that. One of the unexpected joys of parenthood, for me, was reencountering books from my childhood that I had loved and that, much to my relief, I found I still loved. Reading bedtime stories to my kids (daughter Zoë, son Isaac; two years apart) was—not always, but often—like revisiting a favorite old neighborhood after many years and finding not only that it hadn't been chain-stored into submission or paved over altogether, but that it was far more interesting and complex than I knew. I had vivid childhood memories of Dr. Seuss, like every American born in the past sixty years, but I was surprised by just how aggressive some of his stories are—to the point that many Seuss characters seem to be sublimating anger or frustration in a way that might strike a parent as very, even too familiar. (We all have those feelings . . . no?) I had vivid memories of Beverly Cleary's suburban comedies, too, but was struck and moved, as I read the books to my kids more or less sequentially, by the deepening emotional richness of her novels; you could sense her growing as an artist on the page, especially as her focus moves from Henry Huggins and his dog, Ribsy, to the sisters Beezus and Ramona. Her masterpiece, *Ramona the Pest*, a psychologically acute study of a girl struggling against social conventions (in her case, kindergarten's), is like Henry James with much shorter sentences. I'm sort of joking, but I'm sort of not, and a few years after I first had this epiphany I discovered that Beatrix Potter had also garnered comparisons to James, and from no less an authority than Graham Greene, so if you find the reference a bit much, blame him too.

Some reunions disappointed. I had loved *Curious George* and its sequels as a kid but, thirty years on, I discovered the books carried with them a stale, colonial aroma. I also wearied of the series' random, and-then-*this*-happened narratives, which reminded me of the long, rambling, frankly boring stories that young children themselves tell. (In my experience, kids' drawings and paintings tend to be far more engaging than kids' narratives.) A few years post–*Curious George*, my children and I took up Madeleine L'Engle. I remembered *A Wrinkle in Time* as gripping, mind-expanding, and spooky, and it was still all that, though it also proved preachy and on close inspection harbored within its interplanetary adventure a now dated Cold War fable about collectivism—Ayn Rand for kids. That I could forgive, or even find interesting in an archaeological way; a less forgivable problem is that the novel ends abruptly and unsatisfyingly.

Oh well. Taste is always a mystery, and never more so than with children. At one point when my kids were very young and particularly unfathomable, they couldn't get enough of a series of books based on the Disney Winnie-the-Pooh movies. These were clumsily written, banal little stories about being nice to your friends, taking care of the environment, celebrating differences—the twenty-first-century, middle-class American version of *Serve God / Hate lies.*[1] The illustrations, ham-handed takeoffs on Disney's already watered-down versions of E. H. Shepard's original illustrations, were hopeless; and is there any cultural artifact more dispiriting than a shoddy children's book? Less stories than licensing deals, these were a cheap corporate product in the guise of something nourishing. Eventually I got fed up with reading them over and over and decided to force the kids to listen to the original A. A. Milne books, which I found charming and droll and they, shrugging off the whimsy and irony, found only "OK" (their go-to adjective in those days when damning with faint praise).

But then, in the final chapter of *The House at Pooh Corner*, came this curveball:

> Christopher Robin was going away. Nobody knew why he was going; nobody knew where he was going; indeed, nobody knew

---

[1]Again, if any actual children are reading this: being nice to friends, taking care of the environment, and celebrating differences are all good things, but they are not very often the basis for interesting stories.

why he knew that Christopher Robin *was* going away. But somehow or other everyone in the Forest felt that it was happening at last.

Milne never explains precisely what is going on here, but I take it
to mean that Christopher Robin is being shipped off to boarding
school, or maybe some heartless parent or governess has told him that
he is getting too grown up to be talking to stuffed animals. Whatever
the reason for his leaving, the crux of the story is that Christopher
Robin has to break the bad news to Pooh. They go off for a walk
together in the Hundred Acre Wood, discussing the special joys of
doing "Nothing." They keep walking and talking about this and that,
and you start to get the feeling that Christopher Robin is stalling for
time, putting off the painful inevitable. Finally, from out of nowhere,
he blurts:

> "I'm not going to do Nothing anymore."
> "Never again?" [asks Pooh.]
> "Well not so much. They don't let you."

Pooh, the bear of little brain, doesn't quite understand that, well,
Christopher Robin is breaking up with him; he has only an inchoate sense that his world is changing and not for the better. And poor
Christopher Robin, like so many males in this position, can't quite get
the words out, stammering like a Hugh Grant character. It's a wrenching scene, in its way; Pooh's uncomprehending innocence makes it
feel nearly cruel:

> "Pooh," said Christopher Robin earnestly, "if I—if I'm not
> quite—" he stopped and tried again—"Pooh, *whatever* happens,
> you will understand, won't you?"
>   "Understand what?"

"Oh nothing." He laughed and jumped to his feet. "Come on!"

"Where?" said Pooh.

"Anywhere," said Christopher Robin.

As I read this aloud, I couldn't help weeping. It's a story, of course, about leaving childhood behind, which for poor baffled Pooh, the one being left—the one who really exists only in Christopher Robin's imagination—is a kind of death. I naturally thought about my own kids growing up, which for a parent is another kind of death, or, more to the point, an intimation of one's own. Isn't it ourselves we're really mourning when we say, *Oh my God, they grow up so fast?* (My wife counters with a vehement "No.")

All this was swirling through my head as I read, tears spilling down my face, and my heartless kids couldn't have cared less. They were just glad the book, which they had endured to humor me, was almost over. I tried to explain what was going on between Pooh and Christopher Robin, and why that moved me, but they already understood it fine, they just didn't find it particularly sad; I guess they were used to abandoning toys and getting on with the next phase in life.[2] But forget them. I had been moved and provoked when I might have least expected it: reading *The House at Pooh Corner.*

I can't honestly recall if I read or was read Milne as a kid. The books I do remember reading, even the ones that I have cited as childhood favorites over the years, I don't think I gave much thought to before

---

[2]Not that children can't be hugely sentimental about their own childhood. Several years after *The House at Pooh Corner* my kids, now young teenagers, bawled their eyes out when Andy gives away Woody, Buzz, and Jessie in *Toy Story 3*.

reencountering them as a parent and then embarking on this project. Many of us say we loved *Green Eggs and Ham* or *The Lion, the Witch and the Wardrobe* or *Charlotte's Web* when we were young, but that's often where the conversation ends, in a hazy, nostalgic glow—a seminal reading experience reduced to a yearbook page. I hope this book will shed light on *why* we loved the books we loved, and on the social and personal contexts that produced them in the first place; what they meant to their authors and illustrators; and why, too, they sometimes fall short or even veer off into the ditch. You don't have to be an easy mark to appreciate these works; in fact, a hard, skeptical eye is better. The journalist and critic Ron Rosenbaum, whom I've long admired, used to have a column in the *New York Observer* called "The Edgy Enthusiast"; that is a rubric I hope to channel here.

Roughly speaking, this book is organized chronologically, by the ages of intended readerships, beginning with picture books for the youngest children and moving on through chapter books and then to novels that just kiss the border of young adult fiction, maybe crossing over once or twice.[3] I've tried to weave in a parallel narrative showing the way the best authors and illustrators not only address the needs of different age groups but also challenge them, broadening worlds and stretching imaginations. I'd like to think there's an implicit coming-of-age story here—literally by the book.

Start with *Goodnight Moon*, which has probably put more toddlers to sleep than any other book in history; it also prods them to begin making sense of the world beyond their own noses, finding gentle drama in just looking around—and listening. (*Goodnight noises everywhere*). Stories that take love as their subject, such as *The Runaway Bunny* and *The Giving Tree*, reflect children's growing understanding

---

[3]YA, as it's known to the trade, is a world unto itself, and its appeal to adult readers has been well documented, so I leave it to others to grapple with.

of the complex bond between parent and child. Fairy tales, frightening yet soothing, help older children cope with their sometimes conflicting or unacknowledged emotions, while animal stories often turn the lens in the opposite direction, outward, offering insight into the ways of both the natural and human worlds. Dr. Seuss has taught several generations of children how to read while cheerleading for the anarchic power of imagination (especially his own); one moral of his oeuvre: discipline is not the enemy of creativity. Beverly Cleary's comedies of manners speak to the growing complexities of kids' roles as members of families and neighborhoods—as social creatures. L. Frank Baum used fantasy to create a kind of alternative American myth. C. S. Lewis did the same, and more explicitly, for Christianity. Louisa May Alcott and Laura Ingalls Wilder delineate the more personal passage from girlhood to womanhood; they show children how growing up is done, but from the inside, as story, not prescription. And finally there is E. B. White, who, in *Charlotte's Web*, crafted a masterly novel of ideas about what it means to lead a good life and how then to face death with grace.

So cradle to grave, as they say. One disclaimer: this is not intended to be a comprehensive history or survey or guide. It couldn't be; the ocean of children's books, even if you're trying to chart only its friendliest waters, is way too vast, too deep, too fluid, at least for me. One of the more humbling aspects of writing this book was that nearly all those I told about it asked if I would be including some childhood favorite of theirs I'd never heard of. I regret I didn't have room for those books and series, or for many of my own childhood favorites and more recent enthusiasms. Even the following list of authors and illustrators that I wished I'd had time and space to include—beyond passing mention, if that—is incomplete, but I offer it as a mea culpa: Hans Christian Andersen, Ludwig Bemelmans, Quentin Blake, Sandra Boynton, Andrew Clements, Christopher Paul Curtis, Roald

Dahl, Ingri and Edgar Parin d'Aulaire, Edward Eager, P. D. Eastman, Kenneth Grahame, Daniel Handler, S. E. Hinton, Maira Kalman, Jon Klassen, Hilary Knight, Suzy Lee, Grace Lin, Betty Bao Lord[4], Robert McCloskey, Christopher Myers, Kadir Nelson, E. Nesbit, Katherine Paterson, Dav Pilkey, Dan Santat, Richard Scarry, William Steig, John Steptoe, J. R. R. Tolkien, P. L. Travers, Chris Van Allsburg, Mo Willems, Jacqueline Woodson. As of this writing, in early 2017, my newest favorite picture book (and current default baby gift) is *They All Saw a Cat* by Brendan Wenzel, published in 2016; it is his first work as both writer and illustrator, and I can't wait to see what he does next.

A special nod to J. K. Rowling, who created a true monument of contemporary children's literature, one I feel privileged to have experienced in "real time" alongside my kids—the closest thing they and I will come to experiencing what it must have been like to await a new Beatles album or the next installment of *David Copperfield*. But the Harry Potter epic has been so widely appreciated and so thoroughly analyzed I feel I have nothing to add to the conversation, except a piece of advice: if you are planning to read the series aloud to someone, and unless you are a professional actor, do not attempt "voices." You will soon be in over your head, and the whole thing, though spectacular, goes on *forever*.

---

[4]Lord mostly writes for adults, but her children's novel, *In the Year of the Boar and Jackie Robinson* (2008), is a wonderful middle-grade story about a young Chinese immigrant growing up in Brooklyn who finds her way into American culture with the help of baseball.

1

New Eyes, New Ears: Margaret Wise Brown and *Goodnight Moon*

At his daughter Chelsea's high school graduation, in 1997, then-president Bill Clinton addressed the assembled students and parents. "Indulge your folks if we seem a little sad or act a little weird," he told the graduates. "You see, today we are remembering your first day in school and all the triumphs and travails between then and now." Being Bill Clinton, he then went for the emotional jugular. "A part of us longs to hold you once more as we did when you could barely walk, to read to you just one more time from *Goodnight Moon*, or *Curious George*, or *The Little Engine That Could*." Poor Chelsea. She must have died inside, while her classmates likely rolled their eyes, but I bet at least half the parents started sniffling. Bill, so expert at reading crowds and delivering the goods, knew exactly what he was doing in name-dropping those books, all so evocative of bedtime and blankies, sippy cups and night-night. On the other hand, if he was trying to imply an artistic equivalence among the three titles, I would argue that the former president is nuts. *Curious George* and *The Little Engine That Could* have their moments, but *Goodnight Moon* is a transcendent masterpiece.

There isn't anything else quite like it in American letters. *Moby-Dick, The Adventures of Huckleberry Finn, The Great Gatsby*, and *Beloved* might all stake a claim to being the mythical Great American Novel, but *Goodnight Moon* stands alone as the totemic picture book of American babyhood. Here I give it a clear edge over Eric Carle's *The Very Hungry Caterpillar*, its equally popular and brilliant board book rival, because *Goodnight Moon*, suffused with tenderness, joy, and mystery, is in no small sense *about* babyhood, though kudos to Eric Carle for creating his own transcendent masterpiece about a bug.

For many children, Margaret Wise Brown's deceptively simple little volume, with its illustrations by Clement Hurd, is their first exposure to something approaching narrative, and by dint of its sheer ubiquity, *Goodnight Moon* is surely one of the most formative influences on young American lives, up there with *Sesame Street* and the Disney princesses. More than that: from a parent's point of view, it's essential, like Balmex, Pampers, pacifiers, a stroller; it's gear. As happens with many new parents, my wife and I received multiple copies of *Goodnight Moon* (three, if memory serves) when our daughter was born. First published in 1947 to modest success, the book didn't take off until the 1960s and '70s, when, while no one was looking, its popularity seemingly grew overnight, like kudzu. As of 2016, according to the agent for Brown's estate, it had sold 26 million copies in various editions, which might make it the most popular picture book in America, pushing it past the longtime champion, the inexplicably beloved *The Poky Little Puppy.* Every year *Goodnight Moon* sells another 600,000 to 800,000 copies— which means, in a good year, there is roughly one *Goodnight Moon* purchased for every five births in America. It has been translated into twenty languages.[1]

For its author, it was just another book. Brown published more than sixty in her abbreviated lifetime—she died at the age of forty-two, in 1952—and *Goodnight Moon* wasn't even mentioned in her *New York Times* obituary. No one seems to know why it became her preeminent work, but like all of her books it is grounded in a profound empathy for the very young. She is the only author I deal with at length in this book who formally studied to be a writer for children, yet she was also a natural with an intuitive sense of how to speak to them. In one of her earliest stories, "The Shy Little Horse" (from a 1938 collection, *The Fish with the Deep Sea Smile*), she writes that the title character "had brand new eyes and brand new ears, and he heard and saw everything"—which was also Brown's gift, to experience the world like a child, as if both she and it were just off the griddle. This brief excerpt from her poem "Fall of the Year" (also collected in *The Fish with the Deep Sea Smile*) sings with that senses-open freshness:

All in one day
Darkness came before the night
The air grew cold enough to bite

"Her genius came from her extraordinary memory of feelings and emotions way back to her earliest years," Clement Hurd, who aside

---

[1]Brown didn't invent the night-night book, but *Goodnight Moon* has inspired many acolytes, which I quickly grew tired of counting on Amazon. A very partial listing: *Goodnight, Gorilla; Goodnight, Construction Site; Goodnight Pirate; Goodnight Cowboy; Goodnight, Little Monster; Goodnight World; Goodnight Galaxy; Goodnight Fish; Goodnight Owl; Goodnight, Fairies; Goodnight Boats; Good Night Trains; Goodnight,* [Chicago] *Cubs; Goodnight Michigan; Goodnight Darth Vader;* and, inevitably, *Goodnight Already!* (Outright *Goodnight Moon* parodies are a separate and equally legion genre.)

from *Goodnight Moon* illustrated seven other books of Brown's, wrote in a remembrance for the *Horn Book* years after her death. Brown herself described her gift as succinctly and evocatively as she did most things. "The first great wonder at the world is big in me," she once wrote to a lover, trying to explain the source of her creativity. That wonder infuses *Goodnight Moon* with an underlying delight, and even awe. It is there in the book's very first words:

> In the great green room
> There was a telephone
> And a red balloon
> And a picture of—
> [*here we turn the page*]
> The cow jumping over the moon.

A less interesting and less intuitive writer might have started out with something like, "There once was a little bunny who was going to sleep in his little bunny bedroom." Instead, by offering a simple, almost liturgical accounting of the room and its furnishings, Brown instantly and gracefully gives the reader a child's-eye view of things. (The listener, presumably, already has one.) *The great green room*: to a two-year-old, a bedroom—or any room—is an epic space, a Monument Valley full of objects and details that glow with strange newness, having not yet acquired the dull patina of familiarity that allows older children and adults to get on with their responsibilities and not be stopped in their tracks by, say, the miracle of grass. (One of my own earliest memories is of waking from a nap and being fascinated for what now seems like hours by the play of dust motes in the slanting, late afternoon light. On some level, I believe, I go to movie theaters and museums still hoping to be mesmerized in the same way.)

Brown's first great wonder is reinforced by Hurd's illustrations, both in their sense of scale—in the book's spreads the emphasis is on the great green room itself, a place for a child's eye to explore, rather than on the bunny, a small figure tucked away in the corner of most of the drawings—and in the bright, flat, unnatural color scheme, those electric greens and oranges and yellows rubbing against one another on the draperies and walls and floor to almost hallucinatory effect. It's easy to take *Goodnight Moon* for granted—as I said, it's practically gear—but look at it with brand-new eyes and it dazzles.

I had always pictured Margaret Wise Brown as a kindly gray-haired woman with an ample lap; I think I pictured her as my grandmother, or maybe *Goodnight Moon*'s quiet old lady whispering hush. Certainly Margaret Wise Brown, as a name, is the equivalent of a comfy old sweater or a square meal heavy on the potatoes; it *sounds* grandmotherly. In reality, she was less kindly and ample than headstrong and zany, like a madcap heroine in a 1930s screwball comedy, a slender young woman who could have been played by Katharine Hepburn or Carole Lombard, the latter of whom she resembled.

In a 1946 profile—she had forty-odd children's books under her belt by then—*Life* magazine described Brown this way: "She is a tall, green-eyed, ash blonde in her early thirties [she was actually thirty-six] with a fresh outdoors look about her. People who meet her for the first time are likely to think she is extremely sophisticated, which is entirely true. Her striking appearance is usually punctuated by some startling accessory such as a live kitten in a wicker basket or a hat made out of live flowers." Brown was the sort of person who thrived in café society, who was friendly with literary types such as Bennett Cerf, E. J. Kahn, and Leo Lerman; but she was also the sort of person who kept a dog, a cat, a goat, and a flying squirrel in her Greenwich Village apartment. Though she wasn't an heiress or a debutante, she had grown up with money and always had enough of it, along with a casual attitude toward finances: as *Life* observed, "Except for clothes, champagne, and flowers, Miss Brown hasn't much interest in spending." (Years earlier, she blew her first advance on an entire cart of flowers that she brought back to the apartment for a celebration; and she took a lowball $150 advance for another book because the fee coincided precisely with the cost of a wolfskin jacket she had decided she couldn't live without.) Full of schoolgirl enthusiasms, she had a deep reservoir of childhood memories and feelings that she drew on for her work. Ideas for books seemed to occur to her with ridiculous ease: "I finish the rough draft in twenty minutes," she told *Life*, "and then spend two years polishing." The magazine added that she was "currently polishing twenty-three books more or less simultaneously." At the same time she worried that her talents denied her a place at the literary world's grown-up table. Yearning to write for adults, she never found homes for her "serious" short stories and poetry.

"Margaret was the most creative person, male or female, that I have ever known," wrote Hurd.

"She was almost overwhelmingly original," the writer Naomi Bliven once told an interviewer. "Never for a moment did you feel she was lackadaisical about *anything*."

"For ten minutes I was enchanted by what she had to say, and by the eleventh minute I had the need to run away," Bliven's husband, Bruce Bliven Jr., remarked to the same interviewer. The Blivens were friends of Brown's (he had written her *Life* profile), so presumably he was kidding around when he said this, but I'd bet there was more than a grain of truth in it: Brown sounds as if she could be a handful.

Born in 1910, she had grown up on Long Island, where her father was an executive at the American Manufacturing Company, which made rope and twine and sacks, an enterprise so prosaic as to sound almost whimsically prosaic, like a business invented by Roald Dahl for the dull part of a book. Brown was herself a dreamer and a story-teller from the get-go, disappearing into "worlds of her own making," as she later put it, and reading fairy tales to her younger sister while altering the plots to serve her own emotional needs. (In Brown's improvisations, cruel older stepsisters transformed into heroines.) By the time she got to college—Hollins, her mother's alma mater—she was bursting with creative energy but not necessarily focus or discipline. An English composition professor simultaneously praised her and damned her as a "genius without talent."

She moved to New York after graduation—and after breaking off her engagement to a southern boy from a "good" family. Settling into the city, she took some writing courses at Columbia and had a one-session flirtation with painting at the Art Students' League. But she was adrift, pessimistic about a future as any kind of artist. Like many single women of her era, she wound up studying to become a teacher, having enrolled, somewhat ambivalently, at the Bureau of Educational Experiments' Cooperative School for Teachers, a temple of the progressive education movement then known informally (and now officially) as Bank Street, after its original address in Greenwich Village. (Full name: Bank Street College of Education.) Though Brown quickly decided she didn't want to teach, she discovered that she found children fascinating. She loved listening to them, to the inventive and unself-conscious ways they used language. "They tell me stories and I write them down. Amazing. And also the pictures they paint. It must be true that children are born creative," she wrote to a favorite literature professor at Hollins. When she took a course on writing for children she stumbled on her calling.

The class was taught by the school's cofounder and chief administrator, Lucy Sprague Mitchell, an author herself, who sensed something unique in Brown—"crazy, penetrating, blind instincts and feeling for language," Mitchell later said—and took her under her wing.

Like seemingly everything else in the 1930s, the children's book world was riven by absolutist ideologies. Mitchell was the leading proponent of what she called the Here and Now philosophy: the idea that stories drawn from real, everyday settings, informed by careful observations about how children perceive and respond to their environment, were the perfect nourishment for very little kids, for whom, after all, there is no such thing as been there, done that. Here and Now–ists frowned on fantasy, myths, fairy tales, and nursery rhymes, all the stuff of classic children's literature, which they dismissed as inherently unwholesome, more suited to adults' cravings for the sensational and bizarre than to children's simpler needs. For the youngest child especially, the thinking went, a story about a bird or a cup or a truck could be as fascinating as a tale about a fairy or a dragon, if not more so, and had the added benefit of being real and thus, in some sense, instructional. As Mitchell put it in the introduction to the *Here and Now Story Book*, a collection of her own work published in 1921: "It is only the jaded adult mind, *afraid to trust the child's own fresh springs of imagination*, that feels for children the need of the stimulus of magic." (The italics are Mitchell's.) What this meant in practice was stories with titles such as "The Room with the Window Looking Out on the Garden," "Pedro's Feet," "Marni Gets Dressed in the Morning," and "Boris Takes a Walk and Finds Many Kinds of Trains."

Alison Lurie, for one, received a copy of the *Here and Now Story Book* for her fifth birthday and was not impressed:

> [It] was a squat volume, sunny orange in color, with an idealized city scene on the cover. Inside I could read about the Grocery Man ("This is John's Mother. Good morning, Mr. Grocery Man") and How Spot Found a Home. The children and parents in these stories were exactly like the ones I knew, only more boring. They

never did anything wrong, and nothing dangerous or surprising ever happened to them—no more than it did to Dick and Jane, whom my friends and I were soon to meet in first grade.[2]

Mitchell wasn't immune to such criticism. As she wrote in the preface to *Another Here and Now Story Book*, published in 1937 (with editing and contributions from Brown): "If the stories in this book are less lovely than Cinderella or Little Red Riding Hood or Pandora's Box, it is because we lack the requisite artistry, not because we do not value loveliness. The great writer for the young children of the 'here and now' period is still to come."

Brown would prove to be that writer. Her first book, *When the Wind Blew*, published in 1937 when she was twenty-seven, was praised by the *New York Times*—in terms that would apply to most of her work—for its "poetic quality, color, and rhythm." From there she was off, editing and writing for W. R. Scott, a small experimental publisher associated with Bank Street, while also selling books to nearly all the major houses with children's divisions. She was astonishingly prolific, publishing five books in 1941, four in 1942, five in 1943, eight in 1944, and three in 1945. "It's getting so you can't turn around blindfolded in a bookstore without catching a new story by Margaret Wise Brown," the *Chicago Sun* noted in 1947. "The surprising thing is that they always seem to fit the bill." At one point she had contracts with six different houses, under her own name as well as three pseudonyms, and by the end of her career she had worked with most of the era's important illustrators (some of whom she had discovered),

---

[2]Lurie continues: "After we grew up, of course, we found out how unrealistic these stories had been. The simple, pleasant adult society they had prepared us for did not exist. As we suspected, the fairy tales had been right all along—the world was full of hostile, stupid giants and perilous castles and people who abandoned their children in the forest."

among them H. A. Rey, Crockett Johnson, Garth Williams, Esphyr
Slobodkina, and Kurt Wiese. Leonard Wisegard won the Caldecott
in 1946 for illustrating her story *The Little Island*. Though it often
seemed as if she pulled ideas out of the air—she wrote her second
most famous book, *The Runaway Bunny*, on the back of a ski lift
ticket—she worked hard at her manuscripts, took her responsibility
to children very seriously, and always insisted that crafting stories for
kids was harder than it looked. "Children are keen as wild animals,"
she once wrote, "and also as timorous. So you can't be 'too funny' or
'too scary' or 'too many worded.' All these things are not as easy as
they sound for grown people."

Despite her fluency in the language of her own youthful memories, she worked hard at understanding the world from a child's perspective. Amy Gary, in her 2017 biography, *In the Great Green Room:
The Brilliant and Bold Life of Margaret Wise Brown*, describes Brown
taking a Method-acting approach: "She returned to the fields and
woods of Long Island and physically positioned herself to see things
from a child's point of view. She picked daisies, watched bugs crawl,
and gazed at clouds floating by." Before writing a story about a farm,
she picked potatoes on the North Fork. To attempt a story about
ships, she hung out at the then-busy docks of lower Manhattan, and
paddled a canoe around the island.

Her work was informed by Here and Now ideas, but she was too
original and free-spirited to be doctrinaire. What really distinguishes
her books is her sense of poetry and language, and her wit, her ability
to seed simple declarative sentences with peculiarity—all of which, as
her first biographer, Leonard S. Marcus, points out, owes something
to one of her favorite writers, Gertrude Stein, whose lone children's
book, *The World Is Round*, she helped edit.[3]

---

[3]Believe it or not, *The World Is Round* reads as if someone had decided to parody Stein

One of Brown's first "hits" was 1939's *The Noisy Book*, a kind of sensory exercise for kids that tells the story of Muffin, a dog whose eyes are temporarily bandaged:

> "Poor little Muffin," said the people in the street.
> "Muffin has a big white bandage over his eyes and can't see a thing."
> But Muffin could hear. . . .
> MEN HAMMERING
> Bang bang bang. . . .
> Bzzzzzz bzzzzzz
> A bee. . . .
> Then the sun began to shine
> Could Muffin hear that?

The author is making excellent use of her "new ears" here, but her best books also use concrete details to pluck ineffable emotional chords, as in this passage from *The Important Book* (1949), which speaks softly to a child's need for security:

> The important thing about the sky is that it is always there.
> It is true that it is blue,
> And high,
> And full of clouds,
> And made of air.
> But the important thing about the sky is that it is always there.

---

by retelling the story of Leni Riefenstahl's 1932 film, *The Blue Light*, in Stein's voice. It won't be to most children's or adults' taste, but Clement Hurd's illustrations, done in rose pink and deep blue, are gorgeous.

I also love the eloquent final lines of *The Little Island*, almost a haiku, which express feelings of both aloneness and belonging, of the struggle to define a self, really—a topic of no small interest to any child:

> And it was good to be a little Island.
> A part of the world
> And a world of its own
> All surrounded by the bright blue sea.

On its face, *Goodnight Moon*, as a catalog of the furnishings in an idealized child's room, is steeped in Here and Now ideas, but as Marcus points out, it is "supercharged" with so "freewheeling a sense of the fantastic as an aspect of the everyday" that it also serves as a cheeky, even subversive counterpoint to Lucy Sprague Mitchell's orthodox empiricism. The pictures of the cow jumping over the moon and the three bears might be affectionate nods to the more imaginative world of nursery rhymes and fairy tales, an in-joke for children's book professionals of the 1940s, although the imagery also held personal significance for Brown: there had been decorative tiles of the cow and the three bears in her childhood bedroom. The very act of cataloging a room held private meaning, too: while floundering through her early twenties, Brown once told a friend, she would combat depression every morning by looking around her apartment and making note of the various things that gave her pleasure, an intimate accounting she would then commit to paper.

Brown would say she literally dreamed *Goodnight Moon*, writing it down one morning upon waking and then reading it back to her editor at Harper, Ursula Nordstrom, who was instantly taken with it, though one wonders if she realized she had a masterpiece on her hands.[4] (Did Paul McCartney when he dreamed the melody for "Yesterday"?) The anecdote rings true to me because the book has a strange, dreamlike feel in places: for example, the quiet old lady whispering hush who materializes in the middle of the book after we've already been introduced to her empty rocking chair. Again, Brown avoids the obvious choice, which would be having the bunny being put to bed by its mother. But who is this quiet old lady? A nanny? The bunny's grandma? A random caregiver dragged in off the street? Brown doesn't say and it doesn't matter anyway—it's just the kind of odd, open-ended detail, like the red balloon (did the bunny get it at a party? at a shoe store?), that gives *Goodnight Moon* traction with children's imaginations. (Enigma goes a long way: it is one reason we celebrate the *Mona Lisa* over thousands of other very accomplished portraits of pretty young Italian girls.) I think there might be a teasing

---

[4]She might well have, since Nordstrom had plenty of experience with masterpieces. As director of Harper's children's book division from 1940 to 1973, she also edited Russell Hoban, Syd Hoff, Crockett Johnson, Ruth Krauss, Else Holmelund Minarik, Maurice Sendak, Shel Silverstein, John Steptoe, E. B. White, and Laura Ingalls Wilder. Leonard S. Marcus, who edited her letters, rightly calls her "children's literature's Maxwell Perkins" and she will turn up repeatedly in these pages. You can get a sense of her exacting yet empathetic editorial mind, and her wit, in this response to a manuscript by the writer Janice May Udry: "The ending seems a little flat to me, but perhaps that's because I'm not four years old."

One reason for Nordstrom's success was that she was constantly on the lookout for accomplished writers and artists—all sorts—whom she might turn to children's books. As she once wrote to Russell Hoban, "[O]n my ceaseless search for new talent I went late one afternoon to a gallery exhibit of drawings. I was terribly tired that day and sort of depressed, but I pushed myself way up on Madison Avenue to try to find someone NEW who can *draw*, just black and white line, that's all I asked for! Across the room I saw the most magnificent black and white drawings, my fatigue vanished, a large smile covered my large face, I catapulted my large self across the room. Henri Matisse. I was so mad, because everyone knows he is tied up with Simon and Schuster."

little wink in there, too, between Brown and her young audience, an implied dismissal of all adults as old people *always* whispering hush, akin to the offscreen parents and teachers in the animated *Peanuts* cartoons whose voices go *wahwahwahwahwah* like a trumpet played with a plunger. And then there's the book's great overt laugh line, "Goodnight nobody," an absolutely brilliant joke that has served as an introduction to absurdist humor for several generations of toddlers, paving the way for Monty Python and David Letterman. (In our house, "Goodnight mush" usually got a big laugh too, simply on onomatopoetic grounds, my modern children having no idea what mush is.)

The book was originally titled *Goodnight Room* and, by one account, ended with the couplet "Goodnight cucumber / Goodnight fly"—suggesting a daffier, throwaway tone in its initial conception. The finished work takes a beautiful conceptual leap in its final pages. Most night-night books end with the child tucked into a cozy bed, and so does Brown's; but in Hurd's final illustration, with the room darkened and the colors grayed, the focus is not on the comfort and security of bed but rather on the bright, blue, starlit sky outside. This is a response to Brown's final words—"Goodnight stars / Goodnight air / Goodnight noises everywhere"—which take us away from the indoor world of the known and off into the wide world beyond, paralleling the journey into sleep and maybe, for that matter, the journey out of infancy. Or perhaps I'm reading too much into it. But still: lovely. And hmmmm: Would any children's editor today permit a book to end with the potentially unsettling "Goodnight noises everywhere"? What noises? Where? Who's making them? Wolves? Bats? Clumsy monsters? Talkative boogeymen?

There are hints of story here, too, of beginning, middle, and end, enfolded into the bedtime ritual. For some kids, this might be their first encounter with narrative—primitive narrative, perhaps, but a step up from books that merely catalog colors or shapes or baby animals or trucks. It's telling that two other of America's most enduringly popular books for very young children, Eric Carle's *The Very Hungry Caterpillar* and Ezra Jack Keats's *The Snowy Day*, are each in fundamental ways *about* the passage of time, about giving time shape and meaning, which is one way to define "story." I'm being reductive here—there is so much more to these two great books—but I do think their intro-level narratives are one small reason why they, along with *Goodnight Moon*, continue to resonate with kids.

Eric Carle's book could almost be a sequel to Brown's and Hurd's, taking us through the great green room's window and into the world of "noises everywhere." The very first thing we see is the moon, and the words begin, "In the light of the moon a little egg lay on a leaf." The sun comes up on the next spread—we learn it is Sunday—and a caterpillar pops out of the egg. The rest of the book gives a day-by-day account of its eating habits: one apple on Monday, two pears on Tuesday, and so on through to Saturday, when it gorges on cake, ice cream, a pickle, salami, and more.[5] Now fat and no longer hungry, it makes itself "a small house, called a cocoon," and two weeks later, in one of literature's great twist endings (if you happen to be a very young child and don't yet know your insect biology), the caterpillar emerges as "a beautiful butterfly!" Carle's nearly phosphorescent illustration, a collage using his own hand-colored papers (his signature technique), does justice to both adjective and exclamation point, though as a more

---

[5]This comic abundance had personal meaning for Carle, a German who had experienced severe deprivation when, at fifteen, he was put to work on the Siegfried Line in the waning days of World War II, digging antitank ditches alongside prisoners of war and slave laborers. In an autobiography included in *The Art of Eric Carle*, he describes subsequently working as a file clerk for the U.S. military during the occupation. The best part of the job was being allowed to eat in an officers' dining hall. "I surreptitiously stuffed peanut butter sandwiches, lumps of butter, cubes of sugar, leftover bits of steak, and desserts into my pockets." He was essentially feeding his entire family.

scientifically literate friend recently pointed out to me, the butterfly should really be emerging from a chrysalis. (Cocoons are generally reserved for moths.)

The Snowy Day, as the title suggests, confines its action to a single day, with a coda, the following morning. It begins by depicting its young protagonist, a city boy, at another window: "One winter morning Peter woke up and looked out the window. Snow had fallen during the night. It covered everything he could see." The modest story follows Peter's day as he plays in the snow, goes home, is given a bath by his mother, and is put to bed. He has stashed a snowball in his jacket pocket "for tomorrow" and is sad to learn it has melted. He dreams that the sun comes out the next morning and melts all the snow, but he wakes up to—more snow! That's it: a quiet, happy ending to a quiet, simple story. Indeed, its descriptions and details are so homespun and down-to-earth that The Snowy Day could itself be a Here and Now text. The magic is in Keats's illustrations, which mix collage and painting: the seemingly offhand dynamism of his horizontal compositions, the poetry of contrast between vast, white, subtly textured snowscapes and Peter's angular, bright red snow-suit—Keats's art transforms his words much the way snow transforms a city. I should note too that Peter is black, a rarity for the hero of a children's book (or most any branch of popular culture) when The Snowy Day was published in 1962. Keats, who was white, had been bothered by the absence. "None of the manuscripts [by other authors] I'd been illustrating featured any black kids, except for token blacks in the background," he wrote of Peter's genesis in an unpublished autobiography. "My book would have him there simply because he should have been there all along." The Snowy Day took on a life of its own in Keats's mind. Making it, he felt, was a form of play, "different from anything I've ever done. . . . I don't think I will ever experience again a dream of such innocence and awaken to find the book finished." As was also the case with Carle and *The Very Hungry Caterpillar*, *The Snowy Day* was Keats's first as sole author and illustrator. Rookie home runs.

Goodnight Moon was Brown's third collaboration with Hurd; their second, from 1942, was *The Runaway Bunny*. (By way of sly self-reference, or perhaps product placement, the artist reproduced one of the illustrations from the earlier book as a painting on one of the walls in the great green room.) Hurd was a Yale graduate, comfortably well off, who had studied painting with Fernand Léger in Paris, which is perhaps where he got *Goodnight Moon*'s flat, electric colors. Brown had given him his first children's book assignment, in 1938, after admiring a ceiling mural he had executed at the country home of a mutual friend. Typically, Brown would include detailed art instructions with her manuscripts, but for *Goodnight Moon* she attached only a reproduction of Goya's *Boy in Red* (formal title: *Manuel Osorio Manrique de Zúñiga*) as inspiration. The painting depicts a four- or five-year-old boy standing stiffly in the eighteenth-century Spanish equivalent of a Little Lord Fauntleroy outfit, holding a pet bird on a leash while two cats look on hungrily. There is a lost, poor little rich boy quality to the figure—a poignancy echoed in Hurd's illustrations of that tiny bunny nearly adrift in that huge bed in that even larger room. (Am I the only reader wondering where the bunny's parents have run off to? Are they out at some fabulous party with Bennett Cerf and Leo Lerman, or wintering in Palm Beach? Is the bunny a spiritual cousin to Eloise, abandoned at the Plaza?)

Hurd's first sketches for the book depicted an actual little boy going to sleep—at one point he toyed with the idea of making the boy African American—but Brown and Nordstrom decided he was better at drawing rabbits and pushed him in that direction. This was by all accounts a purely practical decision (like Maurice Sendak's decision to rework a proposed book, *Where the Wild Horses Are*, because he felt he was no good at equine anatomy), although I think it had the added value of making the book more universal and timeless, as is usually the case with animal characters. Nordstrom also requested that Hurd deemphasize the udder on the cow jumping over the moon—in the final illustration it looks more like four pimples—lest the art offend some readers, especially librarians, as too biologically frank.

If you think that this level of attention to detail was unusual, Bruce Bliven Jr. in his *Life* profile recorded this exchange between Brown and an unnamed colleague (probably discussing *Goodnight Moon*, which was in production when Bliven was reporting his piece):

> "I like the rabbit, he has real sleepiness."
>
> "Yes, but I'm worried about the yarn; it loses personality and softness."

Hurd's *Horn Book* portrait of Brown was affectionate, but he also made it clear that she was no pushover: "Maybe collaboration on a creative level is always difficult, and maybe the more creative a person is, the more difficult he or she is to work with, but I do feel that all Margaret's main illustrators did their best work in her books," a group in which he included himself.

It would be fun to report that *Goodnight Moon* was ignored or, better yet, reviled upon publication, its genius appreciated only decades later by a new generation of more enlightened parents such as mine. But no. One of three books Brown published in 1947, *Goodnight Moon* was a modest but clear success. It received admiring reviews, most recognizing its artistry while focusing more closely on its efficacy as a sleep aid. *The New York Times* was typical: "The rhythm of the little story is like the sing-song of disconnected thoughts with which children so often put themselves to sleep, and should prove very effective in the case of a too wide-awake youngster." *The New Yorker* praised it as a "hypnotic bedtime litany," although the magazine's children's books critic, Rosemary C. Benet, seemed more excited by another Brown picture book that she reviewed on the same page: *The First Story*, Brown's retelling of Genesis.

Goodnight Moon sold six thousand copies in its first year—nice, but not remarkable. Like most of Brown's books, it was not bought by the New York Public Library and was left off the library's influential list of recommended titles, a commercial blow. (The children's department was led by Anne Carroll Moore, a powerful figure in the era's juvenile publishing scene and a fierce opponent of Here and Now–ism; you could probably write an amusing book devoted to what became known in the field as the "fairy-tale wars" of the 1920s, '30s, and '40s.) In short, there was nothing to suggest that *Goodnight Moon* would one day become a ubiquitous gift at baby showers. By way of a not totally fair contrast, *Five Little Firemen*, a collaboration between Brown and Edith Hurd—Clement's wife, a writer; the two women used the fragrant joint pen name Juniper Sage[6]—would sell 170,000 copies the following year, when it was published by Golden Books, Random House's pioneering mass-market children's imprint. In 1949, that title's sales reached a cool million.

By 1951, *Goodnight Moon* was moving only 1,300 copies and veering toward slipping out of print. After Brown's death, in 1952, her executors put its value at a scant $200 (not quite $1,900 in 2017 dollars). A turning point may have come the following year, when *Goodnight Moon* was praised in "Child Behavior," a widely syndicated parental

---

[6]Brown's genius extended to pen names. According to Clement Hurd, an early draft of *Goodnight Moon* was jokingly credited to "Memory Ambrose with pictures by Hurricane Jones."

advice column, for "captur[ing] the two-year-old so completely that it seems almost unlawful that you can hypnotize a child off to sleep as easily as you can by reading this small classic." By 1955, sales were back up to four thousand copies, and only took off from there. . . .

1960: eight thousand copies.

1966: twenty thousand copies.[7]

1977: 100,000 copies (the year of *Goodnight Moon*'s first paperback edition).

Sales took another leap in 1991, the year of the first board book edition, a now indispensable medium Brown herself had helped pioneer back in 1938 with *Bumble Bugs and Elephants*, her first collaboration with Hurd. And as previously mentioned, *Goodnight Moon* now sells upward of 800,000 copies a year, the numbers periodically goosed by anniversary promotions.

It no doubt aided Brown's work that while she empathized deeply with children she wasn't in the least sentimental about them. Clement Hurd described visiting "Brownie," as friends sometimes called her, in 1951 at her summer home on an island off the coast of Maine with his wife and then two-year-old son, Thacher:

> Very excited at our bringing Thacher, Brownie had made all sorts
> of preparations for his visit. There was a fur rug on Thacher's bed
> and a lion skin on the floor, complete with head and bared fangs.
> Furs were fine in books, but the reality of the furs themselves

---

[7]The leap was partly fueled by a Great Society education bill that pumped nearly $300 million into school libraries over four years—legislation that suggests a government and a body politic entirely alien to the present day's. If you agree that spending public money on children's books is a good thing, the contrast can prompt only awe, tears, or the gnashing of teeth.

was more than Thacher had bargained for, and there was nothing to do but let him share our room during the visit. Seeing that Thacher had a mind of his own and didn't hesitate to show it, Brownie perhaps wasn't so enchanted with him. . . . Maybe it was after his falling from grace that we recognized that Margaret was, in general, not especially fond of children.

"I'm not nice to them like other people," she told an interviewer. "I admire their absolute integrity, their dignity, their strength and individuality. But I am not going to become maudlin about them just because they're little." As she put it on another occasion, "To be a writer for the young, one has to love not children but what children love."

She never married or had kids of her own. Her relationships with men were for the most part haphazard and disappointing. Her steadiest (though not very steady) long-term romantic relationship was with a woman named Michael Strange, a poet, performer, and memoirist who was twenty years older than Brown and is best remembered today for having been John Barrymore's second wife. Strange (neé Blanche Oelrichs) was demanding and condescending—her own daughter once described Strange as "too imperial, too remote" and complained that she "carried herself like a little general"—and the relationship between Brown and Strange was tense and often destructive for the younger woman, very much the emotionally subordinate partner and in both women's eyes the lesser artist. Strange even made fun of Brown's "baby books," though she would herself try her hand at children's books—unsuccessfully. (Reading the passages on this romance in Marcus's and Gary's biographies of Brown is like having drinks with an unhappy friend who doesn't realize the reason for her unhappiness is that she's yoked herself to a miserable, abusive partner; you want to reach through time and shake Brown, tell her to dump Strange and never look back.) Though they spent periods of time apart, the

relationship ended only with Strange's death in 1950, from leukemia;
Brown was at her bedside.

As seriously as she took writing for children, Brown had long felt
like a poor sister to the larger literary world, never giving up on her as-
piration to write for adults as well. Near the end of her life, according
to Hurd, "she became tired of children's books and turned to writing
songs." He continued:

> Her great desire was to do an adult work on Virginia Woolf, but
> she never accomplished it as it required more discipline and stick-
> at-it quality than she had. Her creative work habits were some-
> how perfectly suited to her type of books for the very young. She
> never had certain hours for work but worked only when she felt
> creative—which might be all the time, night and day. And she
> was always somewhat skeptical of what she once called "mysteri-
> ous clock time."

Brown would die an appropriately madcap death at an inappropriately
young age. Not long before her forty-second birthday, she met James
Stillman Rockefeller Jr., then twenty-six, a passionate sailing enthusiast and a great-nephew of John D. Rockefeller's. (Doubly blessed in
his financial bloodlines, he was a descendant of Andrew Carnegie's
as well.) Within a few months he and Brown had fallen in love and
made plans to marry in the Caribbean, where Rockefeller was sailing
in preparation for embarking across the Pacific to the South Seas, a
long-planned trip that would now serve as the couple's honeymoon.
They arranged to meet in Panama and Brown took a pre-wedding
holiday in the south of France, where, felled by abdominal pains, she
underwent surgery for the removal of an ovarian cyst and her appendix. This all went perfectly smoothly, absent complications. Two
weeks later, however, as she was preparing to leave the hospital, she

demonstrated her regained robustness for the nurses with an exuber-
ant cancan kick. She lost consciousness almost immediately: the high
kick had dislodged a blood clot in one of her legs, which traveled
quickly to her brain, and within an hour she was dead. According to
Amy Gary's book, her last word, in response to a nurse's asking how
she was feeling, just before her cancan kick, was "Grand!"

There are two codas to her story. One, Brown had left behind
stacks of finished and unfinished manuscripts, the wellspring for a
steady flow of posthumous publications. (Brown was a pioneer in this
sense, paving the way for the ongoing careers of the late Shel Silverstein and Dr. Seuss.) Two, in keeping with her freewheeling, impulsive
approach to life, she had frequently revised her will, often in whimsi-
cal terms. When she died, the will then in effect bequeathed royalties
from the lion's share of her books—seventy-nine titles in total, including *Goodnight Moon*—to the middle of three young brothers whose
family she had befriended and who had spent many hours hanging
out at her writing studio, which was tucked just behind the family's
apartment building. Albert Clarke, nine years old when Brown died,
was apparently more agreeable than Thacher Hurd. By 2000 he had
received nearly $5 million, and by 2016 his earnings would have
reached well into eight figures.

As in a folktale, this unexpected and seemingly miraculous gift
proved to be an ambiguous blessing. According to a 2000 profile of
Clarke in the *Wall Street Journal*, he spent most of his adulthood living
aimlessly, almost like a drifter, with bouts of homelessness, back in the
days when Brown's royalty checks came to only five figures. By 2000
he had homes on Cape Cod and in Southampton and could afford to
buy new clothes rather than wash his old ones. He also told the *Wall
Street Journal* he believed that Brown was his biological mother. There
is no evidence for this, although some of Brown's friends thought she
may have left Clarke her royalties because, as a boy, he had looked like

the kind of child she might have had, had she ever had children. But no one really knows.

Brown left behind one other interesting directive. According to Garth Williams (in an unpublished memoir quoted by his biographers, Elizabeth K. Wallace and James D. Wallace), the author requested that her friends have a get-together on the first anniversary of her death. "She wanted us to have a gay party and drink champagne," Williams wrote. The idea was that Brown would "attend in spirit," but in the event no one felt much cheer. "It was not gay. . . . [W]e all noted that none of us could really accept the fact that this was not another of her practical jokes—her worst."

A somewhat better one was the laughably modest epitaph she requested for a memorial headstone. It was placed at her summer home in Maine, after her ashes were scattered at sea:

WRITER OF SONGS AND NONSENSE

Cute, though I might have gone with GOODNIGHT NOBODY.

2

Runaways: Family Drama in Picture Books—and Well Beyond

*P*ortnoy's Complaint isn't a children's book—notoriously not—but it is indisputably a child's book. The novel's very first word is "She," she being the mother of Philip Roth's hero and narrator, Alexander Portnoy. He is on his psychiatrist's couch as the narrative begins, dredging up memories of *her*:

> She was so deeply imbedded in my consciousness that for the first year of school I seem to have believed that each of my teachers was my mother in disguise. As soon as the last bell had sounded, I would rush off for home, wondering as I ran if I could possibly make it to our apartment before she had succeeded in transforming herself. Invariably she was already in the kitchen by the time I arrived, and setting out my milk and cookies. Instead of causing

me to give up my delusions, however, the feat merely intensified
my respect for her powers.

Sophie Portnoy is not only powerful; like many omnipotent beings she
is also easily bruised and vengeful. So she makes a habit of banishing
young Alex from the family apartment for transgressions so minor their
nature is not apparent to the perpetrator himself. She cannot love him
anymore, Sophie says, "not a little boy who behaves like you do."

> Because she is good she will pack a lunch for me to take along,
> but then out I go, in my coat and galoshes, and what happens
> is not her business. Okay, I say, if that's how you feel! . . . Who
> cares! And out I go into the long dim hallway. Who cares! I will
> sell newspapers on the street in my bare feet. I will ride where I
> want in freight cars and sleep in open fields, I think—and then
> it is enough for me to see the empty milk bottles standing by our
> welcome mat, for the immensity of all I have lost to come break-
> ing over my head. "I hate you!" I holler, kicking a galosh at the
> door; "You stink!" To this filth, to this heresy booming through
> the corridors of the apartment building where she is vying with
> twenty other Jewish women to be the patron saint of self-sacrifice,
> my mother has no choice but to throw the double-lock on our
> door. This is when I start to hammer to be let in. I drop to the
> doormat to beg forgiveness for my sin (which is what again?) and
> promise her nothing but perfection for the rest of our lives, which
> at the time I believe will be endless.

Endless. Mother and son will be locked in this dance for eternity. Resistance is futile, escape impossible. Roth doesn't let Alex's figuratively
impotent, literally constipated father off the hook. But it is Sophie
who dominates both novel and son's psyche, to the point that the

book reads like an extended, primal scream of a Jewish mother joke. And yet anyone of any ethnicity, religion, or gender should be able to recognize the yin-yang, push-me-pull-you, love-me-let-me-go tension between parent and child that Roth vivisects with such anger and glee. Because just as nearly every culture seems to enjoy some version of a fillable pancake, whether crepe, roti, tortilla, or wonton wrapper, so most of us know Sophie Portnoys, some maybe more neglectful than smothering, others more passive-aggressive than *aggressive*-aggressive, but all, whatever their gender, leaving tire treads back and forth across their offspring. As the British poet Philip Larkin famously put it: "They fuck you up, your mum and dad. / They may not mean to, but they do."

I bring up *Portnoy's Complaint* because it reads like an R-rated antithesis of the work I really want to talk about: *The Runaway Bunny*, which in its own sunny way is as incisive a treatise on the parent-child bond as Roth's novel. I also bring up *Portnoy's Complaint* to highlight the fact that books for very young children occupy a rare literary preserve where mum and dad *don't* fuck you up.

It should take but a minute's thought to compile a list of iconic "bad" or at least "difficult" parents in works for adults. Aside from Mr. and Mrs. Portnoy, I came up with Medea, King Lear, Queen Gertrude (*Hamlet*), Pap Finn (*The Adventures of Huckleberry Finn*), Mary Tyrone (*Long Day's Journey into Night*), Mama Rose (*Gypsy*), Jack Torrance (*The Shining*), Troy Maxson (*Fences*), every single adult in *The Ice Storm*. On the other hand, in trying to conjure an equally extensive list of iconic good parents in adult literature. . . . Well, I came up with Atticus Finch and David Copperfield's mother, though the latter is killed off early and the former lost some of his Gregory Peck shine following the publication in 2015 of *Go Tell a Watchman*.

There are plenty of excellent parents in books for older children, including, as we will see, Ma and Pa Ingalls in the Little House series and Marmee in *Little Women*. (Speaking for myself, I find Marmee insufferable but I realize that this is a minority opinion.) In Beverly Cleary's novels, middle-grade readers will encounter mothers and fathers who are loving, thoughtful, and, in their occasional shortcomings, recognizably human.[1] But these are mostly counterexamples. As soon as kids are old enough for fairy tales, they are exposed to an endless string of evil stepmothers, enabling fathers, and even more murderous parental stand-ins such as witches, ogres, goblins, and giants. I also think it is noteworthy that two of the most popular modern picture-book heroines, Madeline and Eloise, are functional orphans. Adolescent readers harbor even stronger prejudices against parental judgment, so in YA fiction families often become cesspools of pathology and dysfunction; and what is a teen dystopia but a projection of those pathologies onto society at large? President Snow in the Hunger Games books might as well be just another one of Mom's abusive boyfriends who has somehow come to rule an entire nation.

It is among picture books for the very young where you have to look far and wide for withholding mothers and fathers with anger issues. There are a few characters I might accuse of sloppy parenting, such as the Man in the Yellow Hat, who is so laissez-faire he never realizes that merely admonishing Curious George to be a good monkey, and then abandoning him for hours on end, will never not prove a recipe for disaster. And as we will see, the mother in *The Cat in the Hat* is so loopy she leaves her children in the care of a fish; hers will be the house where all the kids go to smoke weed in high school. But most parents in books for the very young are steady, kind, and dull—less like child-services cases and more like presidents in textbooks from the pre-pathography era.

---

[1]Cleary was also ahead of the nontraditional family curve, featuring a working single mother in her 1953 book, *Otis Spofford*.

Why are the literary scales on the rest of the shelves weighted so heavily toward bad parenting? Tolstoy's line about all happy families being alike is the wrongest literary maxim this side of Fitzgerald's claim that American lives lack second acts, but no one would deny that unhappy families make for better stories. Also, what we need from stories changes as we age. When we are very young, what we need are our parents. When we are older, what we need is to pull away from their gravitational field, or at least to try, and in the process kick up a little ruckus.

The Runaway Bunny endures in part because it hits a sweet spot between infancy's abject dependency and a toddler's itch to make some actual use of his or her newfound mobility. Anyone who read *The Catcher in the Rye* or *The Outsiders* as an adolescent will remember how those books crystallize the conflicting emotions, the yearning for security and the need to rebel, so endemic to that stage of life; well, *The Runaway Bunny* serves a similar purpose for the Pull-Ups years (or year).

The text begins, "Once there was a little bunny who wanted to run away." Like most children sniffing at independence, he announces his plan—"I am running away"—to which his mother responds, "If you run away, I will run after you. For you are my little bunny." So begins a lyrical back-and-forth in which the little bunny insists that if his mother does run after him, he will become a fish and swim away in a stream, and she responds that she will become a fisherman; he then says he will become a rock on a mountain "high above you" and she responds that she will become a mountain climber "and climb to where you are"; and so on. Several pages later the bunny has become a sailboat being blown homeward by his mother, who is now the wind itself. It is a beautiful image but also a bit frightening: a parent who has literally become elemental, as necessary to life as earth, water, and fire. The story goes on for a few more exchanges, but it's all diminuendo, and the bunny finally gives up, assured that he has what he really wants. "Shucks," he concedes, "I might as well stay where I am and be your little bunny."[2]

For the readers to whom *The Runaway Bunny* is addressed, this is all very calming. When I said that the mother as wind was a rather frightening idea, I meant for those of us old enough to have already spent our teenage years and young adulthood litigating independence from our parents—and subsequent decades re-litigating it. Toddlers, if I may extend the metaphor, only threaten to sue; they might have their lawyer send a nasty letter (in the form of a tantrum), but they never follow up. At that age, threats to run away are meant to test the resiliency of the child-parent bond: a more advanced form of peeka-boo, a less advanced version of leaving a joint or a birth control device where mom or dad can find it. My daughter, when she was two or three, played a game in which she would announce that she was "taking a trip," then march off with her baby stroller to the kitchen for thirty seconds or so, then rush back and announce that she was "home," then fly across the living room to her mother's arms, laughing with both exhilaration and relief.

Brown's mother rabbit passes her own little bunny's test with quite a bit more flair than most parents muster. Clement Hurd's full-color paintings fill every other spread, alternating with line drawings to give the book an appropriately steady visual rhythm. The paintings tend to foreground the mother rabbit, emphasizing her solidity, her

---

[2]Brown's text originally concluded, "And so he did." Ursula Nordstrom felt the ending was too abrupt and cabled that note to Brown, who was vacationing on the island in Maine where she eventually bought her summer home. Brown cabled back, "'HAVE A CARROT,' SAID THE MOTHER BUNNY." That is how the book now ends—a funny, offhand but sweet coda, and also, perhaps, an acknowledgment that food is at least as important as love when it comes to parenting.

comforting *thereness.* Hurd's work in *Goodnight Moon* is more interesting and sophisticated, to my eye, but I'm not sure any illustrator
ever served a text better than he serves this one.[3]

I don't know if Philip Roth was familiar with *The Runaway Bunny*
when he wrote *Portnoy's Complaint*—probably not, I'm guessing; he
would have been nine when it was first published in 1942. But how
much difference is there between the mother rabbit's becoming the wind
itself and Alex Portnoy's belief that his mother is a physics-defying shape-
shifter who whisks herself to school to become his teachers? The key difference is that what is reassuring to a toddler is a sign of budding neurosis
in Roth's slightly older hero. At some point in our lives we *do* need to run
away, however gingerly or briefly. (Or messily and repeatedly . . .) That
is why leaving home is one of the great primal themes in children's literature, whether that means sneaking into Mr. McGregor's vegetable garden, or wandering through a dark wood with a basket for grandmother,
or setting sail for Treasure Island. But note above how Sophie Portnoy
throws that impulse into Alex's face when he allegedly misbehaves, and
how she turns it into a debilitating, humiliating ritual, drowning any itch
for independence with a tidal wave of guilt and theatrical self-sacrifice.
Portnoy's Complaint is *The Runaway Bunny* turned rancid.

Speaking of guilt and theatrical self-sacrifice, I would like to put
in a bad word for *The Giving Tree,* Shel Silverstein's inexplicably popular retelling of *Stella Dallas* and *Mildred Pierce* for nursery schoolers.
It was the author and illustrator's second children's book, published in
1964, when he was most famous for his cartoons and comic sketches
in *Playboy.* The title character is an anthropomorphized apple tree

---

[3]He had some time with it: Hurd was unsatisfied with his first stab at the book, and
the art we know today was done in 1972 for a new edition made feasible on the book's
thirtieth anniversary by the increasing popularity of *Goodnight Moon.*

who loves an unnamed little boy. She gives him her leaves to play with, her branches to climb, her fruit to eat, her shade to rest in. The boy loves the tree in turn. "And the tree was happy," Silverstein writes. "But time went by."

That "but" is an obvious prompt to find a box of Kleenex before we turn the page. The boy, now a teenager, isn't much interested in the tree anymore. One day, though, he shows up. The tree asks if he still wants to play, like old times, but the boy announces that he is "too big" for that. He doesn't want leaves and shade; he wants cash. So the tree tells him to take all her apples and sell them at the market. "And the tree was happy." The boy turns up once again in middle age, looking for lumber to build a house for his family, and again a decade or so after that, now worn down, looking for more lumber to build a boat and sail away from the mess he has made of his life. The tree keeps giving until, inevitably, she is reduced to a stump. The former boy, now old and bent, shows up one last time. The tree sadly says she has nothing left to give. That's OK, says the old man, "I don't need very much now, just a quiet place to sit and rest. I am very tired." So he sits on the stump. And yes, "the tree was happy."

This sentimental, punishing book leaves me cold—and I am usually a sucker for turn-turn-turn hokum, being someone whose eyes, long into middle age, can still well up for "Puff the Magic Dragon" and "Cat's in the Cradle." And don't get me started on "Sunrise, Sunset." But what lesson does *The Giving Tree* mean to impart? I don't see a wise, ennobling, bittersweet parable about maternal steadfastness. I see two deluded losers engaged in a folie à deux: the Joe Buck and Ratso Rizzo of children's literature. I suppose I can understand why *The Giving Tree* would hold some allure for exhausted, long-suffering mothers and fathers—it is one of the rare children's books that ask us to identify with a parent figure, though I think even Sophie Portnoy might have found it over-the-top. To Silverstein's credit, not once does the phrase "After all I've done for you" pass the tree's . . . lips? But why any kids would respond to the book is beyond me. Some do, however—though if you boil it down, what the book is telling them is that if you leave home it will kill your mother. (Maybe Sophie *would* approve.)

To my mind, a fitting if unintended put-down of *The Giving Tree* came from Ursula Nordstrom, its editor. Several years after the book's publication, when it was showing staying power, she sent a copy to Clifton Fadiman, an influential mid-century literary personality. (He was on the editorial board of the then mighty Book-of-the-Month Club.) In an accompanying letter, Nordstrom told Fadiman, "Ministers write me that they use it in sermons." That is pretty much all you need to know about *The Giving Tree*. Let's remember Silverstein instead for his collections of mordant children's poetry, such as *Where the Sidewalk Ends* and *The Light in the Attic*.

One of the most popular children's books of the last quarter century is *Guess How Much I Love You*, written by Sam McBratney, illustrated by Anita Jeram, and published in 1994. I think of it as a spiritual sequel to *The Runaway Bunny*. In the later book, a young rabbit, Little Nutbrown Hare, engages in a friendly competition with his father, Big Nutbrown Hare. At stake: who loves whom the most? Little Nutbrown Hare stretches his arms out as wide as he can and says he loves his father "this much." Big Nutbrown Hare stretches out his longer arms and declares, "But I love *you* this much." And so on. Each time Big Nutbrown Hare tops Little Nutbrown Hare until finally, as son is being put to bed, he tells father, "I love you right up to the moon." Big Nutbrown Hare appears stumped. "Oh that is far," he says. "That is very, very far." But as his son falls asleep, the father whispers to him, "I love you right up to the moon—and back."

Guess How Much I Love You is a sweet book, but as with *The Runaway Bunny* I find it slightly unnerving from my perch outside its target audience. Certainly if I were Big Nutbrown Hare, I would let my son win a round or two in this who-loves-whom-more cage match. But Big Nutbrown Hare holds firm, a benevolent version of implacably competitive dads such as the Marine officer in Pat Conroy's *The Great Santini*. Daddies dote on their children, *Guess How Much I Love You* seems to say, but daddies also have to get the last word in. I wonder how things will stand between Big and Little Nutbrown Hare in twenty or so years when they face each other on a supposedly friendly tennis court.

But back to mommies. If you share my uneasy admiration for *The Runaway Bunny*, you may not be surprised to learn that the book owes its emotional intensity in part to a medieval Provençal love ballad, "Les Métamorphoses," that Brown came across and decided to plunder. The poetry's "beautiful pattern" might be "applied to our ends," Brown wrote to her mentor Lucy Sprague Mitchell, but she borrowed its emotional currents as well.[4] The ballad, as reproduced in Amy Gary's biography (which credits the translation to Brown) begins with a demurral:

> *If you pursue me*
> *I shall become a fish in the water*
> *And I shall escape you.*

---

[4]Brown would spend more than a year working and reworking the deceptively simple manuscript of *The Runaway Bunny*, even though she had dashed off her first draft on the back of a ski lift receipt. She wrote again to Mitchell, "I wallow in uncertainty about punctuation, wording, and form. . . . [W]hat is consistancy [*sic*] and what makes the best poetry." I think Brown's stroke of genius is the little bunny's concessionary "Shucks," which breaks the text's rhythm and disrupts its hypnotic, even dreamy mood—1940s slang as smelling salts.

The ardent lover responds:

If you become a fish
I shall become an eel
And I shall eat you.

The initial speaker, the prey (love ballad or no, that seems the right word here), now imagines turning into a fox to escape. The pursuer counters by promising to become a hunter, prompting this final exchange:

If you hunt me
I shall be buried deep, deep in the ground
And you will never have my love.

If you are dead, dead and buried
I shall be the dust on your grave
And I will marry you, dead or alive.

So yes, *The Runaway Bunny* evolved from a ballad about obsessive love with an unpleasant ending, one that to twenty-first-century eyes may read like the poem a stalker would leave on his intended's windshield. In a horrible way, this is not altogether inappropriate. According to people who study "attachment"—developmental psychology jargon for what normal people call "love" or "affection"—there is a connection between an infant's overwhelming love for its parents and the swooning, sickly-sweet onset of romantic love, the delicious loss of self in another and the corresponding existential dread in the face of a lover's absence. The late psychoanalyst Selma H. Fraiberg described this quite eloquently in her classic 1959 book on child development, *The Magic Years*:

Like the beginnings of all "real love" the infant's new attachment
to his mother is an exclusive and proprietary love. The baby protests when his mother leaves him. Naptime and bedtime bring the
most anguished cries. . . . All of these disturbances are the result of
love. His mother has become so important to him that her pres-
ence means satisfaction and her absence creates anxiety. . . . The
infant has not yet learned that when mother goes away she comes
back. He behaves at such times as if mother were gone forever and
his world is empty of meaning.

There is [a] parallel to be found in the experience of love in
later life. In the early, very intense stages of love, the absence of
a loved person is experienced like the loss of a part of one's self.
"I have no existence without you!" "I feel that I am not alive." "I
am not a whole person!" The feeling that [the] loved one gives
meaning to existence and intensifies [selfhood] has its counterpart
in the infant's experience in his early attachment to his mother.[5]

Really, it's all one big messy, distressing, insoluble knot. As I understand
how attachment works, babies are born not knowing where they end
and where everything else in the world begins; they don't even realize
that they are *they*—or *I*'s. Rather, they exist as if suspended in a thick
puree of undifferentiated beingness and otherness. What helps them sort

---

[5]Lest you dismiss this as mid-century psychoanalytic guff, the developmental psychologist Alison Gopnik reports in her 2009 book, *The Philosophical Baby*, that, "like
Freud," contemporary researchers have found "the same still-startling equation between the early love of parents and children and the later sexual love we feel for our
romantic partners." She adds, however, that current understanding of the processes
that create that equation is very different from Freud's: "Rather than saying, like
Freud, that children want to have sex with their mothers, it's more true to say that
grown-ups want mothering from the people they have sex with." Is that less morti-
fying, or more so? (I should also note that I owe my definition of "attachment" to
Gopnik.)

things out, what helps them develop a sense of self and a linked sense of the rest of the world as distinct from themselves, is learning to love another person. But in learning to love they are also made aware of their own dependence—their real-life Achilles' heel. As Fraiberg concludes:

> So if we ask, "When does the child first experience anxiety in rela-
> tion to the outer world?" the answer will be "When he first learns
> to love." Here is a riddle for the poets!

And also a riddle for children's book authors and ribald literary novel-ists. You can see what Brown's runaway bunny and Alexander Portnoy and all the rest of us are up against. I wouldn't say either Brown or Roth solved Fraiberg's riddle, but each illuminates it in her or his own way. Another way of putting it: Mom and Dad—can't live with them, can't live without them.

But before we move on, and lest you think all I do in this chapter is find fault with hard-pressed storybook parents who are just doing the best they can (is my own mother's voice intruding here?), I would like to consider the parents in Russell Hoban's series of picture books about a young badger named Frances. They may well be the best mother and father in all of literature; they are *just right*, to borrow from Goldi-locks. (Where, by the way, were *her* parents?) Hoban's series, which eventually numbered seven books, began in 1960 with *Bedtime for Frances*, in which Frances, who seems to be five or six, contrives as many ways as she can to avoid going to sleep. She asks for a piggyback ride to bed. She asks for her doll. She asks for her teddy bear. She asks for kisses. She asks for a second round of kisses. Through it all, Mom and Dad comply with smiles and equanimity. Finally, Frances is put to bed, but soon convinces herself there is a tiger in her room.

She went to tell Mother and Father.

"There is a tiger in my room," said Frances.

"Did he bite you?" said Father.

"No," said Frances.

"Did he scratch you?" said Mother.

"No," said Frances.

"Then he is a friendly tiger," said Father.

"He will not hurt you. Go back to sleep."

"Do I have to?" said Frances.

"Yes," said Father.

"Yes," said Mother.

Many, even most, parents would have blown their stacks by this point—it's possible I myself may have under similar circumstances—but Frances's mother and father remain preternaturally patient, loving yet firm; they give their daughter just enough leeway. For her part, Frances will continue to test her luck, sharing with Brown's runaway bunny an active imagination combined with a hunger for reassurance. Back in bed, she mistakes a robe on a chair for a giant, comes back out, asks to watch television, asks for a piece of cake, goes back to bed yet again, worries about what might come out of a crack in her ceiling: "Maybe bugs or spiders. Maybe something with a lot of skinny legs in the dark." Each time her parents listen calmly, gently deflect her anxieties, and steer her back to bed. They are less helicopter parents than tugboat parents.

They have their limits, however, as all parents must. Frances worries that "*something*" is moving her bedroom curtains, "just to see if I am watching." She marches into her parents' bedroom, where they are now asleep.

Frances stood by Father's side of the bed very quietly, right by his head.

She was so quiet that she was the quietest thing in the room.

She was so quiet that Father woke up all of a sudden, with his eyes wide open.

He said, "Umph!"

Frances said, "There is something moving the curtains. May I sleep with you?"

Garth Williams's drawing of Father's grumpy face, one eye still closed with sleep, the other glaring at Frances, might be the most expert thing he ever did—as funny and sympathetic a distillation of paternal misery as you will find. Now, with an implied testiness in his voice, Father explains to Frances that it is the wind's job to blow the curtains just as it is Father's job to go to his office at nine in the morning, and just as it is Frances's job to go to sleep so she will be wide-awake for school. Furthermore, Father says, if the wind doesn't blow it will lose its job, and if he doesn't go to the office on time he will lose his job, and if Frances doesn't go to sleep right now . . .

"I will be out of a job?" said Frances.

"No," said Father.

"I will get a spanking?" said Frances.

"Right!" said Father.

"Goodnight!" said Frances and went back to her room.

She manages a bit more fretting, but is soon fast asleep and does not get up again "until Mother called her for breakfast."

I don't approve of spanking, or the threat of spanking, but in my view Frances's mother and father otherwise do a wonderful job. I also like that Hoban (who had seven children with two wives) promotes the parents' point of view without pandering, the way Silverstein does in *The Giving Tree*. Frances is meant to be seen as a bit of a pain, a grade-school piece of work—kids can appreciate her as a broadly drawn, gently satiric version of themselves—while Father, in his measured paternal wisdom, is a Ward Cleaver–like role model for burrowing mammals.

Animals have long served as exaggerated stand-ins for various human archetypes (which I'll delve into in a later chapter). But would *Bedtime for Frances* have been as effective if the family had been voles, as Hoban intended? It was Williams who came up with the idea of making Frances and her parents badgers. Voles are basically mice by another name, and it is possible that as a busy children's illustrator Williams had had his fill of mice by that point in his career and simply wanted to draw something new. He later recalled that the story as written could have been about any kind of animal, large or small, even elephants, so he suggested a "much neglected" one. Whatever the impulse, badgers were an inspired choice. There is a Botero-like heaviness to Williams's rendering of Frances's mom and dad, a droll gravitas, which serves as a visual representation of their mostly amused, unflappable parenting (and of Hoban's deadpan text). Voles may have fine qualities, but droll gravitas is probably hard for them to muster.

Frances runs away herself in her second book, *A Baby Sister for Frances*.[6] The family has a new addition, Gloria, and while Hoban never states outright that Frances is jealous or resentful—like Harold Pinter, Hoban is a master of implication—she is clearly aggrieved that her routines have been disrupted and her needs not immediately met. For instance, Mother has been too busy with the baby to iron the blue dress Frances wants to wear to school, so Frances has to wear a yellow one. Mother has also been too busy to shop for groceries,

---

[6]That book, like the rest of the titles in the Frances series, was illustrated by Lillian Hoban, Russell's wife, using Williams's character designs; this understandably irked Williams. Look at Hoban's and Williams's drawings side by side if you want a lesson on the differences between a very good illustrator and a sublime one.

so Frances has to have bananas on her oatmeal instead of her usual raisins.

"Well," Frances announces, "things are not very good around here anymore. No clothes to wear. No raisins for oatmeal. I think maybe I'll run away." It is time for school, so Frances makes plans to run away that evening, after dinner. When the time comes, she packs up a few things and tells her parents good-bye. Where is she running away to, they want to know. "I think under the dining room table is the best place," Frances says. "It's cozy, and the kitchen is near if I run out of cookies." Demonstrating again their admirable equanimity, her parents agree that this sounds like a sensible plan, and so Frances is off.

It all works out fine. Relaxing in the living room, her parents talk loudly enough for Frances to overhear. They note how empty the house feels without Frances; how quiet the house now seems; how they will just have to get used to living in a quiet house; how even baby Gloria misses Frances; how "It is just not a family without Frances"; and how, even though babies are nice, "a family is *everybody all together*." That last is a rare example of Hoban's writing being a little too on-the-nose, to my taste, but then again, to cite Ursula Nordstrom, I'm not four. At any rate, Frances falls for it and "returns" home, her dignity intact, her taste of imagined independence perhaps intoxicating. The bigger point is that her parents have just the right touch, and that she has just the right nerve, and that the Frances books are a perfect bridge between *The Runaway Bunny* and gritty stories about troubled kids kicked out of broken homes—hard cases like Snow White and Hansel and Gretel.

A Baby Sister for Frances ends with the baking of a chocolate cake, as all stories about running away should end. Comfort food. A proffered carrot works too.

3

Once upon a Time and In and Out of Weeks: Fairy Tales and Maurice Sendak

A fairy-tale wedding. We all know what the phrase implies: picturesque setting, lovely afternoon or evening, gorgeous couple, exquisite flower arrangements, towering cake, Pachelbel's "Canon in D," magic in the air, love, happiness, no sibling with a drinking problem or personality disorder "ruining the day for everyone," as greataunts (mine, anyway) have been heard to whisper at less-enchanted nuptials. And yet authentic fairy-tale weddings, the ones celebrated in actual fairy tales, are often unpleasant affairs. For instance, on Cinderella's big day in the Grimm brothers' version of her story, the evil stepsisters have their eyes pecked out by a pair of doves. The entertainment at Snow White's wedding, as also recounted by the Grimms, climaxes with the wicked queen's feet being forced into red-hot iron slippers, an unbearable agony that causes her to dance herself to death. The narrative does not say who did the forcing, but I imagine the wedding party flanked by two hooded dungeon masters out of a Charles Addams cartoon.

It is a tribute to the cultural elasticity of fairy tales that on the one hand, we can stereotype them as simplistic or naive or, perhaps most to the point, childish, while on the other hand, it is not exactly a secret that many of them, in their original, unadulterated, 120-proof versions, are so gruesome and bleak, even barbarous, as to raise the question whether they should be thought of as children's literature at all. If you find the denouement of "Snow White" troubling, try "The Stubborn Child," another of the Grimms' tales. It is a hard little nugget of a story, a shard of narrative obsidian, a mere paragraph in the telling:

> There once lived a stubborn child, and he never did what his mother told him to do. And so our dear Lord did not look kindly on him and let him become ill. Doctors could not cure him, and before long he was lying on his deathbed. His coffin was being lowered into the grave and they were about to cover it with earth when suddenly one of his little arms emerged and reached up into the air. They pushed it back in again and covered the coffin with more earth, but it was no use. The little arm kept reaching out of the grave. Finally, his mother had to go to the grave and strike the little arm with a switch. After she did, the arm withdrew, and the child finally began to rest in peace beneath the earth.

It is hard to imagine Walt Disney making a film out of this—George Romero or David Lynch might pull it off—just as it is hard to imagine anyone thinking this was a story children would enjoy listening to. But there it is, lurking like a moldy berry among the 209 other entries in the Grimms' basket, nestled next to the tales everyone knows and others equally obscure: "The Goose Girl," "The Sea Hare," "The

Devil's Sooty Brother," "Hans My Hedgehog," "The Jew in the Brambles." Some of these stories have earned forgetting. But "The Stubborn Child," though you might think it heavy-handed as a cautionary tale about minding one's mother, does possess a genuine power to disturb and not just appall, striking chords of guilt, fear, and pathos. I wonder if Edgar Allan Poe knew it, whether it served as a seed for "The Premature Burial."

"The Stubborn Child," or "The Willful Child," as the German title, "*Das eigensinnige Kind,*" is sometimes translated, is also, in its way, emblematic of the form: like the arm that won't stay buried, fairy tales themselves are stubborn, willful, unruly. With their bloodletting, mutilation, magic, illogic, matricide, patricide, filicide, casual sadism, hints of incest, threats of cannibalism—with all their rude verve— they occupy a kind of literary danger zone, cherished and yet, in many cases, disreputable, befitting their role as the pulp fiction or B-movies of premodern Europe.

Like fables, they entertain and, at times, delight; they even moralize on occasion; but they are also rife with perversity: eruptions of id, unbidden thoughts and desires, long-ago nightmares remembered all too well. Floating up from the collective unconscious and then polished over centuries into universality, dating from times and places where few if any distinctions were drawn between child and adult listeners, they still retain their rough, strange edges. Even when those edges are further dulled, in accordance with modern child-safety standards, fairy tales cling to the imagination, like burrs you can't pry from a sweater. The recent Hollywood vogue for live-action fairy-tale adaptations such as *Maleficent, Snow White and the Huntsman,* and the improbable *Hansel and Gretel: Witch Hunters* suggests that fairy tales are as vital as ever, and not just noisier.

I referred earlier to fairy tales in their "original, unadulterated" state, but that was misleading shorthand; there really are no such animals. A point of definition: I'm referring to fairy tales that sprang from the European oral tradition, as rendered—faithfully or not—many, many years ago by the Germans Wilhelm and Jacob Grimm, the Frenchman Charles Perrault, and others. There is, of course, a whole world of fairy tales from other continents. There are also so-called "literary fairy tales," written from scratch by the likes of Hans Christian Andersen, George MacDonald, and E. T. A. Hoffmann, or, another step or two removed, L. Frank Baum, C. S. Lewis, J. R. R. Tolkien, and—another step still—J. K. Rowling. (What is it with writers of fantasy hiding behind their initials?)

Folkloric fairy tales—maybe we should call them old, weird fairy tales in tribute to Greil Marcus's "old, weird America" (his name for the font of indigenous music that Bob Dylan and The Band drew on for *The Basement Tapes*)—clearly crawled out of some deep crevices in history and the human psyche, the "last echoes of ancient myths" in the Grimms' formulation. These tales have crossed countries and continents, never taking definitive form, "as fluid as a conversation taking place over centuries," in the words of the fairy-tale scholar Marina Warner. Overheard snippets from a never-ending game of telephone might be another way of putting it. Thus, as mentioned above, the sisters in the Grimms' "Cinderella" have their eyes pecked out by doves while, as the novelist A. S. Byatt has noted, Filipino children are told a version of the story that ends with stepmother and stepsister pulled apart by wild horses. Want more? Indonesians grow up with a grind house finale, in which, Byatt writes, "Cinderella forces her stepsister into a cauldron of boiling water, then has the body cut up, pickled, and sent to the girl's mother as 'salt meat' for her next meal." French palates are perhaps too sophisticated to fall for such a ruse, so in Charles Perrault's more benevolent telling, the heroine—"as good-natured as she was beautiful," and thus less bloodthirsty than her literary cousins—fixes her two stepsisters up with a pair of nobles; the tale ends with all three young ladies well married and no one tortured, blinded, or eaten.

So many Cinderellas. And yet, if you read enough fairy tales, they begin to seem populated by the same revolving cast of princes and princesses, simpletons and evil stepmothers, witches, giants, ogres, talking fish, talking birds, talking cats, talking toads, talking frogs—the Enchanted Repertory Company. In the English-speaking world, the Grimms and Perrault live on in memory as the collectors with the niftiest specimens in their jars, but the stories themselves are essentially authorless. Angela Carter, the novelist and poet who molded fairy tales to her own purposes in stories such as "In the Company of Wolves" (her reimagining of "Little Red Riding Hood"), called fairy tales "the perennially refreshed entertainment of the poor" and compared them to humble foods when she wrote about the impossibility of precision and provenance in this realm: "Who first invented meatballs? In what country? Is there a definitive recipe for potato soup? Think in terms of the domestic arts. 'This is how *I* make potato soup.'" In other words, Walt Disney's *Snow White* and *Cinderella*, whatever you think of them, are as valid as anyone's, even a seventeenth-century Black Forest crone's.

I realize this is a book about children's books, not film, but it is impossible to talk about fairy tales in twenty-first-century America without pausing to consider Disney, since so many of us have our first or most vivid experiences with fairy tales through his lens. To the extent that fairy tales are popularly thought of as pablum, I suspect he is largely to blame, but I would like to stand up for him. He and his colleagues and successors at his namesake studio are often mocked for introducing saccharine or sentimental elements into their adaptations. One Marxist folklore scholar I tried to read accuses him of "managing to domesticate the fairytale and restore its conservative features," a criticism that requires you to regard as progressive a genre where snagging a prince or princess is so often life's be-all and end-all. But Disney doesn't get nearly enough credit for adding humor to the recipe. His seven dwarfs, for instance—they are unnamed and undifferentiated in the Grimms' version—are one of the great comic inventions of twentieth-century cinema, a precisely delineated troupe of knockabout comedians larger in number than the Three Stooges and The Marx Brothers combined (if you don't count Gummo and Zeppo, as you shouldn't). Yes, Disney's Snow White is a sweet-voiced simp of a heroine, a girl with barely more personality than the cheerful, chattering forest animals she is forever befriending, but this wan character represents an improvement over the Grimms' Snow White, who has no personality whatsoever. She is described only in terms of her beauty: "as beautiful as the bright day," and so on, as if she were a human bauble. Cinderella, Rapunzel, and the rest aren't much livelier, and forget about the princes. As Philip Pullman once wrote—exaggerating, but not much—"There is no psychology in a fairy tale. The characters have little interior life; their motives are clear and obvious. If people are good, they are good, and if bad, they're bad. . . . One might almost say that characters in a fairy tale are not actually conscious." So another point for Disney, or maybe half a point. And you can hardly blame him for toning down the violence. Most fairy tales, were they faithfully adapted, would easily earn what Hollywood calls a "hard R" rating.

Disney's critics often betray a weak grasp of the aesthetic and formal differences between premodern folk tales and modern commercial movies, the latter of which need to last at least eighty minutes or so and entertain relatively sophisticated people who may have traveled to another village on occassion or even seen a real prince or princess on TV. Most fairy tales don't take the time to sketch in atmosphere and motivation, and they don't often adhere to tidy, three-act storytelling. "They come in, clobber you over the head, and then go away," Joan Acocella wrote in *The New Yorker* several years ago in an essay on the Grimms.

I have no idea whose versions of the stories I heard as a child, or whether they were read to me or ad-libbed, but I remember being thrilled by "Little Red Riding Hood" and "Jack and the Beanstalk," held rapt by the delicious, mounting suspense contained in the repetitions of *all the better to* and *fee-fi-fo-fum*. In his manuscript of "Little Red Riding Hood," Perrault included a memo to the reader following the climactic "All the better to eat you with": "You say these words in a loud voice so as to frighten the child, as if the wolf were going to eat it." Of course you do. Screams! Laughter! As I said, delicious.

Fairy tales may be where those of us who enjoy scary adult films and stories first develop the taste. For some—Charles Dickens, to cite one example—fairy tales also provoke their first sexual stirrings. In a memoir about his childhood, "The Christmas Tree," Dickens wrote of Little Red Riding Hood: "She was my first love. I felt if I could have married [her], I should have known perfect bliss. But, it was not to be." That the creator of Little Nell, Little Dorrit, and so many other sweet, pure, and unworldly (though also uneaten) heroines would have an erotic fixation on Little Red Riding Hood, herself so emblematic of the type—archetypal, in fact—is too perfect, almost a real-life Rosebud.

The child psychologist Bruno Bettelheim's 1976 book, *The Uses of Enchantment: The Meaning and Importance of Fairy Tales*, is unavoidable here—probably the single most influential work on this subject. Bettelheim posits that fairy tales have survived for so long and remain so potent in our culture because their ogres and wolves and murderous stepmothers confront children's most primal fears in ways both dead-on and fanciful, helping to resolve anxieties about abandonment, becoming sexual, coming into conflict with their parents, finding a mate, finding a place in the world. "This is exactly the message that fairy tales get across to the child in manifold form," Bettelheim writes: "that a struggle against severe difficulties in life is unavoidable, is an intrinsic part of human experience—but that if one does not shy away, but steadfastly meets unexpected and often unjust hardships, one masters all obstacles and at the end emerges victorious."

The Grimms were onto this themselves, writing in the introduction to the second edition of their fairy-tale collection, "Children's stories are told so that the early thoughts and forces of the human heart will awaken and develop in their radiant mildness." The intervening centuries have devalued radiant mildness as a therapeutic goal, but in the post-Freudian era fairy tales make easy marks for armchair psychoanalysts: fatherless Jack growing a towering, erectile beanstalk from a small seed and stealing a golden-egg-laying goose from an angry male giant . . . Snow White's youthful "fairness" arousing her stepmother's murderous jealousy, from which she is protected by little asexual men until an appropriate full-size mate happens along . . . Little Red Riding Hood venturing away from home and safety into a dark, fecund forest where she is attacked and eaten by a predatory wolf, only to be saved by a strapping father figure of a huntsman who splits the wolf open like, well, whatever. . . . Having spent years in therapy unpacking the dismayingly heavy-handed symbolism of my own dreams, I am inclined to agree with Bettelheim generally, though at times it is hard not to be amused by his Freudian orthodoxies, as when he writes that "Hansel and Gretel" is a story about the dangers of "regression" in which the gingerbread house the hungry children find in the forest "stands for oral greediness and how attractive it is to give in to it" and the witch who wants to eat them "is a personification of the destructive aspects of orality." That may be true, but I would add that, on a more literal level, "Hansel and Gretel" is also a story about two children cast out of their home during a famine—as was sometimes the sad custom in premodern Europe, when the story was first making the rounds. "Hansel and Gretel," though, wouldn't be the first work of art to accrue new layers of meaning over the centuries.

I can't say whether I was drawn to the fairy tales I loved as a child because they soothed my anxious psyche, but I was struck recently, when reading the Grimms, Perrault, and others, by the degree to which fairy-tale worlds mimic the real world as kids experience it: the profound strangeness of the new and unfamiliar, the fear of lurking monsters and hidden evildoers, the seeming arbitrariness of adults' demands, the supernatural assumptions about almost everything. When I was two or three, for instance, I thought the sun literally set on the other side of our neighbor's house—and why wouldn't I have? A little older, I believed that our TV worked because there was a troupe of small actors living inside the set, performing *Underdog* and *Captain Kangaroo* just for me. One morning, I mistook the cement mixer that came to pour our backyard patio for some kind of giant defecating rhinoceros. Is it such a great leap—is it maybe even a backward hop?—from that to magic beans and enchanted frogs? And while the original audiences for fairy tales didn't mistake "Rapunzel" or "Rumplestiltskin" for journalism, they did live in a threatening world they believed populated by witches and goblins, sprites and spells—by magic—and they had the scary impenetrable forests and spooky, otherwise inexplicable natural phenomena to prove it.

To a modern adult sensibility with a taste for classic French literature, Perrault's *Contes du temps passé* (Tales of Times Past) is a charming, pleasant read. A poet and panegyrist as well as a high-level bureaucrat attending to cultural affairs under Louis XIV, he reworked old folktales and other literary flotsam, initially in verse and then in prose; presented them in salons and at the Académie Française; and finally published his collection in 1697. (*Tout* Paris was convulsed by

a fairy-tale fad in the 1690s.) Perrault has a droll, assertive voice; Dr.
Seuss was a fan of his witty "Puss in Boots." Not surprisingly, given
Perrault's résumé, he also has a keen eye for social observations, to
the extent that such opportunities present themselves in fairy tales.
For instance, when his Sleeping Beauty wakes from her hundred-year
slumber (not because of a kiss, by the way, but merely because the spell
has an expiration date), Perrault describes her gazing at the inevitable
bedside prince "with greater tenderness in her eyes than might have
seemed proper at a first meeting." The couple of course fall instantly
in love, and the prince is gallant enough "not to tell her that she was
dressed like Grandmother in the old days, with a high starched collar."
Meanwhile, the rest of the castle's population has also woken up, "and
since they were not in love they were all dying of hunger." Indeed, it
is a famished and irritable lady-in-waiting who finally gets Sleeping
Beauty out of bed. Had Balzac ever tried his hand at fairy tales, the
results might have been something like this.[1]

Perrault has his unsavory moments. His tale "Donkey-Skin" is set
in motion by a widowed king's "criminal desire" to marry his daughter; "Bluebeard" is about a serial killer; and "Sleeping Beauty" has
a long second act in which the heroine, now married to the prince,
must protect her two young children, a girl named Dawn and a boy
named Day, from her mother-in-law, the queen, who "came from a

---

[1] Confession: I wrote that last sentence off the top of my head, rather glibly, and when
I thought to make sure Balzac hadn't in fact written any fairy tales, I found that he
had. His 1831 novel *The Wild Ass's Skin* tells the story of a despondent young man
who, on the verge of suicide, comes to possess a magic piece of leather that will grant
him his every wish, with the caveat that each wish shrinks the skin, and that when he
runs out of skin and wishes, he will also die. The book turns out to be a very adult
fairy tale about humankind's troubled relationship with desire in all its forms. It was
a best seller, Balzac's first big success. The French title is *Le peau de chagrin*, and, yes,
there is a pun there, *chagrin* having the dual meaning of leather made from a donkey
or ass and something close to its meaning in English. All in all, highly recommended!

family of ogres" and is whispered to have "ogreish tendencies" herself, meaning she may have a literal taste for children. (Perrault feels obliged to note that the king married her "only because of her great wealth.") It is unclear how much effort the queen puts into restraining her appetites, but she soon falls off the wagon:

> [The queen] said one evening to her steward, "Tomorrow evening for supper, I want to eat little Dawn."
>
> "Alas, my lady!" said the steward.
>
> "That is my wish," said the queen, and her tone was the tone of an ogress who wants fresh meat, "and I want to eat her with onions and mustard sauce."

So French, that last detail! Is it wrong to laugh? Happily, little Dawn is not filleted, nor, despite the queen's subsequent commands, are little Day or Sleeping Beauty herself. Justice is served when the queen, in a fit of frustrated rage, flings herself into a convenient cauldron full of toads and snakes and is "devoured in an instant by the horrid creatures."

Perrault's conclusion is abrupt and, I think, wonderful:

> Despite everything, the [prince] was upset: she was his mother; but he consoled himself with his beautiful wife and children.

How unexpected to find shades of ambiguity and rue at the end of such a preposterous saga, but as noted, fairy-tale endings don't always fulfill the breezy, happily-ever-after stereotype. *She was his mother.* Alexander Portnoy might sympathize.

The same year Perrault bought out his collection, 1697, his contemporary Catherine-Anne d'Aulnoy published *Les contes des fées* (Tales of the Fairies), from which we English-speakers derived the term fairy tale. Even earlier collections had been printed in Italy in the sixteenth and seventeenth centuries; the older still *One Thousand and One Nights*, which like the Bible had no single compiler, first appeared in France in 1704, translated from the Arabic, and was soon after brought out in English as well. So as a literary genre the fairy tale was well established in 1812 when Jacob and Wilhelm Grimm published their own first collection. Born a year apart in a Hessian town outside Frankfurt, they were lawyers by training whose shared interest in literature and philology, alongside a general passion for collecting (there is a German word for that: *Sammlergeist*), led them to become folklorists, with the aim, as Wilhelm once wrote, of preserving "our national poetic heritage."

Lest this set off warning bells, German nationalism no longer resonating with as much wholesomeness today as it might have possessed two hundred years ago, I should note that during the Grimms' formative years Napoleon controlled much of what was not yet a unified country, so their efforts and those of like-minded romantic peers may have had more of a scrappy, underdog esprit than subsequent efforts to promote German culture. In the brothers' view, they were conserving a dying tradition. As they wrote in the introduction to their first edition, "The custom of telling tales is . . . on the wane, just as all the cozy corners in homes and gardens are giving way to empty splendor. One quickly discovers that the custom persists only in places where there is a warm openness to poetry or where there are imaginations not yet deformed by the perversities of modern life." On that latter score, the brothers didn't know the half of it.[2]

---

[2]You can hardly blame the Nazis on the Grimms, but, not surprisingly, the Third Reich embraced the brothers' work, insisting that fairy tales be taught in schools and even restoring the violence and cruelty that had been pruned from some editions. As well, writes the fairy-tale scholar Marina Warner, "No less than twenty-three

The initial 1812 volume of their *Kinder- und Hausmärchen* (Children's and Household Tales) had eighty-six stories; a second volume with seventy more followed, in 1815, as did various revised editions until the final, standardized edition of 1857, with its grand total of 210 tales. Unlike Perrault, who reworked children's stories with an eye to impressing and amusing his literary peers, the Grimms approached their work as scholars, their collections comprising ostensibly faithful transcriptions of tales told by authentic, goat-herding, milk-pail-carrying *Volk* in their natural, unspoiled habitats; in reality, though, as Marina Warner observes in her history of fairy tales, *Once upon a Time*, "many of their sources were literate, even French-speaking, sophisticates and much traveled," so the *Märchen* weren't always as 100 percent *Volk*-pure as advertised. Moreover, as the Grimms' books, which had been intended for specialists, began turning up in nurseries and schools, the brothers revised their stories with an eye to a newly emergent "family market," as we now say. So in came Christian elements and out went digestive-tract jokes and bawdy bits such as when, in an early edition, Rapunzel inadvertently betrays the secret visits from her hair-climbing prince by beseeching the witch who holds her captive, "Tell me, Godmother, why my clothes are so tight and why they fit me no longer." (The weight gain

---

live action [fairy tale] films were made, and included ghastly and dismaying scenes, including Red Riding Hood rescued by an SS officer from an anti-Semitic cartoon wolf."

More benign tales had their ideological uses, too. One Nazi-era writer discerned this moral in "Cinderella": "[Nature] does not let itself be cheated and deceived. It opens itself up to the pure person and the devoted. It reveals its help to him! It fuses the suitable specimens of a species together. . . . The prince finds the genuine, worthy bride because his unspoiled instinct leads him, because the voice of his blood tells him she is the right one." (That interpretation might be the critical equivalent of the evil stepsisters' ghastly efforts to cram their big feet into Cinderella's glass slipper.) The Reich embraced the Grimms so enthusiastically that during the postwar occupation the Allies banned fairy tales for a period as part of denazification efforts.

is not from bratwurst.) The violence, however, mostly remained—
sex, then as now, raising more hackles than bloodshed where tender
young sensibilities are concerned.

Whatever their "impurities," I think the Grimms' tales loom larg-
est in the Western imagination because they tap the old, weird roots
better than most. The famous stories are fine, but it's the more out-of-
the-way, less-well-lit corners of the Grimms' oeuvre that truly make
your hair stand on end or make you laugh. Many stories are swift and
clobbering, as Joan Acocella said, while others go on and on and on,
shifting narrative shape again and again like a long night's dream you
can't wake from. Some have the flabbergasting pleasures of outsider
art or pop-culture flea-market finds: lurid exploitation movies, genre
fiction ripped from forgotten headlines, ambitious but misbegotten
concept albums, your grandfather's dusty erotica—the sort of works
that leave you dumbstruck to think that someone actually put this
down on paper or canvas or celluloid or wax. Many of the Grimms'
tales, obscure and not, don't play by the commonly accepted rules of
well-crafted storytelling: they bestow and dispense with motivations
on a whim, tack on codas that have nothing to do with the rest of the
tale, litter their landscapes with dei ex machina. What might well be
my favorite sentence in the entire canon comes near the end of the tale
"Ferdinand Faithful and Ferdinand Unfaithful," when the narrator
abruptly notes, "However, the queen did not like the king very much
because he had no nose." You sometimes wonder: Were their sources
pulling the brothers' legs?

And yet, as the Grimms hoped, there is poetry here too. Consider the opening of "The Two Journeymen," which begins not "Once
upon a time" but with something more contemplative: "Hill and valley never meet, but God's children do, sometimes even the good and
bad ones." As table-setting maxims go, I think that is an excellent one,
worthy of overuse.

There is also deadpan wit—intentional or not, you can't always tell—in these stories, as in this exchange from "The Fisherman and His Wife," between said fisherman and a flounder he has hooked:

Flounder: "I beg you, let me live. I'm not a regular flounder, I'm an enchanted prince. What good will it do you to kill me? I wouldn't taste right anyway."

Fisherman: "Ah, you needn't go on as much as all that—a flounder that can talk I'd let swim off anyway." He does, and is then berated by his wife for neglecting to ask for a wish, which is what social convention expects you to do, apparently, when you encounter a talking flounder.

That may be the closest thing to consistency in the Grimms' universe: the knack so many of their characters have for accepting all sorts of magic, mayhem, and absurdity with a matter-of-fact shrug or, at most, base self-interest. This blasé affect, this lack of evidence of much internal life, in Philip Pullman's term, can feel like a philosophical stance, a sort of fairy-tale Zen. Or maybe it's a peasant's expression of powerlessness amid harsh circumstances? At any rate, I think it's a key to why fairy tales are so easy to read into and project on, why they serve as such enduring templates and provocative mirrors. However bizarre and specific their external events, they are stories about people who are barely individuals, or even types, and as such they can be stories about everyone.

That might be another reason why some critics resent Walt Disney: the way his name has been seared like a literal brand on universal stories, usurping even the Grimms, who had the grace to downplay their own authorship. But you know who else was a fan of Disney's? Maurice Sendak, who once observed:

> Disney has often been condemned for corrupting the classics, and
> he has, to be sure, occasionally slipped in matters of taste and ab-
> solute fidelity to the original. But he has never corrupted. If there
> have been errors, they are nothing compared to the violations
> against the true nature and psychology of children committed by
> some of the so-called classics.

I took that from a wonderful 1988 essay Sendak wrote on Disney's
Pinocchio, which Sendak felt was far superior to the sadistic Italian
fairy tale the film was very loosely based on. It makes sense that Sendak would admire Disney—Sendak's was originally a child's admiration, but one that he was willing to own as an adult—because, for
my money, he is Disney's chief rival as the twentieth-century artist
who most profoundly channeled the fairy-tale ethos and truly put
his own stamp on the genre, though their achievements could hardly
be more different. If Disney Americanized fairy tales, adding vaude-
ville rambunctiousness along with fancy new cinematic bells and
whistles—and in the process, like so many popular American artists,
created something with global commercial appeal—Sendak's gift,
manifest in the picture books he wrote and illustrated such as *Where
the Wild Things Are* and *In the Night Kitchen*, was to reinvent the fairy
tale by drilling down through his own unconscious and ransacking
his own childhood joys and terrors. In a tradition of less crowd-
pleasing American artists—Sylvia Plath and Mark Rothko come to
mind—Sendak found the universal in the profoundly, even heroically
personal. His fairy tales are songs of the self.

Like those of Perrault and the Grimms, Sendak's stories have provoked debates about whether they are truly appropriate for children.
He is often given credit for single-handedly "wrenching the picture
book out of the safe, sanitized world of the nursery" and plunging
it into "the dark, terrifying, and hauntingly beautiful recesses of the

human psyche," as his *New York Times* obituary put it when he died in 2012, at the age of eighty-four. That tribute is not entirely fair: Sendak's contemporary and friend Theodor Geisel—Dr. Seuss, to you— ventured into some pretty creepy places, though always with a laugh. But sure, Sendak was a more relentlessly introspective author, probed deeper, and never pulled a punch. In that, he found purpose and meaning—safe harbor in an ocean of anxieties, and worse. Eulogizing Sendak for *The New Yorker* shortly after his death, Adam Gopnik described Sendak's characters as "creatures of needs and fears—but ones who like their fears, or are at least fascinated by them. . . . It is a terrible cliché to say that what distinguishes his work is its darkness or its embrace of fear; the Nancy Drew books do that as well. What distinguishes his art is the calm poise that his children possess in the face of darkness." That could also describe any number of fairy tale heroes and heroines (especially the simpletons), so I would only add that a second distinguishing feature of Sendak's art is that his children are people, not archetypes or ciphers. They breathe the same air you and I do, no matter how enchanted or bizarre the worlds they enter.

Sendak often claimed to be writing for no one but himself, and grumbled in interviews—he was a frequent and generous though often cranky profile subject—about being relegated to "Kiddiebookland" (a ghetto he located "next to Neverneverville and Peterpanburg"). "How infuriating and insulting when a serious work is considered only a trifle for the nursery!" he once exploded. On another occasion, sitting down with Larry King in 1991, he groused, "I wrote exactly what was in my head. I never set out to write books for children. I'm no more interested in them than I am in grown-ups. . . . My work is peculiar. I'm a middle-aged elderly man and I have kids swimming in milk, and you can't put it on the same shelf as Norman Mailer or Saul Bellow. What are you going to do with it? You put it in the kiddie section. But it isn't because I intended it to be there. It's how my head works."

I will confess to having struggled over the years—or decades, to be honest—with his 1963 masterpiece, *Where the Wild Things Are*, though the poetic concision of its text, its incantatory lilt, similar to that of *Goodnight Moon*, can move me deeply. If you don't remember: Max, a young boy wearing a wolf costume, makes mischief of one kind and another, is called "wild thing" by his unseen mother, to which he responds, "I'll eat you up!" and is sent to bed without supper. As he stews in isolation, his room transforms into a forest. He finds a boat and sets sail across the sea "through night and day and in and out of weeks and almost over a year"—Sendak's "once upon a time"–like incantation that begins the magical part of the story—and discovers a land full of real Wild Things: monsters, roughly the size of SUVs, with "terrible teeth" and "terrible roars," "terrible eyes" and "terrible claws." Max, as unperturbed as any of the Grimms' heroes, tames them by shouting, "Be still!" and staring into their eyes without blinking. He then leads them in a "wild rumpus" across three marvelous, antic, textless spreads, until he grows bored, sends them to bed without *their* suppers, bids them farewell, and returns home, where he finds his own dinner waiting for him. "And it was still hot," the story concludes; more comfort food for another runaway, if only a runaway in his dreamlike imagination. This may not be quite happily ever after, but at least it is happily for tonight.

As in all great picture books, the effect of Sendak's text is inseparable from the wit and crosshatched richness of his Dürer-meets-*Mad*-magazine illustrations, which feel both timeless and of their early-1960s moment. The Wild Things themselves are simultaneously horrid and silly, giant babies once we get to know them, their claws and fangs and sickly yellow eyes notwithstanding; their anxious faces betray fears of their own. Appropriately enough, since they are in some sense Max's creations, they are monsters with the souls of children. (I wonder too if Sendak here owes a conscious or unconscious debt to Disney's dwarfs.)

My adult response to *Where the Wild Things Are* goes like this: what an empowering, psychologically astute parable about a child learning that anger, while sometimes overwhelming and scary, can be safely expressed and conquered. When I was a child myself, however, the book left me cold. I don't remember precisely why. Maybe I was too literal-minded to be transported by Sendak's dream logic. Not that I didn't like fantasy, but I also liked rules. Traditional fairy tales, with their clear villains, precisely delineated quests, and bloody, well-deserved vengeance: that's what worked for me. It occurs to me now that another reason I didn't respond to *Where the Wild Things Are* may well have been that anger wasn't freely expressed in my buttoned-down family of origin; perhaps I found Sendak's parable less liberating than off-putting or even frightening. (I might have been better served by *Where the Passive-Aggressive Things Are*.) I do remember the book as something to be reckoned with, like the mumps. I was four when it was published in 1963—certainly the right age for it. I was cognizant that teachers and librarians thought it was a "good" book, as proved by the shiny gold Caldecott sticker on its front cover. (A budding critic, I had a premature and probably unhealthy interest in consensus.) I don't think my family had a copy, but I remember seeing it in what I now realize were the more cosmopolitan homes on my cul-de-sac in a Northern California college town; the book resides in memory as an early 1960s progressive totem alongside Danish modern furniture, traditional African art, and the sticky, stale-sweet smell of pipe tobacco. I was aware of *Where the Wild Things Are* as something I *should* like, and I think I felt lacking for not "getting" it.

Speaking of African art and pipes, Sendak was himself a veteran analysand, and his partner of fifty years was a psychoanalyst. He was steeped in it. As he once wrote about his "curious" indifference to Jean de Brunhoff's *Babar* when he was a young man still learning his craft, "This was in the 1950s. I was then a green recruit fresh off the analyst's couch and woe betide any work that failed to loudly signal its Freudian allegiance. With a convert's proverbial fervor, I rushed pell-mell into the very heart of what I considered Babar's unresolved problem: his mother's death, of course." The problem, to Sendak's eyes, was that de Brunhoff dispatches the young elephant's mom— like Bambi's mother, the victim of a wicked hunter—in the course of a single spread; after a brief cry Babar gets on with his life and is soon taking in the sights of Paris. A "useless" death, Sendak remembered objecting: "Why give us a mother's death and then deprive us of the pleasure of wallowing in its psychological repercussions?" Sendak eventually came around to de Brunhoff's "genius," sparking to what he saw as a loving and generous spirit infusing the work despite its French equivalent of a stiff upper lip. (Myself, I remain on the fence with regard to Babar, whose continental airs, such as his green three-piece suit, bowler hat, and two-tone shoes, I found precious even as a child.) I risk this digression because I want to point out once again that (a) Sendak was not just a genius author and illustrator himself but also a wry and penetrating essayist and critic, maybe the best on kids' books I've ever read; and (b) an analytic perspective pervades his work. If you are attuned to it, you get a frisson of acknowledgment from his work, not unlike the way your own shrink might nod at you discreetly when you pass her on a sidewalk.

Sendak was born in Brooklyn in 1928, the youngest son of émigré Polish Jews. His childhood was shadowed by a series of illnesses— pneumonia at age two, scarlet fever at four—as well as what he often presented as a general, overhanging melancholy, no doubt exacerbated by the trials of growing up gay in Brooklyn in the 1930s and '40s, and in a family haunted by news of the cascading horrors in Europe. "I was a miserable kid," he is quoted as saying in the book *The Art of Maurice Sendak*. "I couldn't make friends. I couldn't skate great. I couldn't play stoopball terrific. I stayed home and drew pictures. You know what they all thought of me: sissy Maurice Sendak. Whenever I wanted to go out and do something, my father would say, 'You'll catch a cold.' And I did. I did whatever he told me."

Sendak often told the story of how he dredged the Wild Things up from childhood memories. Here is the version he gave Terry Gross, of National Public Radio:

> I didn't want [the Wild Things] to be traditional monsters, like griffins and gorillas and such like. I wanted them to be very, very personal. It had to come out of my own particular life. . . . And it was only when I had them all that I realized they were all my Jewish relatives.
>
> They were all the adults who treated us in such silly fashions when we were kids. And these were the real monsters of my child-hood. You know, people come on Sunday and wait to get fed; un-cles and aunts and they all say the same dumb thing, where you're beating time until food gets put on the table: how big you are and how fat you got, and you look so good we can eat you up. In fact, we knew they would because my mother was the slowest cooker in Brooklyn. So if she didn't hurry up they would eat us up.
>
> So the only entertainment was watching their bloodshot eyes and how bad their teeth were. You know, children are mon-strously cruel about physical defects; you know, hair curling out of the nose and the weird mole on the side of the head. And so you would glue in on that and then you'd talk about it with your brother and sister later. And they became the Wild Things.

The book itself, Sendak told the writer and critic Nat Hentoff in a 1966 *New Yorker* profile, "was a personal exorcism. . . . It went deeper into my childhood than anything I've done before." He added, "When I write and draw, I'm experiencing what the child in the book is going through. I was as relieved to get back from Max's journey as he was." To Ursula Nordstrom, Sendak's editor at Harper, *Where the Wild Things Are* was nothing short of revolutionary. True, she was probably biased, but given her backlist she was also well qualified to judge. As she wrote to Hentoff:

> I think *Wild Things* is the first complete work of art in the picture book field, conceived, written, illustrated, executed in entirety by one person of authentic genius. Most books are written from the outside in. But *Wild Things* comes from the inside out, if you know what I mean. And I think Maurice's book is the first picture book to recognize that children have powerful emotions, anger and love and hate.

Nordstrom's "inside out" gets at the real genius of the book, and what it is I think Sendak did for the fairy-tale genre. (If *Where the Wild Things Are* isn't a fairy tale per se, it's certainly in the neighborhood—a neighborhood where the borders are amorphous to begin with.) In the old stories, to the extent characters have needs they tend to be motivated not by emotion (female jealousy aside) but by circumstance: hunger, poverty, needing a mate, some arbitrary task or quest. Max's voyage, on the other hand, though humming with mythic, magical overtones, is spurred by his own roiling, contradictory feelings. This might sound fanciful, but I believe Sendak restored a measure of reality to fairy tales with *Where the Wild Things Are*, an immediacy that had gone missing in the centuries since people—most people—had quit believing in witches or stopped fearing that their parents would dump them in a forest, or worse, when the porridge ran out. Sendak repotted the genre and moved it to a recognizable space, interior though that might be.

•   •   •

The punch line of my own up-and-down relationship with *Where the Wild Things Are* is that once it finally clicked for me, after I reencountered the book in my late thirties, when someone had given it to my family as a baby gift, I was as eager as any convert to read it to my own kids, as soon as they were old enough. And yet when that time came, and with an ironic circularity real life rarely achieves on its own, they didn't like the book any more than I had. They found it—this was all I could get out of them, one of the rare times in their younger days when they were willing to venture an opinion more negative than just "OK"—"boring." Perhaps they had already internalized Sendak's lessons about not fearing your anger (in their New York City apartment unlike my childhood ranch house, yelling at one another is a virtual hobby), or maybe they simply agreed with the anonymous reviewer for *Publishers Weekly* who, back in 1963, had dismissed Sendak's book as "pointless and confusing."

Sendak himself, though he could be tetchy about criticism, readily acknowledged the book wasn't for everyone. He once described an encounter he had at a library conference:

> A woman stood up and said, "You know, I read *Where the Wild Things Are* to my daughter, and every time I read it to her, she puts her hand over her ears and screams." I was stunned. And I said, "Well, why are your torturing your child? Do you not like her?" . . . And she said, "But it won the Caldecott. She's supposed to like it." There you go. Poor kid. She's probably in some home at this point.

Yet another person who didn't immediately see the greatness in *Where the Wild Things Are* was Bruno Bettelheim. The author who would do more than anyone else to rehabilitate fairy-tale trauma pronounced himself "skeptical" about Sendak's book, owing to its presumed scariness, although he qualified his opinion by admitting he hadn't read it. This was in a 1969 column he wrote for *Ladies' Home Journal*, a dialogue with three mothers who were concerned about the story's effect on their children. The psychologist, relying on the mothers' descriptions, fretted about the fearsome monsters, but even more he fixated on the detail of Max's mother sending him to bed without his supper, which Bettelheim feared would aggravate a child's "basic anxiety" regarding "desertion." He concluded: "If I were writing the book, where the child said, 'I'll eat you up (Mommy),' maybe I'd first let the mother explain why children want to eat up their mothers and not have her send them to bed without supper." That might be good parenting advice, but it's a truly lousy editorial suggestion. Bettelheim's fixation here seems especially odd: Max's mother's withholding a single meal is small potatoes next to, say, the deprivations in "Hansel and Gretel," a story Bettelheim would be championing in a few years in *The Uses of Enchantment*. Sendak resented the criticism. Though *Where the Wild Things Are* was already a celebrated bestseller of several years' standing when Bettelheim's article came out, Sendak nursed a grudge for the rest of his life, bringing up Bettelheim repeatedly in interviews, even referring to him as "that creep" and "Beno Brutalheim" on NPR during an interview in 2005. Which, by the way, was fifteen years after the creep's death.

Bettelheim did make a provocative point in the *Ladies' Home Journal* piece regarding stories that seek to engage children's most primal emotions:

> In many cases [the book] comes out of the psychology of the writer . . . it doesn't come out of the psychology of the child. The old-fashioned fairy tale, which was gruesome enough, had one redeeming feature. It came out of the fantasy of the adult, not out of what the adult thought was the fantasy of the child, and in this

way it was more or less authentic. Storybooks like [*Where the Wild Things Are*] . . . come out of the fantasy of adults who believe they really know the fantasy of children. But the child's fantasies are quite different from the adult's.

An educator and children's book critic I once spoke to who *had* read *Where the Wild Things Are* criticized it in similar terms, as having the processed feel of "something arrived at years later to understand the writer's own anger." I very much don't agree, though I might have agreed if she had been talking about the two picture books that Sendak viewed, along with *Where the Wild Things Are*, as part of a loose trilogy: *In the Night Kitchen*, from 1970; and *Outside Over There*, from 1981.[3]

The former is another tale of nighttime transformation, even more surreal than its predecessor, and the illustrations, which pay explicit homage to Winsor McCay's dreamy comic strip *Little Nemo in Slumberland*, are among Sendak's most playful and inventive. The story begins

---

[3] I am writing here about an extremely small slice of Sendak's total output—just a sliver, as adults say when birthday cake is being passed around. All together, he wrote and illustrated over twenty books, and illustrated seventy-plus more for other authors. I haven't read everything he ever did, but everything that I have seen is worth your attention. I am particularly fond of his drawings for Else Holmelund Minarik's Little Bear series, and for several books he collaborated on with Ruth Krauss, including *A Hole Is to Dig*, published in 1952—his first big critical and commercial success. These titles contain some of his liveliest, wittiest character illustrations, with personalities and emotions exquisitely calibrated. (Sendak once drew Little Bear on a scrap of paper for a friend of mine and I am eternally, horribly jealous.) *The Moon Jumpers*, written by Janice May Udry, features some of his most gorgeous color illustrations, a series of moonlit landscapes. It came out in 1960, and in hindsight seems like a dry run for the nightscapes of *Where the Wild Things Are*, though the earlier illustrations might be even more ethereal. No artist has ever captured as luscious a moon as Sendak, and this was a motif he returned to throughout his career. Strictly out of curiosity and with no disrespect intended toward Clement Hurd, I wish there were a parallel universe where Sendak had also illustrated *Goodnight Moon*.

with Mickey, who could be Max's slightly chubbier brother, woken up by a "racket in the night" that isn't explained, though comic sound effects indicate a rhythmic thumping and bumping coming from another room in the apartment. (*Hmmm.*) After shouting, "Quiet down there!" we are told that Mickey "fell through the dark / out of his clothes past the moon & his mama and papa sleeping tight / and into the light of the night kitchen." There, a now naked Mickey—his penis and scrotum have been a flash point for censorious adult readers ever since (school librarians have been known to take bottles of correction fluid and dab on pairs of tighty-whities)—meets three identical bakers who look like Oliver Hardy and attempt to bake Mickey into a cake. He escapes this mild peril by jumping into a pile of bread dough "all ready to rise." Sendak then tells us, "He kneaded and punched it and pounded and pulled," until he's fashioned the dough into an airplane, in which he flies off, telling the bakers, who are now in need of milk for their cake, that he will "get milk the Mickey way." That involves flying "up and up and up and over the top of the Milky Way" and then diving headfirst into a giant phallic milk bottle, inside which Mickey swims joyously while singing, "I'm in the milk and the milk's in me." This liquid revel then ends with Mickey standing on top of the milk bottle in a modified chest-pounding Tarzan pose and shouting, "Cock a doodle doo!"

I think *In the Night Kitchen* is a story about sex.

Plenty of people, children and adults, love the book; Ursula Nordstrom deemed it "the masterwork of [Sendak's] life." Myself, I was past the picture-book phase in 1970, so I can't say what I thought of it as a child; today, though I am delighted by the art, the story strikes me as opaque and arbitrary, dreamlike but lacking true dream logic. I also find the rising dough and the ejaculatory milk bath and the cock's crow, I don't know . . . risible? There, I said it, though this reaction may well indicate a failing on my part, the residue of a stubbornly puerile sense of humor.

I think a bigger problem with *In the Night Kitchen* is that there isn't much *there* there aside from the symbolism: if you're not parsing what's happening down below, you're not left with much on the surface. Or, to put it another way: I don't think many kids are dying to find out what happens to Mickey next. Which is not to say that you can't write a children's story about children's sexuality—as we've seen, many fairy tales ply those waters—or that you can't write and draw a comparatively explicit one, such as *In the Night Kitchen.* The problem is that the book reads as if that's precisely what Sendak set out to do, and then reverse-engineered the tale—from the outside in, as it were. And yet, if there is an implicit suggestion here that children should not be afraid or ashamed of awakening sexuality, that moral is all to the good; and again, plenty of people, young and old, love and respond to *In the Night Kitchen.* I reiterate this due to critical modesty as well as a fear that Sendak, who also held a lifelong grudge against "flaccid fuckhead" Salman Rushdie for a respectfully mixed review of one of Sendak's later books—"I called up the Ayatollah, nobody knows that," Sendak once joked—might have left behind a ghost.

Outside Over There is more accessible than *In the Night Kitchen.* You can lose yourself in its lush, exquisite illustrations, painted in a romantic style perfect for a story in which Sendak plants both feet firmly in a traditional fairy-tale world: "Grimm country," as he put it. The story, set more or less in the Grimms' own era, concerns a young girl, Ida, who is charged with looking after her unnamed baby sister "when Papa was at sea, and Mama in the arbor." Alas, baby is kidnapped by some goblins when Ida isn't paying close enough attention, but with help from a magic horn, a gift from Papa, Ida rescues her sister from becoming "a nasty goblin's bride" and all is set right. Sendak told interviewers that the tale drew on his childhood fears about the Lindbergh baby kidnapping and, closer to home, his terror when his older sister briefly lost him one day at the 1939 World's Fair. As he had with *Where the Wild Things Are*, he called *Outside Over There* an "exorcism" and pronounced it his "most personal" book, which was surely saying something. You sense the story's deep meaning for Sendak even without his explications, but the effect, for me, is like listening to a detailed description of someone else's dream: curious, but maybe not involving. For all we know, that may be how plenty of fairy tales got started, too: with some plowman or village busybody going on about a dream he or she couldn't shake. If so, centuries of retellings surely served a Darwinian purpose, honing and shaping and improving the story like an out-of-town tryout.

But I came to praise Sendak. He was never reticent about discussing his work and the work of other authors and illustrators he admired, and I think his most eloquent statement of purpose was the speech he gave in 1970 when accepting a Hans Christian Andersen Medal, a biannual award that functions more or less as the Nobel Prize of children's literature:

> In a way, I'd rather have been a composer of operas and songs, and I must turn to music to describe something of what I am after. The concentrated face of Verdi's Falstaff or a Hugo Wolf song—where music and words mix and blend and incredibly excite—defines my ideal. Here words and music form a magic compound, a "something else," more than music, more than words. My wish is to combine—in words and pictures, faithfully and fantastically—my weird, Old Country–New Country childhood; my obsession with shtetl life, its spirit; and the illuminating visions especially loved artists have shown me. All this, mixed and beaten and smoothed into picture-book form that has

something resembling the lush, immediate beauty of music and all its deep, unanalyzable mystery. Most of all, the mystery—that is the cherished goal.

The fusion of mystery and immediacy lies at the heart of fairy tales' power, too (and probably that of any worthwhile art, if you get right down to it). I would wager this insight explains why, when Sendak illustrated a 1973 collection of the Grimms' tales translated by the poets Lore Segal and Randall Jarrell, the collaborators titled it *The Juniper Tree*, after a fairy tale that is one of the most immediate and visceral in the Grimms' canon but also one of the most unfathomable.

"It is a long time ago now, as much as two thousand years, maybe," the story begins quietly. A couple yearn for a child. One winter day, the wife pricks her finger while standing in the snow under a juniper tree that grows in their front yard. Blood falls on the snow; the woman sighs and says, "If only I had a child as red as blood and as white as snow." Nine months later she does—a son. She immediately dies from happiness, and, per her request, is buried under the juniper tree. An ironic tragedy, and that is only the preamble.

The man remarries and has a daughter with his new wife, but the wife is jealous of her stepson and one day, after "the evil one got into her," she kills the boy by slamming the lid of a trunk on his neck and cutting off his head. In a rare introspective moment for a fairy-tale character, she expresses guilt about the murder, or at least fear that she will be caught. So she puts the boy's head back on his neck; sits the body in a chair so it looks alive; and then, when her daughter comes into the room, instructs her to box the boy's ears when he doesn't respond to a question. His head flies off his neck and the daughter, whose name we now learn is Ann Marie, believes it is she who has killed him. (The boy doesn't have a name.) Her mother tells Ann

Marie, "You just keep quiet and nobody will know. After all, it can't be helped now; we will stew him in a sour broth."

Ann Marie weeps but keeps her mother's secret when her father comes home and the mother claims the stepson has gone on a trip to visit relatives. She then feeds the father the stew made of his own son. He, unknowing, relishes it:

> "Ah wife, what good food this is! Give me some more." And the more he ate the more he wanted, and said, "Give me more. You can't have any of it; it's as if all of this were for me." And he ate and ate, and threw the bones under the table, and finished it all up.

As Joan Acocella observes, "You can hardly believe what you're reading." And the story goes on! Poor traumatized Ann Marie takes her brother's bones and buries them under the juniper tree, which magically grows to new heights, and then from out of the tree flies "this lovely bird that sang oh, so gloriously sweet and flew high into the air." This is the bird's "sweet" song:

> *My mother she butchered me,*
> *My father he ate me,*
> *My sister, little Ann Marie,*
> *She gathered up the bones of me*
> *And tied them in a silken cloth*
> *To lay under the juniper.*
> *Tweet twee, what a pretty bird am I!*

The bird sings first for a goldsmith, then a cobbler, then a miller, each time receiving a gift in exchange: a gold chain, a pair of red shoes, and a millstone. (Why everyone is delighted by the song rather than alarmed or outraged is not explained.) The bird flies back to the house, somehow carrying all three gifts, and sits outside in the juniper tree, continuing to sing its song:

> Inside the father, the mother, and Ann Marie were sitting at the table and the father said, "Ah, suddenly my heart feels so easy. Why do I feel so wonderfully good?" "No," said the mother, "I'm just so frightened as if there was a great storm coming." But Ann Marie sat and cried and cried.

Father continues to feel good, Ann Marie continues to cry, and the stepmother grows increasingly tortured.

> "I'm so frightened! My teeth are chattering and it's as if I had fire in my veins." And she tore at her bodice to loosen it, but Ann Marie sat in a corner crying and held her plate in front of her eyes and cried so hard she was getting it wet and messy. And so the bird sat in the juniper tree and sang:
> "My mother she butchered me."
> And so then the mother stopped her ears up and squeezed her eyes shut and did not want to see or hear, but in her ears it roared like the wildest of storms and her eyes burned and twitched like lightning.

The bird keeps singing its song, over and over. The father eventually goes outside and the bird gives him the gold chain. Ann Marie follows and receives the red shoes. But the stepmother remains rooted inside, suffering Dostoyevskian torment. The narrative gains a relentless fury and—unusually if not unprecedentedly for a fairy tale—descends into harrowing psychodrama:

But the woman was so frightened she fell full length on the floor and the cap fell off her head. And still the bird sang.

"My mother she butchered me."

"I wish I were a thousand miles under the earth so I didn't have to hear it."

"My father he ate me."

And the woman lay there as if she were dead.

How the storyteller ratchets up the drama here! It's like crosscutting in a film, and a century before D. W. Griffith. Finally, with her "hair standing straight on end like flaming fire," the stepmother can bear the agony of her guilt no longer and runs outside to see what present she will get:

And as she came out of the door, crunch! the bird threw the millstone on her head and she was squashed. The father and Ann Marie heard it and came out. There was steam and flames and fire rising from the spot, and when they were gone, there stood the little brother.

What does "The Juniper Tree" mean? I couldn't begin to say. Is it a story for children? Not mine. (Obviously, the answer in this and all such cases is: know the kids. They are people, not a category.) Bettelheim declined to grapple with "The Juniper Tree" in *The Uses of Enchantment*, not mentioning the tale even in passing, though it certainly explores some very primal family dynamics. I admire the story's narrative cunning in starting out with some standard fairy-tale tropes—the couple yearning for a child, the pinpricked finger, the dead good mother, the evil stepmother—and then leaping into such strange and alarming territory. I realize I'm about to commit the critical sin of anachronistic backfilling here, but I can't help feeling that the story has a postmodern prankishness lurking beneath its surface, as if the narrator is saying, "So you think you know fairy tales, do you?" In highlighting this one, Sendak and his collaborators seem to be answering, *No*, we can never know fairy tales. They remain wild things at heart.

For all that, the ending of "The Juniper Tree" is disarmingly sweet, if characteristically abrupt:

> [The boy] took his father and Ann Marie by the hand and the three of them were so happy and went into the house and sat down and ate their supper.

The end. The narrator doesn't mention whether or not the supper was still hot.

4

Why a Duck? The Uses of Talking Animals from Aesop to Beatrix Potter to Olivia the Pig

B eatrix Potter rarely deigned to be impressed. As a teenager, growing up in an emotionally stifling home in Victorian-era London, she turned a merciless eye toward all. Her tart appraisals of the paintings and drawings she saw on visits to museums and galleries—written in code in a private journal she never expected to be read by you or me or her several biographers—are almost as entertaining as the children's books she would begin publishing two decades later. "I say fearlessly that the Michelangelo is hideous and badly drawn," she wrote when she was eighteen of one work at the National Gallery, adding "I wouldn't give tuppence for it except as a curiosity." A Rubens fared only a little better. Though she admired the figures, she thought his overall composition "seems rather to want shadow and purpose." It was, she concluded, "rather higgledy-piggledy." She swooned over Leonardo's *Virgin of the Rocks*—"most marvelously painted"—but all the same felt it had "one or two ugly points, particularly the Virgin's head." The land- and seascapes of J. M. W. Turner she seems to have liked most wholeheartedly—she herself was most at home out of doors—though some of his drawings she deemed "enigmas to every eye but their author." Then again, this may have been a compliment.

Lest you think she had a thing only against Italian and French masters, she was no less impertinent toward her own work. Writing to a friend whose yellow tomcat she had used as a model for her paintings of the feline shopkeeper Ginger in her 1909 book *The Tale of Ginger and Pickles*, she observed of the friend's cat, "His colour is so unusual, I thought it was rather a shame to cover him up in clothes for the pictures, but unfortunately there is a demand for comic animals in coats, and *trousers*.[1] I generally refuse to supply trousers on any terms; but it is an unfortunate fact that animals in their own natural pretty fur coats don't sell so well as dressed up—and one has to consider the bills."

She was thirty-six when she published her first commercial book, *The Tale of Peter Rabbit*, in 1902, and though new to the trade she was nervy enough to bicker with her editor over whether the illustrations should be in black and white or color. She had already self-published a successful edition of *Peter Rabbit* with her own black-and-white drawings, and when the editor suggested she redo them in color for commercial publication she initially held firm, insisting that the added expense was not justified for reasons both economic (unlike most authors, she was canny about the business side of publishing from the get-go) and aesthetic. The palette would be hopelessly dull, she wrote with characteristic asperity, given "the rather uninteresting colour of the subjects which are most of them rabbit-brown and green."

---

[1] Italics Potter's. Perhaps, like many of us, she found the word *trousers* inherently silly and so gave it iconic topspin.

As everyone knows who grew up with the finished book and its winsome, tartly comic watercolors, Potter relented. (She found ways to liven her color scheme, adding splashes of red and orange with the help of radishes, goldfish, and an orange-throated bird that stands as silent witness to the hero's misadventures.) *The Tale of Peter Rabbit* was an instant success, selling out its first printing and going on to become one of the most popular children's books of all time, translated into more than thirty-five languages. And yet, despite those lovely watercolors, despite Peter's "quite new" blue jacket with its smart brass buttons, despite his cute little slipper shoes, and despite Peter's siblings being named Flopsy, Mopsy, and Cotton-tail, the book, like its author, is a tough cookie—cute at times but never sentimental. The story is set in motion with a fairy-tale prohibition, as Mrs. Rabbit warns her four children to stay away from Mr. McGregor's nearby garden. "[Y]our father had an accident there; he was put in a pie by Mrs. McGregor," she explains. Though somewhat delicately stated—after his "accident," Mr. Rabbit was merely "put" in a pie; we are spared the skinning and mincing—this is an alarming start for a bunny-rabbit story. Children's literature bleeds absent parents, but few are missing because they became dinner. Aside from Mr. Rabbit, the only others I can think of are James's mother and father in *James and the Giant Peach*: They are eaten on the book's first page by a rhinoceros at the London Zoo. Does Little Red Riding Hood's grandmother count?

An illustration of Mrs. McGregor serving her husband the horrid pie did not survive the transition from Potter's self-published edition, but this was due to her unhappiness with her rendering of Mrs. McGregor's figure rather than to any fear of traumatizing young readers. Nevertheless, the pie in question announces the story's life-and-death stakes: when Peter sneaks into the forbidden garden and gorges on lettuce, radishes, French beans, and parsley, and when Mr. McGregor finally spots him and starts chasing him hither and yon with a sharp-looking rake, Peter's punishment for disobeying his mother is potentially several degrees more dire than a scolding or even a spanking. He flees, is momentarily caught in a gooseberry net, hides in a watering can, just misses being crushed under Mr. McGregor's boot, and finally catches his breath in a doorway, now realizing he has no idea how to find his way home. He is exhausted, scared, and, worst of all, lost, which for a child, so dependent on home and parents, is no mere annoyance but an invitation to existential terror. Potter pauses here to underscore Peter's aloneness—not flinching, maybe even luxuriating in it:

> An old mouse was running in and out over the old stone door-step, carrying peas and beans to her family in the wood. Peter asked her the way to the gate, but she had such a large pea in her mouth that she could not answer. She only shook her head at him. Peter began to cry.

As Maurice Sendak, who considered himself a "true-blue Potterite," once wrote: "The tiny scene has the exact quality of a nightmare: the sense of being trapped and frightened and finding the rest of the world . . . too busy keeping itself alive to help save you." Tough cookie Beatrix, however, isn't done putting Peter through the wringer, though as with the mother mouse rendered mute by a large pea, her details remain delightfully wrought:

> Presently, [Peter] came to a pond. . . . A white cat was staring at some gold-fish, she sat very, very still, but now and then the tip of her tail twitched as if it were alive. Peter thought it best to go away without speaking to her; he had heard about cats from his cousin, little Benjamin Bunny.

We have all of us seen this cat before, if not from a rabbit's perspective; among her many talents, Potter was an astute observer of animal behavior. In the end, she allows Peter to find his way to safety, though minus the new blue jacket and slipper shoes. Even here the book maintains a certain flintiness. Having finally found his way off the McGregor property, Peter is stripped to his animal essence, running on four legs instead of toddling upright on two. He sprints home and collapses on his mother's kitchen floor, spent. "I am sorry to say that Peter was not very well during the evening," Potter reports. While he is dosed with a tablespoon of chamomile tea and sent to bed, "Flopsy, Mopsy, and Cotton-tail had bread and milk and blackberries for supper." That is the final line of the tale, aside from "THE END."

I remember fixating on that supper as a child. I think I felt that despite his misbehavior, Peter deserved a happier ending following his ordeal. And for a child is there anything more unhappy and unjust than your siblings enjoying a treat without you? Even Max, in *Where the Wild Things Are*, finds his still-hot supper waiting for him—despite threatening to eat his own mother and then sailing off to carouse with monsters. And yet, though parent-eating in Sendak should be taken as a symbolic rather than a literal threat, it is Potter's most famous book rather than Sendak's which is deemed so sweet and cuddly that you can outfit an entire nursery in Peter Rabbit gear, from the usual blankets, sheets, and night-lights to window valences and special ceramic boxes for storing first locks of hair and lost baby teeth. (This is not a recent development; Potter, who designed Peter Rabbit dolls and wallpaper herself, was what we now call an early adopter when it came to merchandising.) But which book, in the end, offers more succor? Sendak wears his anxieties on his sleeve, but he has a big, sloppy heart. Potter can come off as a bit of a Mary Poppins figure: magical, but also stern and exacting. Sendak himself refers to the "hard Potter stare." The hero of her first book had been "very naughty," she writes, which

is fair; but does Peter deserve the scared-straight treatment? What are
we to make of this story in the end? It is a cautionary tale, even a kind
of horror story in its way, and yet it is also sweet and hugely charming.
The closer you look at it, the odder it gets.

Animal stories have long had a special hold on the human imagination. Aesop, who knew something about the subject, is credited with
the following anecdote:

> Demades, a famous Greek orator, was once addressing an assem-
> bly at Athens on a subject of great importance and in vain tried
> to fix the attention of his hearers. They laughed among them-
> selves, watched the sports of the children, and in twenty other
> ways showed their want of concern in the subject of the discourse.
> Demades, after a short pause, spoke as follows: "Ceres one day
> journeyed in company with a swallow and eel." At this point there
> was marked attention and every ear strained now to catch the
> words of the orator.

On the one hand, this is a self-serving anecdote. (It also implies that
swallows and eels commanded more interest among the ancients than
they generate today.) On the other hand, the fact that we are still reading Aesop proves his point. The fact that contemporary advertisers
resort to using animal characters to sell boring insurance products—
think of the Geico gecko or the Aflac duck—also proves his point.[2]

---

[2]Aesop may or may not have been an actual person. No one seems to know. If he did
exist, he is said by some traditions to have been born around 620 BCE, possibly in
Asia Minor, or in Ethiopia (from which the name Aesop may be derived). Allegedly a
slave, he was said to have been freed because of his great wit and storytelling skills. He
is also said to have had a hunchback, a misshapen head, a potbelly, bandy legs, and a

If fairy tales often echo otherwise unspoken psychological fears and conflicts, animal stories, very broadly put, can serve a somewhat opposite purpose, looking outward and shining a not always flattering light on the real world. Consider the very hard truths contained in some of Aesop's fables—an important influence on Potter, who loved them as a child and who as an adult wrote and illustrated her own version of "The Country Mouse and the City Mouse." Like that fable, the ones most people remember tend to be gentle satires of human foibles such as "The Dog and His Reflection" (greed), "The Grasshopper and the Ant" (laziness), or "The Fox and the Grapes" (spite). Others celebrate humble virtues, such as "The Tortoise and the Hare" (slow and steady wins the race) and "The Mouse and the Lion," in which the arrogant king of all beasts scoffs at the notion that a tiny mouse could ever be of service to him but learns otherwise when the mouse chews him free from a hunter's net.

Perhaps these fables have endured in the West because they promote vaguely Christian values, like humility. But there are other fables in Aesop's canon, such as "The Lion, the Fox, and the Donkey," with lessons more like those we associate with Machiavelli or the realpolitik of, say, Henry Kissinger:

A lion, a donkey, and a fox formed a partnership and went out hunting. When they had taken a quantity of game the lion told

---

speech impediment. By one account he became an ambassador for King Croesus of Lydia, traveling all over Greece and meeting his end when he angered the people of Delphi (for policy reasons too complex to go into here) and was thrown off a cliff. The fables attributed to him originated as long ago as 2000 BCE and possibly even earlier. The first written collection, now lost, is believed to date to 300 BCE. The oldest surviving collection, numbering ninety-four fables, in Latin, dates to 100 CE. A different collection of more than two hundred fables, in Greek, survives from the second century. Other fables have been accrued under Aesop's name over the centuries, and there is no definitive text.

the donkey to share it out. The donkey divided it into three equal parts and bade the lion choose one—on which the lion leaped at him in a fury and devoured him. Then he told the fox to divide it. The fox collected nearly all of it into one pile, leaving only a few trifles for himself, and told the lion to make his choice. The lion asked who taught him to share things in that way. "What happened to the donkey?" he answered.

That last is a rhetorical question. Aesop's moral: "We learn wisdom by seeing the misfortunes of others." Though harsh, that is a positive spin on the story; its moral could just as well have been "Might makes right," which is in fact the moral from another of Aesop's fables, "The Donkey and the Lion," in which, to poach all the spoils of another joint hunt, the lion has only to *threaten* to kill the donkey. (Perhaps a third lesson to be drawn here is that donkeys should forgo hunting altogether and stick to being herbivores.)

My favorite fable of Aesop's is "The Wolf and the Lamb," because its power politics are so naked, ghastly, and amusing:

A wolf, seeing a lamb drinking from a river, wanted to find a specious pretext for devouring him. He stood higher up the stream and accused the lamb of muddying the water so that he could not drink. The lamb said he drank only with the tip of his tongue, and that in any case he was standing lower down the river and could not possibly disturb the water higher up. When this excuse foiled him the wolf said, "Well, last year you insulted my father." "I wasn't even born then," replied the lamb. "You are good at finding answers," said the wolf, "but I'm going to eat you all the same."

If this were a story about humans, you would take it as a scene from *GoodFellas* or *The Sopranos*. The moral: "When a man is determined to get his knife into someone, he will turn a deaf ear to any plea, however just." It is hard to argue with the truth of that, though it might seem a dark, even amoral lesson for a children's story.[3] Then again, Aesop's fables, like fairy tales, originated in an age when the demarcation between childhood and adulthood wasn't nearly as distinct and impermeable as we like to think it is today, and no one saw a need to shelter children from the world's nastier realities, such as the tendency of the powerful to take advantage of the weak, and the tendency of the weak to be unable to do much about it. This is another way animal stories often differ from fairy tales: the latter, however crazy and horrific they get, tend to deliver some form of justice, however rough. Many classic animal stories have no more concern for justice than does a lion or wolf; if they reflect human behavior, they reflect us at our most Hobbesian.

In his 1962 book *Totemism*, the French anthropologist Claude Lévi-Strauss famously observed that humankind had learned early on that animals weren't just "good to eat" but also "good to think" with. Given that they come in all sizes and shapes, attributes and habitats, winged, legged, finned, and tentacled, animals dovetail with the human instinct to sort, compare, and label; for toddlers, they are right up there with colors, shapes, and numbers as essential objects of fascination. Animals also served for millennia as nifty canvases for the deep-seated human need to color the world with our own prejudices and preoccupations. Thus the lion, when not terrorizing donkeys, came to represent nobility and courage, the fox cunning, the mouse humility, the snake evil. At the same time, given that animals' essences are even more unknowable than ours, they could also appear touched by the divine. People told

---

[3]Aesop's (and nature's) basic premise here underlay as well the best cartoon of the 2016 presidential campaign: Paul Noth's *New Yorker* panel in which a pair of sheep gaze admiringly at a billboard for a wolf politician with the slogan I AM GOING TO EAT YOU. Says one sheep to the other, "He tells it like it is."

stories about animals, created myths around animals, identified with animals, worshipped animals. Along with the sun, the moon, and the stars, they provoked longing and sparked dreams.

Blame science; industrialization; urbanization; monotheism; the fact that many twenty-first-century Americans have almost no contact with animals aside from pets, pigeons, and roadkill—but for whatever reason they have become far less central over recent centuries in religion, art, and storytelling, at least in Western culture. If you want to chart how far birds and beasts and even fish and insects have tumbled in human estimation, imagine how Bastet, the ancient Egyptian cat goddess—variously, across dynasties and kingdoms, a warrior goddess, a protector of other gods and of Egypt itself, a goddess of motherhood and fertility and the moon; not the most powerful Egyptian god, but still a biggie—would feel today if she could go on YouTube and scroll through its endless trove of silly cat videos: cats getting stuck in Kleenex boxes and hamster balls, cats pretending to play keyboards, cats making funny faces and falling off shelves, cats throwing up. The fact that some of these videos have received upward of fifty million views suggests animals still have a hold on a corner of the human imagination, though this corner is flattering neither to them nor to us.

Animal stories do retain pride of place on children's bookshelves, where you can still find not just Aesop but also more recent works that were originally written for adults—*Black Beauty*, *The Call of the Wild*, and *Watership Down*. Expand the age range a bit and the list would also include George Orwell's anti-Stalin allegory from 1945, *Animal Farm*, now a middle-school staple. It sure *sounds* kid-friendly; at least it must have sounded so to the mothers in my elementary school's PTA, who booked an animated version of *Animal Farm* to keep the student body occupied in the multipurpose room one afternoon during parent-teacher conferences. I remember being puzzled by an entertainment that looked for all the world like a Disney movie, with cartoon pigs, sheep, geese, and dogs, but that told a grim, violent, and (to me at the age of six or seven) not very interesting tale about power, corruption, and sophistry in which some of the animals were not just naughty but cruel and vengeful. There were some frightened tears in the audience, and letters of apology were sent home with us the next day.[4]

For kids, animal characters are avatars—stand-ins reflecting their literal smallness and relative powerlessness in the face of adult omnipotence. This is probably one reason there are many more picture books about bunnies and mice and kittens than there are about elephants and rhinoceroses and great white sharks. (Dinosaurs, being both huge and extinct, frightening but dumb, are sui generis.) There is also a bit of a high-low trick going on here: conjuring animals that speak and dress and behave and misbehave like people seems to scratch a long-standing anthropomorphic itch, a wish to extend kinship at least as far as our fellow mammals, if not so far as bugs and fish; and yet, at the same time, there is inherent comedy when animals act like people, a party-trick inappropriateness, as anyone knows who has ever put a hat on a dog or felt guilty about laughing at a chimp riding a tricycle. We want to feel solidarity with animals and yet flaunt our large-brain, opposable-thumb superiority.

There are more naturalistic animal stories. I myself liked Potter and Aesop well enough—the animal characters I *loved* were Snoopy and Bugs Bunny—but as a kid I was also drawn to books such as *Black Beauty* and *Bambi*, which take place in worlds not too unlike our own.

---

[4]Here's a fun fact: The film was a 1954 British production that, twenty years later, was revealed to have been underwritten by a CIA office under the leadership of future Watergate burglar E. Howard Hunt.

I was a particular fan of dog books, devouring *Lassie Come-Home,* *Old Yeller, Lad: A Dog,* and that infamous boy-and-his-bloodhounds weepie, *Where the Red Fern Grows,* in which not just one but *two* dogs die at the end. All of these books exert a lurid, even sadistic undertow, as their four-legged heroes are beaten, whipped, lost, put down— noble sufferers, like pretty ringlet-haired mothers in silent movies. As Margaret Blount points out in her history of the genre, *Animal Land: The Creatures of Children's Fiction,* novels like *Black Beauty* are descendants of books that began to appear in English in the early 1800s, aimed at encouraging children to be kind to animals—titles such as *The History of a Field Mouse, The Escapes of a Hare,* and *The Adventures of Poor Puss.* These stories' "descriptions of quite refined animal torture mostly carried out by cruel children may have had some moral effect" on their readers, Blount writes, though she is skeptical: "One feels kind children would have been made unhappy by them while cruel or amoral children would have been merely given ideas." Indeed, I shudder to think what inspiration certain childhood acquaintances of mine, who were known to put salt on slugs and burn ants with magnifying glasses, might have drawn from this passage from *The Life and Adventures of Poor Puss*—not to be confused with the previously mentioned but unaffiliated *The Adventures of Poor Puss* (IP laws were not as robust in the 1800s as they are today)—which picks up as its beleaguered heroine is returning home after narrowly avoiding being torn apart by hunting dogs:

> Three boys who had been to school, were playing in the fields. Each boy had a large stick on his shoulder, and as soon as they saw Puss, they ran after her. She again took refuge in a tree, but the boys threw stones at her and hit her so hard, that she at length fell senseless to the ground. One of the boys seized poor Puss; and they were going to have some rare sport as they said, by fastening

the cat on a board and then launching it on the pond after which they would set the dogs after her. . . . Everything was in readiness: Puss was bound upon the board, and they were just going to sail it into the middle of the pond, when the schoolmaster came past, and the boys were obliged, after receiving a good flogging, to set poor Puss at liberty.

You will be glad to learn that the drawings in this short book do not provide any useful instruction in knot tying or cat immobilization; and the boys' flogging would seem to fulfill the author's obligation to portray animal abuse in a negative light, just as the old Hollywood Production Code insisted that movie mobsters receive their come-uppance no matter how entertaining their crimes.

Written in 1877, *Black Beauty* is the first great landmark of this genre. Anna Sewell's inspiration was to tell the story in the horse's own voice:

What I suffered with that rein for four long months in my lady's carriage, it would be hard to describe. . . . Before that, I never knew what it was to foam at the mouth, but now the action of the sharp bit on my tongue and jaw, and the constrained position of my head and throat, always caused me to froth at the mouth, more or less. . . . Besides this, there was a pressure on my windpipe, which often made my breathing very uncomfortable; when I returned from my work, my neck and chest were strained and painful, my mouth and tongue tender, and I felt worn and depressed.

Sewell's story and characterizations were strong enough that *Black Beauty*—handed out free to carriage drivers, grooms, and stable boys—transcended its role as polemic and has endured to this day.

Though its horses understand human speech, and though they talk among themselves with proper Victorian stiffness, they otherwise behave more or less as actual horses do, and *Black Beauty* is often cited as the first "realistic" animal novel. But enough of that. Unrealistic animal stories are much more fun, and their mayhem, visited upon fantasy characters, is more entertaining and happily guilt-free.

Aesop's fables had a successor of sorts in *The History of Reynard the Fox*, a European folk epic that dates to the twelfth century. Various editions of *Reynard* began to be published throughout the continent nearly as soon as printing was invented—they were some of the first bestsellers in history. The book is an episodic, loosely knit political satire in which the lion, the king of the beasts, and members of his court try to bring the disreputable title character to heel for a multitude of sins. If Aesop tends to shrug at abuses of power—the fables are no more interested in questioning the lion's and wolf's prerogatives than they are in questioning the wind's—*Reynard* suggests a European culture groping toward humanism with its celebration of a hero who not only pushes back against power but bests it. Unfortunately, the fox's main "virtues"—cunning, ruthlessness, and borderline sociopathy—proved Enlightenment was still a ways off.

The book can be surprisingly rough reading. As Stephen Greenblatt, a critic and literary historian, writes in his introduction to James Simpson's 2015 translation of *Reynard* from Middle English into a vaguely modern idiom, "The hero is not only an inveterate liar but also a sadist, a rapist, and a murderer. Apart from his immediate family, anyone who comes too near to him is grievously injured—scalded, bitten, scratched, mutilated, and (if tasty) eaten." In one raucous, representative episode, Reynard sets an elaborate trap for one of the king's emissaries, Tybert the cat, which not only causes Tybert to lose an eye but also robs a human priest of his right testicle. Don't worry, Reynard assures the priest's wife (whoever first told these stories was far naughtier than Peter Rabbit), "Even if the priest has lost one of his stones, it won't hinder his congress with you. There's many a chapel in this world in which only one bell is rung." *The History of Reynard the Fox* ends with its antihero not in chains but installed as the king's highest-ranking counselor—as dark and ironic an ending as that of *Chinatown* or *Nashville* or any other disillusioned Watergate-era Hollywood masterpiece.

In my view, it is never too early to begin teaching children to be cynical about politics; back in the day, *Reynard* was packaged for young nobles and children of the merchant classes as a book of moral instruction (by negative example, one hopes). But the violence, more gratuitous than in most fairy tales, as gleeful as an Itchy and Scratchy cartoon, occasionally as ugly as a torture porn horror film, will put off many parents if not necessarily youngsters.

More overtly kid-friendly are the Brer Rabbit stories, which were a huge influence not only on Beatrix Potter but also on Kenneth Grahame, A. A. Milne, and Rudyard Kipling. In besting the larger, stronger, carnivorous likes of Brer Fox, Brer Bear, and Brer Wolf, Brer Rabbit makes good use of his native smarts. Like Reynard he preys on his foes' vanity and appetites. Unlike Reynard, he makes for a genuinely sympathetic hero, being so much lower on the food chain. His best-known tale is the one in which Brer Fox sets a trap by fashioning a homunculus out of turpentine and tar and leaving it by the side of the road—the so-called Tar Baby. Brer Rabbit, who is usually smarter than this, tries to engage the Tar Baby in conversation. When it doesn't respond, Brer Rabbit gets angry, accusing the thing of being "stuck up" and punching it in the head. He himself is now "stuck up," as Brer Fox jokes when he shows up to claim his prey, at which point Brer Rabbit regains his wits. *I don't care what you do to me*, he tells Brer Fox. *Hang me, drown me, skin me, pluck my eyeballs, tear out my ears by the roots, cut off my legs, but please, please, don't fling me in the briar patch.* Naturally that's what Brer Fox does: he flings Brer Rabbit into the Briar Patch, which is exactly what Brer Rabbit wanted. He taunts Brer Fox while making his escape through the brush: *Born and bred in the briar patch! Born and bred in the briar patch!* This story might well be the foundational text of reverse psychology. (Why Brer Fox is canny enough to foresee that Brer Rabbit would get into a physical altercation with the Tar Baby, but not canny enough to see through Brer Rabbit's ruse, is one of literature's great mysteries.)

I paraphrased the dialogue just above because the stories, in the versions that were first set down in print, are, let us say, problematic. Likely originating in Africa—there is some intriguing overlap with both Aesop and *Reynard*, suggesting all sorts of narrative cross-pollination[5]—and retold and refined by African Americans, the stories as many people know them today were written down in the late 1800s by a white newspaperman, Joel Chandler Harris. He first heard them from enslaved men and women when he was a poor teenager in Georgia working on an antebellum plantation as a low-level hand, occupying a middle ground in the era's racial and class hierarchies. Harris has received praise as a folklorist, from W. E. B. Du Bois among others, and he wrote the stories in a Georgia plantation dialect that some linguists have said is accurate—he himself sought to distinguish his work from what he called "the intolerable misrepresentations of the minstrel stage"—but nevertheless it is a dialect that is hard on twenty-first-century eyes and ears. Harris also chose, as a framing device, to put the tales into the voice of a character he named Uncle Remus, an elderly black storyteller who entertains the unnamed young son of the plantation owner, "Marse John," and his wife, "Miss Sally." Uncle Remus, Harris once said, "was not an invention of my

---

[5]Some folklorists see that overlap as evidence of an African origin for Aesop, if he was an actual person, or at least for "his" fables.

own, but a human syndicate, I might say, of three or four old dark-ies whom I knew. I just walloped them together into one person and called him 'Uncle Remus.'" In his introduction to his first collec-tion, *Uncle Remus: His Songs and His Sayings*, Harris further notes that the "venerable" Remus is of the type who has "nothing but pleasant memories of the discipline of slavery," along with "all the prejudices of caste and pride of family that were the natural results of that system." Harris, who died in 1908, was a relatively enlightened man for his time when it came to racial issues—he spoke out against lynching and for educating blacks—but I think it is fair to say, at least, that he was still a man of his time, with his own prejudices of caste. In the words of the African American critic and philosopher Alain Locke, from a 1940 essay, Harris "rendered as much poetic justice to the Negro as an orthodox Southerner could."

Across several volumes, Harris wrote down nearly two hundred stories. For all their humor, the tales reflect a lot of hard-won wis-dom. In one, a descendant of Aesop's "The Tortoise and the Hare," Brer Terrapin challenges Brer Rabbit to a race that Brer Terrapin only pretends to run, stationing his identical-looking wife and children at markers along the way to fool Brer Rabbit into thinking the turtle is faster than he. It works—you *can* trick a trickster—and Brer Ter-rapin collects a fifty-dollar bet. *But Uncle Remus, that was cheating,* says the little white boy at the end of the tale. *Of course it was,* says Uncle Remus, who is far more caustic and interesting in the books than he was in the awful 1946 Disney adaptation, *Song of the South,* by which most people remember him.[6] *Animals began to cheat,* Uncle Remus continues, *and then men took it up, and it kept spreading. It's*

---

[6]The film's opening title card sets its lamentable tone: "Out of the humble cabin, out of the singing heart of the Old South have come the tales of Uncle Remus, rich in simple truths, forever fresh and new."

mighty catching, so keep your eyes open, honey. This is not a world where
slow and steady wins the race. But it is also not a world where Brer
Wolf can just gobble up lambs or whoever else catches his eye. Here
the vulnerable often triumph over the powerful—which to modern
tastes feels more like justice than the bullying and butchery in Aesop
and *Reynard.* That these stories were told and embellished by enslaved
people speaks for itself as an act of imaginative defiance.[7]

Animal stories in the twentieth century took on, deliberately or not,
the political and social colorations of their own era. You can, if you
want, read the original Babar and Curious George books, which were

---

[7]The debate over Harris's appropriations has continued through the civil rights era
and into the present day. Thanks to numerous rewritten editions of the tales that
have been scrubbed of dialect and of Uncle Remus, including one by Margaret Wise
Brown, Harris himself is rarely read these days. But some scholars and critics, and
not just antebellum apologists, have found redeeming virtues in Uncle Remus. See
"Black Father: The Subversive Achievement of Joel Chandler Harris," a 2004 essay
in *African American Review,* in which the author, Robert Cochran, declares that the
Uncle Remus books' "multiple ironies were not only not lost upon [Harris] but were
in fact something of his stock-in-trade." In Cochran's estimation, Uncle Remus "is
revealed as a secret hero of Harris's work, a figure wholly worthy of comparison with
Brer Rabbit himself"—an even subtler and more subversive trickster, perhaps.

But the last word here will go to Alice Walker, who grew up in Harris's
hometown—Eatonton, Georgia—and first heard the Brer Rabbit tales not from Harris but from her parents, who had heard them from their parents and grandparents. In
a 1981 essay, "The Dummy in the Window," Walker writes of her hometown, "There
is now and has been for several years an Uncle Remus museum. There was also, until a
few years ago, an Uncle Remus restaurant. There used to be a dummy of a black man,
an elderly, kindly, cotton-haired darkie, seated in a rocking chair in the restaurant
window. In fantasy, I frequently liberated him using Army tanks and guns. Blacks,
of course, were not allowed in this restaurant." She then discusses *Song of the South*:
"Uncle Remus, in the movie, saw fit largely to ignore his own children and grandchil-
dren in order to pass on our heritage—indeed our birthright—to patronizing white
children, who seemed to regard him as a kind of talking teddy bear." She concludes,
"There I was, at an early age, separated from my own folk culture by an invention."

written by Europeans and date to 1931 and 1939 respectively, as coded defenses of colonialism. *The Story of Ferdinand*, published in America in 1936 on the eve of the Spanish Civil War, was an instant success but the hero, a bull who refuses to fight, was condemned by dissenters as a stooge for whatever ideologies they happened to be irked by. "Too-subtle readers see in Ferdinand everything from a fascist to a pacifist to a burlesque sit-down striker," *Life* magazine wrote in 1938.[8] During World War II, Margaret Wise Brown worked on a manuscript, *Bomb Proof Bunnies*, intended to comfort British children during the blitz. She also wrote *The War in the Woods*, which, according to Amy Gary, was "a comical story in which a bear declares that all the animals in the forest must behave like him." (*Heil*, Yogi.) Neither manuscript was finished.

E. B. White's *Stuart Little*, the story of a mouse born to a human family, published in 1945, could be read as a parable of modernist alienation, albeit a drily funny one. Or not. As Leonard Marcus writes, echoing Lévi-Strauss and referring to animal tales in general, "Does not the imaginative distance at which fantasy-animals stand from the reader both put the story's lessons into clearer relief, *and* leave the reader free to dismiss—or enjoy—the whole thing as sheer nonsense?" Sometimes. Hypersensitive racists neither dismissed nor

---

[8]Ernest Hemingway published a silly, unintentionally self-parodic riposte to *The Story of Ferdinand* in 1951 entitled "The Faithful Bull." It begins: "One time there was a bull and his name was not Ferdinand and he cared nothing for flowers. He loved to fight and he fought with all the other bulls of his own age, or any age, and he was a champion. . . . He was always ready to fight and his coat was black and shining and his eyes were clear." This bull is so magnificent that his owner decides not to sacrifice him in the ring and instead puts him to pasture as a stud, but the bull falls in love with one cow and refuses to mate with the others—thus the story's title. Now useless for breeding, he ends up in the ring after all. "He fought wonderfully and everyone admired him and the man who killed him admired him the most." Make of this what you will; I'm sure Hemingway's wives did.

enjoyed *The Rabbits' Wedding*, a 1958 picture book written and illustrated by Garth Williams, which depicted a marriage between a white and a black rabbit. Efforts to ban the book in Alabama failed, though in some southern libraries it was hidden away on reserve shelves. Williams insisted his rabbits had been drawn black and white strictly for graphic reasons. "I was completely unaware that animals with white fur, such as white polar bears and white dogs and white rabbits, were considered blood relations of white human beings," he said. "I was only aware that a white horse next to a black horse looks very picturesque—and my rabbits were inspired by early Chinese paintings of black and white horses in mist landscapes."

Roald Dahl's *Fantastic Mr. Fox*, from 1970, could be read as a less brutal update of Reynard, recast as an ecological parable rather than a political one. But many of the most popular American animal series of the last fifty years—Little Bear, Frances, Arthur—take place in what appear to be fairly typical suburban or urban settings, indistinguishable from human cities and suburbs aside from being populated by talking bears, mice, badgers, aardvarks, and dogs. These are mostly gentle stories, far removed from Reynard's world or Brer Rabbit's or even Peter Rabbit's, but they still benefit from the distancing effect Marcus describes.[9] Ian Falconer's Olivia is bright and passionate but also flighty and spoiled; being a pig softens her harsher edges. The author and illustrator Kevin Henkes has created an alternative Middle America populated by mice characters in picture books such as *Owen*, *Chester's Way*, *Chrysanthemum*, *Wemberly Worried*, and the incomparable *Lily's Purple Plastic Purse*. Aside from having fur, big ears, and

---

[9]The wonderful picture book *No, David!*—a Caldecott Honor book written and illustrated by David Shannon—neatly reverses this formula. David, a high-energy, mischievous boy given to writing on walls and tipping over fishbowls, hears literally nothing but "No, David!" from his mother, as if he were a misbehaving puppy, until the final spread, where Mom tells him she loves him.

long, hairless tails, Henkes's mice behave pretty much the way human children do, with the same joys and anxieties. These books are among the most acute social comedies for children this side of Beverly Cleary. Some of them deal with emotions and themes that are unusual for picture books—shame, for instance, in *Lily's Purple Plastic Purse*—or plumb some of the more familiar ones, such as individuality in *Chrysanthemum*, but with far more nuance and depth than the usual knee-jerk, self-esteem-building, "pro-social" fare kids are often stuck with. The fact that Henkes's stories are about mice rather than humans does make them easier going for very young readers than they might otherwise be. Hearing a story about a first-grader who in a fit of pique writes her favorite teacher a mean letter that she can't undo is discomforting when the first-grader is a mouse; it might be unendurable if the first-grader were an actual girl, as would a tale about a real little boy sneaking into a garden and then losing all his clothes and being chased by a mean old man with a rake.

So back to Beatrix Potter. Her stories really exist on a plane of their own, poised between the wilder, more feral nature of Aesop's lions and Reynard and the more civilized likes of Frances, Olivia, and Lily. Like those latter-day characters, Potter's rabbits, kittens, mice, and hedgehogs dress and act like humans and yet they cling to their animalness, sometimes living in cottages, sometimes sleeping in burrows, sometimes drinking tea, sometimes eating the repulsive stuff animals actually eat. "Neither fish nor fowl . . . this work of the imagination defies pigeonholing," Sendak wrote of *The Tale of Peter Rabbit*. "Amazingly," he continued, "Peter is both endearing little boy and expertly-drawn rabbit. In one picture he stands most unrabbitlike, crying pitifully when there seems no way out of his dilemma. In another he bounds, leaving jacket behind, in a delightful rabbit bound, most unboylike, proving what we already know . . . that Beatrix Potter drew from careful observation of her subject." By way of contrast, I'm guessing even Ian Falconer and Kevin Henkes would admit that, as keen as each author's knowledge of children is, they are less well versed in the ways of actual pigs and mice. A key aspect of Potter's genius is that she keeps one foot firmly planted in each world, human and beast; her stories are familiar yet strange, cozy yet haunted by Darwinian menace. In her view, anthropomorphism had well-defined limits, as she noted by way of criticizing her contemporary Kenneth Grahame's *The Wind in the Willows*: "A frog may wear galoshes; but I don't hold with toads having beards and wigs."[10]

As in *Peter Rabbit*, death lurks as a matter-of-fact threat in many of her books, just as it does in the natural world—and as it most often doesn't in modern books for the very young, outside of fairy tales and therapeutic books about sick grandparents. A passionate outdoorswoman her whole life, and the owner of a large working farm that became her primary home in later years, Potter never shrinks from the "good to eat" side of Lévi-Strauss's equation. In *The Tale of Pigling Bland*, for instance, the hero and his brother are dressed in their Sunday clothes, their tails specially curled, and sent "to market" by their mother as if they were being shipped off to boarding school. (Potter is also on hand for the farewells, inserting herself into the action as she does on occasion.) What will happen at the market is never specified, but we adults can assume it will not be to Pigling Bland's advantage. (No one buys pigs for the milk.) In the end, after a series of scrapes and adventures on the road, Pigling Bland dances away into the sunset with a love interest, the fetching Pig-wig, "a perfectly lovely little

---

[10]I suspect her graphic approach to creating animal characters on the page may have been something like that of Garth Williams. He once wrote: "I start with the real animal, working over and over until I get the effect of human qualities and expressions and poses. I redesign the animal, as it were."

black Blackshire pig" with a double chin, but the couple's happiness is more tenuous and much harder-won than, say, that of the Owl and the Pussycat. I don't know what children make of *The Tale of Pigling Bland*—I don't remember hearing it when I was young—but as an adult, and a parent, I find the hero's trusting naïveté and the brusque way in which he is prematurely thrust into the world heartbreaking. He reminds me of the loving robot boy abandoned by his parents in Steven Spielberg's film *A.I.* We never learn what becomes of Pigling Bland's brother, lost along the way and supposedly returned to his mom by a policeman. Supposedly.

Potter herself grew up in London in a comfortable home, but one that she detested—her "unloved birthplace," as she later referred to it. Her father was a barrister with some artistic and social pretensions and a sizable fortune, thanks to his own father's textile plant in northern England. Beatrix's childhood seems to have been fairly cloistered, even by the standards of her class and era; as an unmarried woman—she was thirty-nine when she entered into her first romantic relationship, with her first editor (a man who died a month after they became engaged)—she remained under her parents' thumb for too much of her adult life, suffering at times from various fatiguing illnesses that were not then diagnosable. One biographer suspects she endured a serious bout of rheumatic fever. I'd guess depression figured in there, as well.

Her main escapes from her "Kensington prison" (Sendak's phrase) were her family's annual summer sojourns on pastoral properties in Scotland and the Lake District. She became an ardent and scrupulous student of nature, drawing animals from life as early as age eight or nine. She was allowed to take a few art classes but didn't like them, feeling they constricted her style, and so was mostly self-taught. Sir

John Everett Millais, the Pre-Raphaelite painter (his drowned *Ophelia* is probably his best-known work), told her when she was still a young woman, "Plenty of people can *draw*, but you . . . have observation." She not only sketched animals from life; she boiled dead ones and then assembled their skeletons to get a better understanding of their anatomy. In one of those snappish teenage journal entries, she dismisses a work by Raphael as proving that the artist "had never looked at a horse."

If I have made it sound as if Potter's was a ghoulish, morose, Wednesday Addams sort of childhood, that is probably not right. She and her younger brother, Bertram, kept what sounds like a small petting zoo's worth of beloved pets, shuttling them between London and the Potters' various summer homes. In *Beatrix Potter: A Life in Nature*, her biographer Linda Lear offers an inventory that promises there must have been a few high-spirited moments in the family's London home:

> The third floor nursery menagerie included, at various times, rabbits (Benjamin Bouncer and Peter), a green frog called Punch, several lizards, including Judy who was a special favorite, water newts, a tortoise, a frog, salamanders, many and different varieties of mice, a ring snake, several bats, a canary and a green budgerigar, a wild duck, a family of snails, several guinea pigs and later a hedgehog or two.

Potter continued to keep and travel with numerous pets throughout her life, basing some of her most beloved characters on creatures she herself had doted on, among them Peter Rabbit and his cousin Benjamin Bunny; the "two bad mice," Tom Thumb and Hunca Munca; Jemima Puddle-Duck; and Mrs. Tiggy-Winkle the hedgehog washerwoman. You get a sense of her working methods—and her patience with her less domesticated pets—from this letter she wrote while working on the book about the latter character:

> Mrs. Tiggy as a model is comical; so long as she can go to sleep on my knee, she is delighted, but if she is propped up on end for half an hour or more, she first begins to yawn pathetically, and then she *does* bite!

Writing and illustrating children's books was in fact a second career for Potter. In her twenties she had wanted to be an amateur naturalist—"amateur" in the Victorian sense of being rich, dedicated, though probably not formally educated in the subject, and definitely not employed. Through her own studies and forest explorations, she became an expert on fungi, collecting rare mushroom specimens and painting illustrations of them that were published in a mycological textbook twenty years after her death—not to cash in on her name but because the renderings were expert. She also made an important discovery about how fungi reproduce. (It has something to do with lichen is all I can say; I've read several accounts and still don't understand it.) However, she grew discouraged after her paper laying out her theories was presented on her behalf at the all-male Linnean Society of London, then one of Britain's leading scientific organizations, and the work dismissed without much if any serious consideration. (Her hypothesis was proved correct decades later.)

She had some success over the years selling witty illustrations of animals ice-skating and such for greeting cards. As a hobby she also wrote illustrated letters with made-up stories about her pets for children she knew, sons and daughters of friends. One friend, her former governess, suggested she try working the letters into books. She did. This was in 1900, and British publishers were chasing a boom in children's books set off in part by the success of *Little Black Sambo*, out the year before. The first result of Potter's efforts was *The Tale of Peter Rab-bit*. Eleven years later, on the eve of the Great War, she had nineteen books to her name, batting out two in most years. She slowed down after that, publishing only four more "tales" in her lifetime, ending in 1930 with *The Tale of Little Pig Robinson*, a riff on both *Robinson Crusoe* and "The Owl and the Pussycat." Her considerable energies had by then been redirected from books to tending and expanding the Lake District farm she had bought in 1905, having finally achieved independence with her earnings from her books. Her menagerie now included a husband, a local solicitor, whom she had married in 1913, at the age of forty-seven. She died thirty years later, leaving most of her property and much of her original artwork to Britain's National Trust for Places of Historic Interest or Natural Beauty, the great pas-sion of her later years.

Potter's tales are of such a high order that it is hard to pick a favor-ite, but everyone seems to have one. *Peter Rabbit* gets primogeniture points. Sendak cites his fondness for *The Tale of the Pie and the Patty-Pan*, a social satire about a cat named Ribby who invites a dog named Duchess to tea; with a touch of prop comedy, it plays out something like a Victorian version of *I Love Lucy.* I am fond of *The Tale of Jeremy Fisher* not so much for its story, which isn't all that eventful—Jeremy goes fishing to provide supper for his friends, a newt and a tortoise (who eats only salad anyway)—but for Potter's paintings, which I think are her best work. Jeremy, who seems to be a frog of the early nineteenth century, dresses in a waistcoat and breeches like an am-phibian Mr. Darcy, though in the Potter manner he also leaps with all due frogginess. The illustrations' luscious, liquid backgrounds, full of reeds, lily pads, and other water plants, demonstrate that Potter took her flora as seriously as her fauna. One painting of Jeremy lounging on a lily pad and eating a butterfly sandwich is proto-psychedelia, a nursery vision for opium eaters. As well, the text includes what I think is the single funniest passage in all of Potter, after Jeremy, having caught not a single fish, has to improvise for his guests:

> And instead of a nice dish of minnows—they had a roasted grass-hopper with lady-bird sauce; which frogs consider a beautiful treat; but *I* think it must have been nasty!

I wouldn't say that *The Tale of Jemima Puddle-Duck* is a favorite, but it is to my mind Potter's most compelling story, possibly because it is also her saddest, flirting with genuine loss. Jemima is frustrated because the farmer's wife won't let her hatch her own eggs. "She tried to hide her eggs," Potter writes, "but they were always found and carried off. Jemima Puddle-duck became quite desperate." Searching for a place to nest away from the farm, she encounters "an elegantly dressed gentleman" who we can see from the illustration is in fact a fox. With obvious ill intent, he suggests Jemima nest in his own woodshed. "But before you commence your tedious sitting," he adds, "I intend to give you a treat. Let us have a dinner-party all to ourselves! May I ask you to bring up some herbs from the farm-garden to make a savoury omelette? Sage and thyme and mint and two onions, and some parsley. I will provide lard for the stuff—lard for the omelette." The offer is taken at face value. "Jemima Puddle-duck was a simpleton; not even the mention of sage and onions made her suspicious," Potter observes coldly. Fortunately, Kep, a good-hearted collie—another real-life pet—gets wind of the plot and rounds up a couple of foxhound puppies who make short work of "the polite gentleman with sandy whiskers." Kep frees the still oblivious Jemima, but the rescue is not joyous: "Unfortunately the puppies rushed in and gobbled up all the eggs before [Kep] could stop them. . . . Jemima Puddle-duck was escorted home in tears on account of those eggs." The tale's coda:

She laid some more in June, and she was permitted to keep them herself: but only four of them hatched.

Jemima Puddle-duck said that it was because of her nerves; but she had always been a bad sitter.

THE END

Here is a rare example of Potter's toughness turning into hard-heartedness, even cruelty. She seems contemptuous of the poor blockhead Jemima, though her paintings of the white duck, who looks charming in her blue bonnet and pinkish shawl, betray grudging affection.

This is one thing I love about Potter: she took a genre, talking animal stories, with roots in myth and social satire and refashioned it as something singular and far more personal—a precursor to what Sendak would do with fairy tales. (No wonder he was a devotee.) In many of her stories you get a faint, tingly sense of emotions being worked out somewhere deep down below the surface, but Jemima's story fairly screams with it. Did Potter harbor conflicted feelings about not having had children, or bitterness about the early, sudden death of her fiancé, three years before *The Tale of Jemima Puddle-Duck* was published? Was she sublimating her anger at her parents, with whom she frequently clashed and who had opposed her engagement to a man "in trade"? Graham Greene, in a perceptive 1933 essay on Potter, wrote that he detected a "dark period" in her work:

> At some time between 1907 and 1909 Miss Potter must have passed through an emotional ordeal which changed the character of her genius. It would be impertinent to inquire into the nature of the ordeal. Her case is curiously similar to that of Henry James. Something happened which shook their faith in appearances. From *The Portrait of a Lady* onwards, innocence deceived, the treachery of friends, became the theme of James's greatest stories.

Is this true? Greene unaccountably dismissed *The Tale of Jeremy Fisher* as "a failure," so I would view everything he says on this subject with skeptical side-eye. On the other hand, *The Tale of Jemima Puddle-Duck* was published in 1908, in the middle of the supposed dark period, and it may well be what he had in mind. The tale really does have a strong Jamesian theme of innocence exploited, though here the story balances on a fulcrum of dinner rather than money, sex, and Old-World corruption. I will confess that these undercurrents and tensions make Potter's books far more interesting to me as an adult than I found them as a child, when they struck me as just a little bit twee—a word I wouldn't have used then, but an expression of a prejudice I surely harbored given my gravitation toward the funny pages and *Mad.*

Greene viewed *The Tale of Mr. Tod*, published in 1912, as the book in which "Miss Potter's pessimism reached its climax." Mr. Tod is a well-dressed fox, perhaps the very same whiskered gentleman who bedeviled Jemima. His frenemy, a badger named Tommy Brock, steals the babies of the now adult Benjamin Bunny, who has married Peter Rabbit's sister Flopsy. (The effect of seeing these characters age is a bit awkward, as it often is in real life. The tale may remind some readers of the regrettable final chapter of *Harry Potter and the Deathly Hallows*, in which Harry, Ron, Hermione, and Ginny, fully but unconvincingly grown in the turn of a single page, send their own children off to Hogwarts.) Tommy Brock takes the kidnapped bunnies back to Mr. Tod's shabby home, to prepare a feast, with Benjamin and Peter in pursuit. They arrive just in the nick of time, as Benjamin realizes when he peeps through the window:

> There were preparations upon the kitchen table which made him shudder. There was an immense empty pie-dish of blue willow pattern, and a large carving knife and fork, and a chopper.

That may be the closest thing to a description of an abattoir in children's literature, though the blue willow pattern adds a wryly genteel note so characteristic of Potter. As in much of her work, even most of it, there is a tug-of-war going on between civility and other, more literally bestial urges; in that sense, her animal tales couldn't be more human. In Greene's view, "But for the nature of [Potter's] audience, *Mr. Tod* would have certainly ended tragically." Maybe so; Potter was no prissier about the appetites of carnivores than Aesop was. On the other hand, the tale could have been much, much, much worse: as Potter surely knew, mother rabbits are known on occasion to eat their young. Happily she left those sorts of stories to the Greeks.

When Greene's piece on Potter was subsequently republished in a collection, he added this footnote:

> On the publication of this essay I received a somewhat acid letter from Miss Potter correcting certain details. . . . She denied that there had been any emotional disturbance at the time she was writing *Mr. Tod*: she was suffering however from the after-effects of the flu. In conclusion she deprecated sharply "the Freudian school" of criticism.

That's Potter in a nutshell, siding with nature—or at least a flu virus—over nurture.

5

You Have to Know How:
Dr. Seuss vs. Dick and Jane

Dr. Seuss wrote the first book I read by myself. What magic: the letters, unherdable cats at first, suddenly lining up nose to tail to form decipherable words—wow! Could solving Fermat's last theorem have been any more exhilarating? Undoubtedly. But still, for me, this was a very big deal.

The book, *Ten Apples Up on Top!*, was part of the Beginner Books imprint Seuss had launched in partnership with Random House in 1958, following the bestselling success of his first book aimed at novice readers, *The Cat in the Hat*. Published in 1961, *Ten Apples Up on Top!* is no *Cat in the Hat*, but it has its charms and it got me, a stubbornly illiterate first-grader assigned to the "baby bear" reading group, off the stick. The story is simple: a lion, a dog, and a tiger compete to see who can balance the highest stack of apples on his head while jumping rope, walking a high wire, drinking milk, and roller-skating.

I remember my mother reading the book aloud to me and pointing out each word with a patience she didn't always possess in those days. (Years later she confessed to having been alarmed by my "slow start.") I wish I could remember exactly which passage set me off on a road that would lead to *The Golden Bowl* and the first chapter and a half, maybe, of *Ulysses*. Was it: "And I can hop / up on a tree / with four apples / up on me"?

I know I liked the way the story builds upon its silly premise, topping itself, then topping itself again. I still like that. By the end of the book, the lion, bear, and tiger, each now with ten apples perched atop his head, are riding a single bicycle while being chased by three hungry birds and a pack of angry bears wielding bats, mops, tennis rackets, and tire irons. Is this the first angry mob in picture-book history? It might be the last, too, publishers for the very young not wanting to model antisocial behavior these days, though I've certainly seen worse on playgrounds. Seuss's 1961 story ends in a further spasm of violence when pursuers and pursued collide with a horse-drawn cart full of apples. *Kapow!* Fruit and fur fly across a bold, wordless, two-page spread, but when everyone falls back to earth a miracle of physics has left ten apples up on top of everyone's head—bears, birds, tiger, lion, dog, and dray horse alike. "Look! / Ten apples / on us all! / What fun! / We will not / let them fall." A happy ending.

As I said, *Ten Apples Up on Top!* is no *Cat in the Hat*, but in the way it blends imagination, humor, rhyme, rigor, silliness, aggression, and chaos theory, it is quintessential Seuss. As he understood, if kids are going to learn to read, they have to *want* to learn to read, which means they need stories worthy of their attention and sympathetic to their sometimes outré tastes. One of Dr. Seuss's many gifts as an author was that, like Margaret Wise Brown, he shared those tastes. As his wife described him to *Life* magazine in 1959, "His mind has never grown up. . . . He doesn't sit down and write for children. He writes to amuse himself. Luckily, what amuses him also amuses them." He seconded the thought: "Ninety percent of failures in children's books come from writing to preconceptions of what kids like. When I'm writing a book I do it to please [my wife and myself]. But when it finally comes out I take one look and say, 'Oh my God!'"

Seuss's friend and admirer Maurice Sendak believed that he appealed to "the animalistic nature of children," telling Larry King after Seuss's death, in 1991, "He was a revolutionary. . . . He said, 'The hell with propriety. The hell with sentence structure. The hell with how it ought to be. Let me show kids what they know already, which is how cuckoo their world really is.' He's against toilet training. He's against order. He's an uncivilized genius and the kids know it."

Sendak might better have said *deceptively* uncivilized. Seuss, whatever his true feelings about toilet training, was quite thoughtful about his work and cognizant of his responsibility as a children's author. As he once explained in a series of lectures, he believed kids' books should have moral underpinnings and that they needed to be rooted in some understanding of the psyche of their intended audience. "Children are thwarted people," he said. "Their idea of tragedy is when someone says you can't do that." But above all, he believed, "They want *fun*. They want *play*. They want *nonsense*." He often referred to his stories as "logical insanity."

As mentioned earlier, Dr. Seuss was a pseudonym used by Theodor Seuss Geisel, Seuss being his mother's maiden name. (His German-American family pronounced it as rhyming with "Joyce," and some sources say the initial *s* had a *z* sound—so either "soyce" or "zoyce." He acceded to the Americanized "sooss" early in his career.) He wrote *Ten Apples Up on Top!* under a second pseudonym, Theo. LeSieg (his surname spelled backward and garnished with a sprig of continental flair), which he often used for books he gave others to illustrate. Roy McKie did the honors here, quite nicely, as he did for later LeSieg titles such as *The Eye Book* (1968) and *In a People House* (1972). All told, Geisel published upward of sixty children's books under various guises; another half dozen have come out since his death, at eighty-seven. This was after a relatively late start: he didn't publish his first children's book, *And to Think That I Saw It on Mulberry Street*, until 1937, when he was thirty-three and already making a healthy living in advertising; he didn't embrace writing for kids as a full-time calling until he was in his late forties; and he didn't really become the brand name and publishing institution he remains today until 1957, when he was fifty-three and in that year published both *The Cat in the Hat* and *How the Grinch Stole Christmas*, a one-two for the ages.

That was the talent half of the equation. On the luck side, it was Geisel's good fortune that his banner year coincided with the peak of America's post–World War II baby boom: 4.3 million kids were born in 1957, still the biggest cohort in U.S. history (though we've come close several times since). Within weeks of publication, *The Cat in the Hat* had gone into multiple printings, and was soon selling ten thousand copies a month; by 1960 it had sold a million copies—unheard-of numbers, then, for a picture book. In a 1960 *New Yorker* profile of Geisel, E. J. Kahn Jr. noted that the only books with a comparable list price which had generated as much revenue as *The Cat in the Hat* were paperback editions of the famously smutty potboilers *Peyton Place* and *God's Little Acre*. Geisel's feat was all the more impressive, Kahn added, because "*The Cat in the Hat* is aseptic."

The book is so familiar, the Cat himself such an iconic character, reproduced to Mickey Mouse levels of near-generic ubiquity on merchandise and shoddy pseudo-Seussian apocrypha, it can be easy to lose sight of just how singularly weird the original work is. As Louis Menand once observed, also in *The New Yorker*, on the occasion of the book's fiftieth anniversary (and this is possibly my single favorite sentence in the history of criticism): "Every reader of *The Cat in the Hat* will feel that the story revolves around a piece of withheld information: what private demons or desires compelled this mother to leave two young children at home all day, with the front door unlocked, under the supervision of a fish."[1] That is a reference to the book's opening, which finds the unnamed narrator and his sister, Sally, cooped up on a rainy day, alone, staring miserably out a window: "Too wet to go out / And too cold to play ball / So we sat in the house / We did nothing at all." Things liven up on the next page when the Cat arrives on the doorstep with an all-caps BUMP!—"How that bump made us jump!"—and then begins demonstrating the many ingenious ways the two children can have, as he puts it, "lots of good fun that is funny." With that, this beloved but unlikely book about a potentially terrifying home invasion, written to make kids want to learn to read, is off and running.

The impulse to educate, whether in the three R's sense or in the loftier, more vaporous realms of moral, cultural, or personal uplift, is almost always the enemy of good children's literature. Of adult literature, too. But kids especially, since they spend so many of their waking hours in school, can sense a lesson coming a mile off; they can hear the gears turning, spot the deck being stacked. *Incoming!* Another of Geisel's gifts, manifest in his Beginner Books as well as in social and political fables such as *The Sneetches* and *Yertle the Turtle*, was an ability to take projects that in lesser hands might have carried the whiff of a lesson plan or a sermon and spin something delightful. The task actually became him: his imagination was so rich, so bountiful, so ready to fly off in any direction that a bit of ballast or drag steadied him. Without it, at times, he seemed capable of fabricating beasts, birds, customs, contraptions, names, and nonsense words with

---

[1] The writer and artist Alexandra Day went Dr. Seuss one better by depicting a mother leaving her infant in the care of a Rottweiler in the winningly irresponsible *Good Dog, Carl* (1985).

such alacrity that the resulting rhymes and stories could feel as if they were less thunderbolts of genius than by-products of a nervous tic. For instance, this snippet from *The Lorax*, his environmental parable from 1971:

> *Then he hides what you paid him*
> *Away in his Snuvv,*
> *His secret strange hole*
> *In his gruvvulous glove*

It might not be clear what a Snuvv or a gruvvulous glove is, even in context, but they verge awfully close to what Geisel criticized in others as "convenience rhymes," just the sort of business that makes Dr. Seuss so easy to parody, and often so poorly. As Alison Lurie writes, "Seuss's verbal inventions can become as shaky and overblown as the structures in his drawings." But there is much less of that contrivance in the Beginner Books, where working with limited vocabulary was a tonic for him, I think, in the way that some modern poets find inspiration when corseted by fussy classic forms, or jazz musicians summon fresh life from the tired DNA of standards. For Geisel, it was a list of some two hundred to three hundred vocabulary words, and a dare of sorts, that pushed him to conjure a book that then barged into American homes with as much brio and disregard for boundaries as the Cat himself. Speaking of DNA, I also think it's fair to say that creator and character shared a few strands.

As far as the public was concerned, Dr. Seuss was presumed to be such an unfettered madman that the *Saturday Evening Post*, in a 1957 profile, felt compelled to observe that "in suburban La Jolla," the rather stuffy (for Southern California) beach community where Geisel had lived since 1949, "he is considered a paragon of propriety. . . . His hair is cut regularly, his shoes are always shined, and he gives his chair when ladies are standing." He was tall, lean, beaky, bespectacled, bow-tied, and, for the last several decades of his life, bearded—a little bit owlish, a little bit Amish. He could be shy, especially in large gatherings, and he was terrified of public speaking, but in small, congenial groups he could become an animated center of attention. By all accounts he liked kids fine but wasn't particularly natural around them or even very interested in them. He had no children of his own. His boilerplate response when asked about that: "You have them, I'll amuse them."

Like everyone, he hit speed bumps and suffered some devastating personal losses. Like most artists, he wrestled with muses and demons. But tortured? Not so much; not judged on the same scale as Vincent van Gogh or Virginia Woolf or even Maurice Sendak. He lived long and well, loved mostly well, knew a lot of interesting people, achieved more success than most in a number of difficult creative fields, and entered one medium's pantheon. After reading three biographies of Geisel and a thick sheaf of profiles and interviews from across several decades, I was left with the overall impression: *Dr. Seuss led a pretty great life. . . .*

He was born in Springfield, Massachusetts, in 1904, and could have been a third-generation beer maker had not Prohibition intervened, shutting down the brewery cofounded by his grandfather and taken over by his father. (Some savvy real estate investments kept the Geisels afloat through the 1920s and '30s.) The family spoke German at home, and this gave Ted, as he was known throughout his life, a cockeyed relationship to English from the start. Early on, he displayed a talent for drawing and an ear for rhyme. He was able to indulge a fascination with exotic animals thanks to his father's position on the board of the Springfield parks department, which afforded the son easy access to the city's zoo. "Young Ted had often entered the lion cages, and had played with the kangaroos and cub bears," the *Saturday Evening Post* would report, not altogether credibly. (Geisel was both a prankster and a fabulist, and readers are advised to read colorful old profiles of him with a skeptical eye.) He was also obsessed with the newspaper comics, especially Krazy Kat—George Herriman's surreal, wide-open landscapes are a clear influence on Dr. Seuss's—and, according to an interview his older sister once gave, any room in the family home with a bare plaster wall had at least one Ted Geisel cartoon drawn on it. Basically, he was Dr. Seuss from the get-go. As he would write years later, "My mother over-indulged me, and seemed to be saying, 'Everything you do is great, just go ahead and do it.'"[2] Which sounds like a recipe for raising either a genius or a monster.

By high school he was such a prolific cartoonist and joke writer that he started experimenting with pseudonyms (including T. S. Le-Sieg) to disguise his hegemony in student publications. At Dartmouth College, he edited the humor magazine, the *Jack-O-Lantern*, where, during his senior year, he first began signing his contributions "Seuss," a subterfuge necessitated not by modesty but rather by his suspension after he was caught serving bootleg gin at his off-campus boarding-house. The very first cartoon published by "Seuss" doesn't promise future glory, but it well captures what undergraduates hoped was the arch, café-society sophistication of the era's college humor: A man and a woman are riding through a desert in a small howdah on the back of a camel. He: "Kiss me." She: "Whaddaya think this is—a taxi?" It's not Peter Arno, but it's not bad.

Geisel graduated from Dartmouth in 1925 and enrolled at

---

[2]The armchair psychoanalyst in me wonders why the most noteworthy mothers in Dr. Seuss are felt largely through their absence: the cavalier mom in *The Cat in the Hat* and Mayzie, "a lazy bird," who abandons her egg to Horton the elephant's care in *Horton Hatches the Egg.*

Oxford intent on getting a PhD in English literature and becoming an academic, which in hindsight sounds like a rotten idea for everyone concerned—Geisel, Oxford, and posterity. Fortunately, he found the university hidebound and his course of study tedious. He hated the food, too. One bright spot was that lectures gave him ample time for sketching in his notebooks. Another bright spot was meeting his future wife, Helen Palmer, a fellow American and Wellesley graduate also studying literature at Oxford. She helped nudge him toward his true vocation. His biographers Judith Morgan and Neil Morgan describe the moment:

> [Helen] stared over his shoulder, astonished, as Ted busied himself in his own world through each lecture. . . . One day she watched Ted undertake to illustrate Milton's *Paradise Lost*; he drew the angel Uriel sliding down a sunbeam, oiling the beam as he went from a can that resembled a tuba.
>
> "You're crazy to be a professor," she blurted after class. "What you really want to do is draw." She glanced at another page and smiled. "That's a very fine flying cow!"

Palmer and Geisel were soon engaged; her insight about his natural talents was an early sign of the smart counsel she would provide not just as wife but also as longtime editorial first responder and eventual partner in Beginner Books. The dons at Oxford apparently agreed with her read on Geisel's academic future, counseling him to take a hiatus from his studies. Characteristically, he would tell different stories about what finally prompted him to flee academia. Whatever the reason, "I threw in my doctoral towel and took the next freighter to Corsica."

That may not have been precisely true, but after half a year of traveling around the continent, he sailed home. Within another half year he was launched professionally, selling cartoons and "casuals" to magazines such as the *Saturday Evening Post*, *Vanity Fair*, and *Life*. (This was the old humor magazine, founded in 1883, not Henry Luce's photo-driven *Life*, from the late 1930s and beyond.) He eventually moved to Manhattan, where he found a staff job at *Judge*, another of the era's thriving humor magazines. Now employed, he was soon married as well. He continued using "Seuss" as a pseudonym—later claiming, "I was saving the name of Geisel for the Great American Novel"—and eventually added the "Dr." (sometimes even more elaborately he was Dr. Theophrastus Seuss) in ironic salute to his abandoned PhD. It stuck, and became something of a household name, long before its owner even thought about writing for children, thanks to a series of cartoons he executed for the bug spray Flit, an early example of what we now call native advertising. One recurring caption, typically affixed to a drawing of someone calling for help while menaced by comically huge mosquitoes—"Quick, Henry! The Flit!"—became a national catchphrase. Geisel would go on to create campaigns for Brevo Brushless Shave, Doggett & Ramsdell beauty products, Essolube, and Hankey Bannister Scotch; he also had clients with names that didn't sound as if he himself had invented them, including General Electric and the American Can Company.[3] Ad

---

[3]I don't think it's a coincidence that Eric Carle, with his own talent for camouflaging educational ideas between the covers of his books, also worked in advertising. Like it or not, there is an affinity between that discipline and the art of creating picture books: both place a premium on terseness and clarity, on making every word and image not only count but resonate—and all with a deceptive lightness of touch. If you squint a little, you might also see that the aims are not dissimilar: advertising, at its best, makes its points while entertaining (we might not approve of the points, but that's another story); so do the good children's books. Take *The Very Hungry Caterpillar*. It tells a charming story for the very young with some excellent visual jokes; it also weaves in the days of the week; counting to five; and, at the end, its lovely biology lesson about caterpillars, cocoons, and butterflies. There is a lot going on there (and yes, it should have been a chrysalis), but everything is fitted together plainly, organically, elegantly; it is as close to

money enabled the Geisels to take a big apartment on Park Avenue, where, running with a tony social set, they numbered among their best friends the heiress Zinny Vanderlip—a detail not at all germane to this consideration of Dr. Seuss, but a name so irresistible and evocative I had to shoehorn it in.

Geisel's college cartoons had been graphically rough-hewn, often with a kind of generic funny-pages look—more Mutt and Jeff or Blondie than Krazy Kat. But by his mid-twenties his artwork displayed a now familiar fluidity, wit, and seeming ease of invention. He had also learned how to make the best of his shortcomings as a draftsman, abandoning any pretense of anatomical correctness, animal or human, and allowing limbs, joints, feet, and fingers to bend and twist any which way they chose.[4] A *Life* cartoon from 1930, depicting pairs of weird but genial creatures boarding an ark as hallucinated in a drunken stupor by "Noah's dissolute brother, Goah," is clearly the work of the same artist who would later create Horton, Yertle, and the recombinant pet store menagerie of *One Fish Two Fish Red Fish Blue Fish*. The subject matter might not sound like what we think of today as Seussian, but elaborate cartoons riffing on the d.t.'s (delirium tremens) were Geisel's stock-in-trade during the 1920s and '30s—so reliably that he was parodied by a rival as "Dr. Souse." Indeed, had he died prematurely, Geisel might still retain minor fame among cartoon scholars for his contributions in expanding the iconography of drunk

---

perfection in its design and construction as any work of art can be. To me, Carle is the Mies van der Rohe of kids' books, though he works with far more colorful materials.

[4]One of his rare failures as an author-illustrator was his mildly risqué 1939 adult fairy tale, *The Seven Lady Godivas*. "I tried to draw the sexiest-looking women I could," he later said, "and they came out just ridiculous." It's true: his heroines' torsos tended to be twice as long as their legs; they looked malformed. But more to the point of the book's failure, its story was labored and unfunny. "I think maybe it all went to prove I don't know anything about adults," Geisel concluded.

tank visions far beyond the usual snakes and pink elephants (the latter already a cliché in the 1920s, though they would yet achieve a magnificent apotheosis in Walt Disney's *Dumbo* of 1941).

Inspired more by the potential for steady royalties than any particular urge to entertain children, Geisel made his first foray into the "brat book" field—his term—after illustrating the U.S. editions of a pair of British bestsellers, *Boners* and *More Boners*, which collected malapropisms from English schoolboys. ("Adolescence is the stage between puberty and adultery. . . . Acrimony, sometimes called holy, is another name for marriage.") His first attempt at an original children's book, an animal ABC, failed to sell. His second was rejected by somewhere between twenty and forty-three publishers, depending on the telling, and for reasons ranging from its lack of an obvious moral to its cartoonish artwork. (The then-cloistered children's book world considered itself a rampart between the nursery and pop culture's degrading vulgarity.) One day, when Geisel was wandering dejectedly down Madison Avenue with the manuscript and artwork under his arm, ready to give up, he happened to run into an old Dartmouth classmate who just three hours earlier had been named children's book editor at Vanguard Press—a double coincidence, if strictly true. The friend, whose office building they were standing in front of—triple coincidence!—invited Geisel upstairs, took a look at his manuscript, and promptly bought what was then called, appropriately, *A Story That No One Can Beat*. "If I had been going down the other side of Madison Avenue, I'd be in the dry-cleaning business today," Geisel said later, one aspect of the tale that is verifiably untrue.

Geisel claimed the germ of the book had come to him during a transatlantic crossing in the summer of 1936, when the ocean liner's engines were thrumming with a rhythm that in poetry is called anapestic meter: da da DA da da DA da da DA da da DA—poetry's version of waltz time. (Aside from much of Dr. Seuss, *The Night Before*

Christmas is also written in anapestic meter. Byron and Shelley were fond of it too.) Geisel became obsessed with the rhythm, started jotting down words to it, and eventually came up with the lines "And that is a story that no one can beat / And to think that I saw it on Mulberry Street." Though not quite sure, at first, what to do with this couplet, he clearly possessed the germ of a great idea, not to mention a hokey scene for a Dr. Seuss biopic if one is ever filmed.

I have been emphasizing Geisel's knack with a tale, his gifts for embellishment, exaggeration, and outright invention, because so many of his best books are celebrations of exactly that. The retitled *And to Think That I Saw It on Mulberry Street*, published in 1937, is a perfect example, practically a manifesto. It tells the story of a boy named Marco whose father tasks him with recounting what he sees on his walks to and from school. When Marco exaggerates a bit for effect, Dad admonishes him for "telling such outlandish tales." In other words, *Entertain me, but don't entertain me too much.* (This is what Marco's future psychotherapist will call "sending conflicting signals.")

So what is Marco to do? He doesn't want to fib but he's bored by the quotidian:

All the long way to school
And all the way back,
I've looked and I've looked
And I've kept careful track,
But all that I've noticed,
Except my own feet,
Was a horse and a wagon
On Mulberry Street.

Obviously, that won't do.

This can't be my story. That's only a start.
I'll say that a ZEBRA was pulling the cart!
And that is a story that no one can beat,
When I say that I saw it on Mulberry Street.

Soon enough, the cart becomes a chariot, the zebra becomes a rein-deer, then two giraffes and a blue elephant; now the chariot is a parade float with a brass band; soon there is a police escort and an airplane flying overhead dumping confetti on the whole thing, plus "a Chinese man / Who eats with sticks"—not the first or last example in his early work of Geisel treating non-whites as exotics or worse—and "A big magician / Doing tricks."

Marco races up the steps to his house eager to tell his father everything he's "seen" but Dad's forbidding reserve—he may have had a bit of Geisel's stereotypical German-American father in him—puts Marco off his game:

There was so much to tell, I JUST COULDN'T BEGIN!
Dad looked at me sharply and pulled at his chin.
He frowned at me sternly from there in his seat,
"Was there nothing to look at . . . no people to greet?
Did nothing excite you or make your heart beat?"

Pffft. Marco deflates.

"Nothing," I said, growing red as a beet,
"But a plain horse and wagon on Mulberry Street."

And that's the last line—a down note, I think. There are other Seuss books that end ambiguously or even darkly, among them *The Lorax* and *The Butter Battle Book*, Geisel's Reagan-era parable about the nuclear arms race, which reads as if the Sneetches had invaded Dr. Strangelove's war room. ("All we need is some newfangled kind of gun. / My Boys in the Back Room have already begun / to think up a walloping whizz-zinger one!") But even readers (like me) who find those books heavy-handed[5] can agree that they are true to themselves. Marco's embarrassment ends *And to Think That I Saw It on Mulberry Street* on a rare Seussian false note, at least as I read it. Not everyone feels that way. Alison Lurie sees a sympathetic warning for children "that it is sometimes, perhaps always, best to conceal one's inner imaginative life from adults." My wife thinks Geisel is pointing kids toward the beauty in the here and now, Marco's plain horse and wagon viewed with a contemplative eye not unlike William Carlos Williams's in "The Red Wheelbarrow." Maybe. But I don't see much in Geisel's work to suggest it ever occurred to him that one might conceal one's inner imaginative life; nor do I see much if any appreciation of the commonplace, except as a jumping-off point. (Margaret Wise Brown was more the "Red Wheelbarrow" type.) The detail that stops me is Marco's blushing. I just can't believe the writer and artist whom Sendak called an uncivilized genius, the man who knew children craved *fun* and *play* and *nonsense*, really wanted Marco to feel ashamed for having let his imagination run riot. Perhaps it would have strained convention in 1937 to end the book with either Marco getting away with his fibs or a team of giraffes showing up on the lawn? At any rate, this was a misstep Geisel wouldn't repeat: in a series of subsequent Dr. Seuss books centered on dreamers and tellers of tall tales, among them *McElligot's Pool* (1947), *If I Ran the Zoo* (1950), *Scrambled Eggs Super!* (1953), *On Beyond Zebra!* (1955), and *If I Ran the Circus* (1956), the characters' flights of fantasy are treated more like performance art or acts of

---

[5]Though Geisel frequently cited *The Lorax* as his favorite of his books, even he admitted, "It was one of the few things I ever set out to do that was straight propaganda."

self-assertion—they're heroic, even if Geisel implies a raised eyebrow here and there. He well understood that fun, play, and nonsense are among the few ways aside from throwing tantrums and running away that children can assert control over their world, at least imaginatively.

He felt he hit his stride with his fourth kids' book, *Horton Hatches the Egg*, published in 1940, in which he returned to anapestic meter after a pair of fairy tales in prose, but in terms of money, children's publishing was a backwater in the pre–baby boom era; even successful books didn't generate much in the way of royalties. Geisel remained restless both creatively and professionally, continuing to pursue advertising work as well as the occasional odd business venture.[6] He tried his hand at a syndicated comic strip and during the run-up to the war he drew political cartoons for the lefty New York newspaper *PM*, though his and the paper's progressive politics didn't stop him from contributing to the era's vast gallery of racist Japanese caricatures. In 1942 he received a commission to join the Hollywood Army Signal Corps unit, led by Frank Capra, where Geisel made training and propaganda films alongside the likes of John Huston, Irving Wallace, Meredith Wilson, and Chuck Jones (the Looney Tunes animator who would later direct the 1966 TV version of *How the Grinch Stole Christmas*). Geisel stayed on in Hollywood for a time after the war as a screenwriter, first at Warner Bros., then at RKO. (My favorite piece of Dr. Seuss trivia: at Warner he worked on an early treatment of *Rebel Without a Cause*.) He had some success with shorts—he wrote the story for the influential,

---

[6]One such was the Infantograph, a dual-lens camera he helped invent that was designed to superimpose the features of a man and woman onto a baby's face in order to show them what their offspring might look like. Geisel and his partners, including the industrial designer Norman Bel Geddes, had planned to debut the Infantograph at the 1939 New York World's Fair, but abandoned the project because even though it was meant to be a novelty, the results, Geisel complained, "tended to look like William Randolph Hearst."

Oscar-winning cartoon *Gerald McBoing-Boing* (1950)—but grew disenchanted with the movie business while finding himself drawn more and more to writing for kids. Researching the imperial Japanese and Nazi school systems for his wartime films had impressed upon him how vulnerable young minds are to abuse by ideologues. At the same time, the insipid nature of so much American children's literature, what he often dismissed as "bunny bunny bunny books," offended him. (I trust he was slagging neither Brown nor Potter, but only their imitators.) Writing and drawing for kids, entertaining them, giving them a laugh or a jolt, but also giving them something more nourishing than pulpy comic books and crummy TV shows, was, he realized, important work.

It was also work he enjoyed, though not without a certain defensiveness. In 1952 he wrote an essay for the *New York Times Book Review* entitled (ellipsis his) " . . . But for Grown-Ups Laughing Isn't Any Fun," about the benefits of writing humor for kids as opposed to adults. Pros: unlike their self-conscious elders, children laugh genuinely and easily. Cons: low pay, low status. The *Times Book Review* piece was graced by a Dr. Seuss cartoon of a depressed-looking sad sack trudging past a pair of alley cats, one of whom remarks, "Him . . . ? Oh, he's a nobody. They say he writes for children." Nevertheless, the following year Geisel decided to turn his full attention to "the so-called Brat Field" after his agent assured him he'd be able to earn the annual $5,000 in royalties (roughly $45,000 in 2016 dollars) that Geisel figured he'd need on top of what he already had for a comfortable if modest life. Seven years later, E. J. Kahn Jr. would report in *The New Yorker*, he earned $200,000 ($1.3 million today), which was only a start.

The Cat in the Hat came about because American education was in crisis, or so it seemed in the 1950s to people who hadn't yet lived

through another seventy years of administrative dysfunction, ideo-
logic conflict, and ever-worsening test scores. Commentators and
educators fretted that children's attention spans were being squeezed
to near-nothingness by movies, radio, and especially comic books and
TV—big 1950s bugaboos. This irresistible candyland of lurid pop
culture had taken kids' "natural love of excitement [and] quickened it
at an earlier age," as the children's book editor and critic Louise Sea-
man Bechtel warned in 1949, decades before video games and social
media were invented. She was speaking to an assemblage of literati
celebrating the twenty-fifth anniversary of the *New York Herald-
Tribune Weekly Book Review*, which had been one of the first outlets
to review children's books, and which wouldn't live to see its fiftieth.

In 1954, the journalist John Hersey published an influential article in *Life* (the Henry Luce version) titled "Why Do Students Bog
Down on the First R?" (that would be the "reading" in "reading, 'rit-
ing, and 'rithmatic"). Hersey observed:

> Many a college has blamed high schools for passing on students
> with average or better I.Q.'s who could not read adequately to
> study college subjects; high schools have had to give reme-
> dial reading instruction to boys and girls who did not learn to
> read properly in elementary schools; the sixth-grade teacher has
> blamed the fourth-grade teacher; the fourth, the first; and all the
> teachers have now and then blamed parents, and with justice.

Torn from today's headlines, as they say. Hersey blamed TV and
comic books, too. But the prime culprits in his eyes were the "namby-
pamby" primers featuring "abnormally courteous and unnaturally
clean boys and girls" which were used to teach reading in the 1950s:
the famous Dick and Jane books, which dated to the 1930s; or, as was
the case in Hersey's local school district in Fairfield, Connecticut, a

rival series that substituted Tom, Betty, and Susan for Dick, Jane, and
their younger sister, Sally, but otherwise offered more of the same.
Both series were based on a pedagogical belief that reading was best
taught through brief, sketchlike stories recounting bland suburban
escapades and composed of carefully selected vocabulary words which
were repeated *bam bam bam*, ad infinitum, as if they were being shot
out of a staple gun. Thus: "Go, Dick, go!" and "Look, Betty, look!"
and "See funny Sally! Funny, funny Sally!"

Then as now, problem readers tended to be boys. Hersey felt they
were particularly ill served:

> Little boys trying to learn to read . . . witness a lone boy named
> Tom condemned to play endlessly, and with unnatural control of
> his manners, with two syrupy girls, Betty and Susan. This fright-
> ful life that poor Tom leads is bound up inextricably with the cru-
> cial first stages of reading. It is not entirely surprising that some
> boys draw back from the experience.

As it happens, my school district used the same primers, the Ginn
Basic Readers, as Hersey's did—*My Little Red Story Book*, *My Little
Green Story Book*, and so on. Was Tom's "frightful life" stuck with
Betty and Susan in a *No Exit* backyard limbo the reason I myself was
slow off the mark? I can't say, but having tracked down some of the
old primers on eBay and reread them, I have renewed respect for those
of my classmates who got through them at a more rapid clip. Also,
pursuant to Hersey's sexist critique, I should note that Tom is himself
no great shakes as a literary character; if he had enough personality to
be described as even "syrupy" it would be a step or two up for him.

Hersey's complaints were amplified the following year when Rudolf Flesch, a writing teacher and language expert, published the bestseller *Why Johnny Can't Read—And What You Can Do About It*, an

attack on the then ascendant "look-say" method of teaching reading, which relied on memorization rather than traditional phonics—the reason for the *bam bam bam* word repetitions in the Dick and Jane and Tom and Betty primers.[7] As pedagogical treatises go, Flesch's is amusingly vituperative, even hotheaded; six decades on, and its emphasis on Johnny rather than Johnny and Suzie aside, it is still a fun read, or quasi-fun. Flesch's main beef was with the mechanics of look-say, but he had plenty of contempt left over for the "totally unexciting middle-class, middle-income, middle-I.Q." content of "those series of horrible, stupid, emasculated, pointless, tasteless little readers." He added, "Don't underestimate their importance in the life of your child. They are all he has to read—all he *can* read—during the first two or three or four years that he comes in contact with books. For all he knows, this is what books look like."

These jeremiads inspired William Spaulding, the head of Houghton Mifflin's educational division, to propose to Geisel that he try writing a non-boring book for beginning readers. Hersey had cited Dr. Seuss,

---

[7]Critics of the look-say primers in the 1950s and '60s often referred with nostalgic fondness to the phonics-based McGuffey readers, which had dominated American education through the second half of the nineteenth century and into the twentieth. But this was a bit of an apples-and-oranges comparison. The McGuffeys served multiple purposes in an age of one-room schoolhouses, also providing text for instruction in subjects we'd cover separately today in English, history, and civics classes. Thus the readers for older students are rich with excerpts from Shakespeare, Milton, Dickens, Longfellow, Thomas Jefferson, Daniel Webster, and on and on. But the McGuffeys with which the youngest students were taught to read, while they may present more challenging vocabulary than the Dick and Jane books, aren't much of an improvement, content-wise. For example, this reading lesson from 1879, which I quote in its entirety: "Did you call us, Mamma? I went with Tom to the pond. I had my doll and Tom had his flag. The fat duck swam to the bank, and we fed her. Did you think we might fall into the pond? We did not go too near, did we, Tom? Can we go to the swing, now, Mamma?" (So many generations of Toms condemned to so many decades of unfulfilling play. . . .)

alongside Walt Disney—and, for some reason, Sir John Tenniel, illustrator of *Alice in Wonderland*, although Tenniel had died in 1914—as creative types who might be able to do better by America's pupils than the
writers and artists behind Tom and Betty and Dick and Jane. "Write me
a story that first-graders can't put down," Spaulding supposedly asked,
and Geisel took him up on the challenge, starting with a vocabulary
list Spaulding gave him of somewhere between two hundred and three
hundred words that educators considered digestible by fledgling readers.
The puzzle, and it was a knotty one, was to somehow discern a story in
a list. "At first I thought it was ridiculous and impossible," Geisel would
later say. Writing in the *New York Times Book Review*, with his tongue
not entirely in his cheek, he recalled his struggles coming up with a story
that would enthrall Spaulding's hypothetical first-grader, whom Geisel
personified here as an aspiring rhinoceros hunter named Orlo:

> After the first couple hours of staring at my Word List, I did dis-
> cover a few words that might come in handy in writing a story.
> Words like *am* and *are* and *is*. But when you want to thrill the
> pants off a rhinoceros hunter, that takes a bit of doing with words
> like *daddy* and *kitten* and *pot*.

Over the years, as usual, he would offer multiple versions of how he
finally broke through. This one seems credible:

> I was about to get out of the whole thing; then I decided to
> look at the list one more time and to use the first two words
> that rhymed as the title of the book—*cat* and *hat* were the ones
> my eyes lighted on. I worked on the book for nine months—
> throwing it across the room and letting it hang for a while—but
> I got it done.

In the end he summoned his narrative from a mere 222 words.[8] To get a sense of the challenge he faced and the magnitude of his achievement (and, I suppose, to engender stray sympathy for the drones at Ginn and Scott, Foresman) take a look at those 222 words as they might have appeared in alphabetic order on the original list Geisel was given. *You* try finding a story in this:

a about after all always and another any are as asked at away back bad ball be bed bent bet big bit bite book bow box bump but cake call came can cat cold come could cup day dear deep did dish do dots down fall fan fast fear fell find fish fly for fox from fun funny game gave get give go gone good got gown had hall hand has hat have he head hear her here high him hit hold home hook hop house how I if in into is it jump kick kind kite know last let like lit little look looked lot made make man mat me mess milk mind mother my near net new no not nothing now of oh on one our out pack pat pick picked pink play plaything plop pot put rake ran red rid run sad said Sally sank sat saw say see shake shame she shine ship shook should show shut sit so some something stand step stop string sun sunny tail take tall tame tell that the their them then there these they thing think this those thump tip to too top toy trick two up us wall want was way we well went were wet what when white who why will wish with wood would yes yet you your

The story Geisel ultimately pruned from that thicket couldn't be simpler; it's really more an incident than a story. The Cat only wishes to entertain the children on this cold, cold, wet day despite the

---

[8]Most sources give the number as 223, but after counting and recounting I could only reach 223 by presuming *mother's* to be a distinct word from *mother*.

protestations of their de facto guardian, the talking fish, a pill who insists,

"No! No!
Make that cat go away!
Tell that Cat in the Hat
You do NOT want to play.
He should not be here.
He should not be about.
He should not be here
When your mother is out!"

Undaunted—cats don't typically pay much heed to the opinions of fish—the Cat entertains the children by standing on a ball with one leg while balancing an increasingly impossible number of objects on his head, hands, tail, and free foot. The kids aren't quite sure how to take this, but for Geisel, this stunt has the advantage of not only being funny, and fun to draw, but also allowing him to cross off a number of words on his list—*cake, rake, toy, man, ship, ball,* and, inevitably, *fall.*

Back on his feet and no worse for wear, though his rake is bent and his cake is no longer presentable, the Cat raises further alarms by declaring he will show the kids "another good game that I know." This is when he releases his famous longhaired sidekicks, Thing One and Thing Two, from a big red box. They go on a rampage, flying kites in the house and wreaking all manner of havoc "with big bumps, jumps and kicks / And with hops and big thumps / And all kinds of bad tricks." Whipsawed between feline id and fishy superego, the young narrator finally decides he's had enough—and not a moment too soon because the fish spies Mom approaching on the sidewalk. The boy nabs Things One and Two with a big butterfly net, as if they were lunatics in one of Chuck Jones's cartoons, and insists the Cat pack them up and get lost. For once, the Cat is taken aback:

> *"Oh dear!" said the cat,*
> *"You did not like our game. . . .*
> *Oh dear.*
> *What a shame!*
> *What a shame!*
> *What a shame!"*

He departs with "a sad kind of look"—remember Geisel's remark that tragedy for a child is being told no?—leaving behind an impossible mess, but he returns almost instantly, now smiling and driving what looks like a housekeeping Zamboni. Order is restored and the children are back at their seats by the window as their mother—who, it must be said, is an agonizingly slow walker, taking thirteen pages to traverse the five or so steps to the front door from the square on the sidewalk where the fish first spotted her—strides in and asks how their day was.

The book was an instant hit. Hersey, its literary godfather, pronounced it "a harum-scarum masterpiece . . . [a] gift to the art of reading." It was also a raspberry directed quite pointedly at Dick and Jane and Tom and Betty: the well-groomed, well-behaved brother and sister we meet at the beginning of the book could just as easily be the stars of a 1950s primer, if those characters ever experienced normal childhood emotions such as ennui, anxiety, and exasperation. (Coincidentally or not, Sally, the girl in *The Cat in the Hat*, shares her name with Dick and Jane's younger sister.)

Another aspect of the book that amuses me is the way it reverses the formula of so many fairy tales, such as "Little Red Riding Hood," "Hansel and Gretel," and "Jack the Giant Killer," in which young heroes and heroines leave home and are forced to navigate the world's temptations and dangers—its chaos. Here, chaos makes an unscheduled house call. Leonard S. Marcus has observed that the Cat, with his tall red-striped hat, bears resemblance to an Uncle Sam "gone agreeably haywire," and I don't think it's ludicrous to detect, as others have done, a few radioactive clicks of Cold War angst in the book—not to suggest that it's a parable of any sort; but it is a product of its time and place.

I'm less convinced by the argument of one of Geisel's biographers, Philip Nel, a professor at Kansas State, that the Cat has deep roots in minstrelsy and other racist or at best ambivalent representations of African Americans in the pop culture of Geisel's youth, not to mention his own early cartoons, though certainly you can divine hints of minstrelsy in pretty much any broad American comedy in any medium. Looked at from yet another angle, the story might reveal a glint of coded autobiography. The Cat is lanky and lean, like his creator, and he favors a bow tie, also like his creator. His compulsive need to entertain, those repeated pleas to "Look at me! Look at me! Look at me NOW," mirror a man fond of pranks and play, often described, even by himself, as an overgrown child, who every time he finished a book flew from his home in La Jolla to New York to give a theatrical reading of the new work to the assembled staff at Random House. I don't know that Geisel consciously projected himself into the book—I haven't come across any writings or interviews where he suggested he did—but the Cat burns with such sui generis intensity that it suggests psychological tinder, whether conscious or not.

That hunch is also due to the fact that the book, its commercial success aside, marked an important creative turn in the context of Geisel's previous work. If Marco's imagination was tamed and shamed at the end of *And to Think That I Saw It on Mulberry Street*, if in the intervening Dr. Seuss books set in a recognizably "real" world (as opposed to his fairy tales and animal fables) imagination is safely confined to the realm of tall tales, here it bursts through the front door in all its manic, messy, covertly hostile splendor.[9] Is the Cat a golem, a Frankenstein's monster, an author's postmodern invasion of his own story? *Something* is in play here. The Cat's tricks might be a mixed bag; the fish thinks so, and, like Sally and her brother, many actual kids are made anxious by the Cat. (I remember responding to the story with a kind of delicious, excruciating dread, similar to what I experienced watching one of Lucille Ball's schemes unravel during the theater of humiliation that was *I Love Lucy*.) But it is telling—and of course a key to the book's comedy—that the Cat remains gloriously oblivious to propriety, manners, taste, personal space. Whatever his trespasses, he feels bad only that no one has enjoyed his tricks; he never apologizes, and certainly never blushes, unlike poor Marco.

In fact, the ending of *The Cat in the Hat* is almost an exact inverse of the earlier book's. There a boy decides not to tell his father a fantastic story he's made up. Here, a boy and girl contemplate whether or not they should tell their mother a far crazier story that has actually happened:

> *Sally and I did not know*
> *What to say.*
> *Should we tell her*
> *The things that went on there that day?*
> *Should we tell her about it?*
> *Now what SHOULD we do?*
> *Well . . .*

---

[9] A free idea for an American studies thesis: Space Invaders—The Semiotics of Doorways in *The Cat in the Hat* and John Ford's *The Searchers*.

What would YOU do
If your mother asked YOU?

That Geisel leaves the question hanging—that he allows for the possibility that the kids might not tell their mom about the Cat; that they
might, in a word, *lie*—could be this radical book's most radical moment. People like to say the 1960s began with Martin Luther King Jr.'s
"I Have a Dream" speech, or the assassination of President Kennedy,
or the Beatles' appearance on *The Ed Sullivan Show*, all of which is a
silly but interesting parlor game; and it is no sillier and no less interesting to propose that the 1960s began when Dr. Seuss first engaged
baby boomers in a conspiracy of silence against their clueless parents.

Did Dr. Seuss revolutionize the teaching of reading? That might be
an overstatement, but Louis Menand says that the first book he ever
read was *The Cat in the Hat*, and I got my start with *Ten Apples Up on
Top!*—so that makes two of us on Team Seuss. It is true as well that
the Dick and Jane and Tom and Betty series were put out to pasture
within a decade of the Cat's appearance; that was due not only to
Geisel, Hersey, and Flesch but also to the increasing attention being
paid to the primers' lack of diversity. (Not that Geisel or his peers in
the loftier precincts of children's publishing had much to boast about
in this regard.) With new editions in 1964 and 1965, the Dick and
Jane series welcomed to the neighborhood a family of equally uninteresting black children, Mike and his not very mischievous twin sisters,
Pam and Penny; but the series went out of print not long afterward,
doomed in part by a Great Society education bill, the same legislation
that helped prime the pump for *Goodnight Moon* by funding libraries, which also mandated that textbooks more credibly reflect local
communities. (From what I have seen, contemporary reading primers

are still bland, but at least they are more culturally diverse than they were in my day, and the illustrations are sometimes lively. Perhaps a smidgen of life is the best that can be hoped for from books that are literally written, designed, and purchased by committee.)

As mentioned earlier, the success of *The Cat in the Hat* prompted Random House, Geisel's regular publisher (which had negotiated the lucrative trade rights to the book while Houghton Mifflin issued classroom editions), to launch the hugely successful and lucrative Beginner Books imprint, in which Helen Geisel was a cofounder and an editor alongside her husband and Phyllis Cerf, the wife of Random House publisher Bennett Cerf.[10] The imprint would issue my beloved *Ten Apples Up on Top!* along with equally enduring titles such as P. D. Eastman's *Are You My Mother?* (1960) and *Go, Dog, Go!* (1961; another poke at Dick and Jane?); *A Fish Out of Water* (1961), illustrated by Eastman, written by Helen under her maiden name, and based on an old idea of Ted's; and Dr. Seuss's own *One Fish Two Fish Red Fish Blue Fish* (1960), *Hop on Pop* (1963), and *Fox in Socks* (1965). In 1974, someone at Beginner Books had the inspired idea to commission the *New Yorker* cartoonist George Booth to illustrate another Theo. LeSieg story, *Wacky Wednesday*—a meeting of greats from separate but allied spheres that I only recently happened upon, and one that thrilled me at least as much as the old video clip I had seen on YouTube a couple of weeks earlier showing Mick Jagger and Keith Richards sitting around a hotel room somewhere in the mid-1960s and having a ball singing Beatles songs.

Being a couple who by both inclination and good fortune seem

---

[10]In an honest-to-God instance of great rather than mediocre minds thinking alike, 1957 also saw the launch of Harper's I Can Read series, conceived by Ursula Nordstrom, which would publish Else Holmelund Minarik's and Maurice Sendak's Little Bear books; the Frog and Toad series, by Arnold Lobel; and Syd Hoff's *Danny and the Dinosaur.*

never to have worried much about money, the Geisels found their post–*Cat in the Hat* wealth to be more a puzzlement than anything else. "Geisel is staggered and a bit frightened by his opulence, but he has never learned to come to grips with money," Kahn wrote in *The New Yorker.* Helen told him, "Ted has no extravagances. I can't think of anything he likes except cigarettes and rocks." (Not a joke: he was an ardent gemologist.) On multiple levels the couple had enjoyed a long and successful partnership. But after a series of illnesses and, apparently, a growing distance in the marriage, Helen took a deliberate overdose of barbiturates one night in 1967 and died, at the age of sixty-nine. Ted mourned for six months, then traveled to Reno, where Audrey Dimond, soon to be the ex-wife of a close friend of his, was getting a divorce after telling her husband that she and Ted were in love. The couple married soon afterward and remained together for two and a half decades until Ted's death, in 1991.

The last Dr. Seuss book published in his lifetime—*Oh, the Places You'll Go!*—came out a year earlier. A sentimental, souped-up riff on a Hallmark graduation card, it is enduringly popular, widely considered wise, and my least favorite thing he ever wrote; it strikes me as what you might get if you asked Mitch Albom to ghost a Dr. Seuss book, but I realize many people might like the sound of that, too.

The Cat himself returned, a year after his first appearance, in *The Cat in the Hat Comes Back.* Sally and her brother have been abandoned once again by their mother, who, blithe as ever, has skipped off "down to the town for the day." Worse, she has added Dickensian cruelty to her arsenal of bad parenting skills by forcing the siblings to dig out the house from what looks to have been several feet of snow. The thoughtful, cautious fish is no longer in evidence—perhaps this is not surprising given the life expectancy of pet fish—so now the children are truly on their own when the Cat shows up on skis with bells on their tips and begins making merry with a transferable pink bathtub ring.

The Cat in the Hat Comes Back is a worthy enough sequel, and its twenty-six new costars, Little Cats A through Z, are a nice addition to the cast and also a clever way to work the alphabet in. But the book lacks the purity of concept and demented originality of its predecessor. The truer sequel, to my taste—and perhaps to many others', since it has become the bestselling Dr. Seuss book of all time—is *Green Eggs and Ham*, published in 1960. Here, the Cat's needy, counterproductive drive to be "fun" is distilled into Sam-I-Am's monomaniacal quest to get an answer to a simple question: Does the tall, shaggy, unnamed figure quietly reading his newspaper at the start of the story like green eggs and ham? The premise is absurd—what *are* green eggs and ham? what is Sam-I-Am's investment in anyone's liking them? who cares?— and Geisel honors that absurdity by ignoring it as he sets Sam-I-Am loose to pursue his quarry with the indefatigable relentlessness of a Terminator, albeit a cheerful and bright-eyed one. What Sam-I-Am really is, I suppose, is a salesman, that ultimate American profession.

Green Eggs and Ham was the result of another challenge: Bennett Cerf had bet Geisel fifty dollars that he couldn't write a book using only fifty words. Geisel not only won; he trumped Cerf by using only one-syllable words—*anywhere* being the sole exception. ("I do not like them in a house. I do not like them with a mouse. I would not like them here or there. I would not like them anywhere.") From such unpromisingly arbitrary origins, Geisel wrought a book with such propulsive rhythms and rhymes, and of such pure, sublime ludicrousness, that anthologists should be ashamed for not including it alongside the usual entries by Mark Twain, Dorothy Parker, James Thurber, Fran Lebowitz, and David Sedaris in treasuries of classic American humor. I suppose there is a moral to *Green Eggs and Ham*: that we should be open to new experiences, as the tall, shaggy fellow learns when he finally gives in and takes a tentative bite. ("Say! I like green eggs and ham! . . . Thank you! Thank you, Sam-I-Am!") And I suppose in Sam-I-Am's hopeful persistence there may be echoes of a kid's trying to capture a distracted parent's attention. ("Hey Daddy . . . Hey Daddy . . . Hey Daddy. . . .") But rather than risk flattening its effervescence, I would prefer to read no more into *Green Eggs and Ham* than I do into "Who's on first?"

In the course of writing this book, I was often asked what my favorite children's book is. I really couldn't say—not out of coyness; it's an impossible question. But I do know that *Green Eggs and Ham* is the one book that never fails to make me smile. Reading aloud to my kids at bedtime nearly every night for years, I grew sick of almost everything, even the masterpieces. But I never, ever got sick of *Green Eggs and Ham*. I didn't really get sick of *The Cat in the Hat*, either, except for the rake and the cake bit. That right there may have been Dr. Seuss's greatest talent of all: he not only made kids want to read; he kept them reading. I, for one, still owe him.

6

Kids Being Kids:
Ramona Quimby, American Pest

There were two kinds of children who went to kindergarten—those who lined up outside the door before school, as they were supposed to, and those who ran around the playground. . . . Ramona ran around the playground.

—Beverly Cleary, *Ramona the Pest*, 1968

I had the good fortune to interview Beverly Cleary, author of *Henry Huggins*, *Ramona the Pest*, and forty-odd other books, on the occasion of her ninetieth birthday, in 2006. We spoke on the phone and her voice had a cheerful yet no-nonsense tone—just what you might expect from a woman who grew up on a farm in rural Oregon, came of age in Portland during the Depression, and began professional life as a children's librarian in the small town of Yakima, Washington. At the behest of my daughter's fourth-grade class, I asked her if she had a favorite among her books. "I like them all or I wouldn't have written them," she replied, which might read as snappish on the page but wasn't at all on the phone; rather, she sounded perfectly sensible. "I have started books," she continued, "and thought, Well, this isn't any fun. So I threw it in the wastebasket."

That lack of sentimentality is one of Cleary's signal virtues as a writer. It's a residue, I think, of the flinty modesty she imbibed during her Oregon girlhood, especially from a mother who constantly admonished her to, in essence, suck it up the way her "pioneer ancestors" had. As a westerner myself with my own very distant pioneer ancestors (there are covered wagons and unlucrative silver mines decorating one branch of my family tree), I recognize this almost reflexive need never to make a fuss or draw attention to oneself; and to be honest, in life it is often a hindrance. (When I was very little I thought the painting *American Gothic* was a portrait of my paternal grandparents.) But as a writer Cleary distills that spirit, retaining the cool-eyed practicality and discarding the thin-lipped dourness. As Cleary told me, she's a woman—and, relevantly here, a former girl—who likes fun. No fun? Throw it in the wastebasket.

I don't think it is too big an exaggeration to call her the first great contemporary realist in children's literature. Her favorite subject: normal, unexceptional kids doing normal, unexceptional kid stuff in normal, unexceptional neighborhoods. At the same time, Klickitat Street in Portland, Oregon—the setting for many of her best-known books, home to Henry Huggins and Beezus and Ramona Quimby—is as richly realized in its way as Middle Earth or Hogwarts, though light-years from either. There are no orphans, no wizards, no talismans, no goblins in Cleary's books—no pirates or cowboys or heroic lifesaving horses and dogs, either—just bratty siblings and recalcitrant pets, skinned knees and neighborhood pecking orders, difficult teachers and well-meaning if uncomprehending parents; and without Cleary's gift for finding the drama and humor in those precincts, I doubt we'd have successors such as Judy Blume or Katherine Paterson or Andrew

Clements, not to mention characters like Junie B. Jones, Judy Moody, and Greg Heffley.

But to call Cleary a realist, the godmother of fiction about quirky but essentially normal kids, is to limit her achievement. Her best books are gems of emotional insight and also, most important of all, they are very, very funny, though never jokey—they're comedies of manners for children. Cleary made me laugh at the age of eight and still makes me laugh nearly half a century later. Slapstick comedians aside, the only other person I can think of who has managed that is Charles Schulz. Though his kids speak with adult inflections, the *Peanuts* neighborhood isn't all that far from Klickitat Street, but Schulz, for all his genius, harbored side-by-side sappy and cruel streaks that Cleary would never stand for. I can imagine her discreetly rolling her eyes at *Happiness Is a Warm Puppy*, and she would never abuse any of her characters the way Schulz punishes poor Charlie Brown. Not that she's a softie; she's a straight shooter, with just a glint of Beatrix Potter's hard stare in her gaze.

I loved Cleary before I knew anything about her, but I loved her even more after reading her two memoirs—*The Girl from Yamhill* and its sequel, *My Own Two Feet*—and learning that her career was to some extent fueled by her pique at insipid children's books, the kind that treat kids as if they were mush-headed or shallow, rather than just young. I haven't read every word Cleary has written, but I've read most of them and I've never known her to condescend to children or anyone else. Her books are warm but they have backbone. Her pique has served several generations of readers well.

Cleary's career as a "real live author"—as the children she meets often put it, she says—began in 1949, when she was thirty-two. She had long harbored an ambition to write for children, going back to her own girlhood. (She reworked a story she had composed in high school as a chapter for her first book, *Henry Huggins*.) But she set writing aside in her twenties to work as a librarian; that period included a wartime stint running libraries for the army, first at a Northern California base and then at a nearby military hospital. It took until after V-J Day, plus several more years and an epiphany about the mediocrity of most children's books, before she sat down at her typewriter and finally banged something out. She had been working at a bookstore in Berkeley during the 1948 Christmas season when, as she writes in *My Own Two Feet*: "One morning, during a lull, I picked up an easy-reading book and read, '"Bow-wow. I like the green grass," said the puppy.' How ridiculous, I thought. No puppy I had known talked like that. Suddenly I knew I could write a better book, and what was more I intended to do it as soon as the Christmas rush was over."

Even then, Cleary needed a second epiphany before she got anywhere, having no actual story in mind, only the ambition to be an author. "*Write*, and no backing out, I told myself. In all my years of dreaming about writing, I had never thought about what it was I wanted to say." She initially considered "the usual first book about a maturing of a young girl" but that notion failed to spark either imagination or memory. Veiled autobiography, she feared, would have been too boring: "I seem to have spent my own childhood reading library books or embroidering tea towels" (an assertion at odds with her portrait of herself as a freethinking, quietly mischievous child in *A Girl from Yamhill*). Still racking her brain for a subject or story, she thought about the "nonreaders," mostly boys, she had known ten years earlier working as a children's librarian.

> I soon learned there was very little in the library these boys wanted
> to read. "Where are the books about kids like us?" they wanted to
> know. Where indeed. There was only one book I could find about

kids like them, kids who parked their earmuffs on the circulation desk in winter and their baseball mitts in summer. That book was *Honk the Moose*, by Phil Stong, a story about some farm boys who found a moose in a livery stable. All the boys liked that book because it fulfilled another of their requirements. It was funny. As I listened to the boys talk about books, I recalled my own childhood reading, when I longed for funny stories about the sort of children who lived in my neighborhood. What was the matter with authors? I had often wondered and wondered again.

Reflecting on all this, she decided she would write about boys like those she had known growing up and as a librarian, "the kinds of boys who did not have scary adventures but who made their own excitement. . . . Forget about girls. I would write a book about a boy, a boy named Henry Huggins, a name that seemed to be waiting in my mind." An anecdote she'd once been told about a family trying to take a dog in a box onto a streetcar suggested the plot for the first chapter of her book, where Henry meets the stray mutt who becomes his pet (and eventually the title character of another book), Ribsy. And yet Cleary still found herself blocked until she discarded the notion of "writing" per se and decided to "tell" her tale the way she would have told it to the story-hour crowd at her library in Yakima.

When I first read that account I wondered if she was being unduly humble about her craft as a writer—to be honest, the anecdote sounded a little too cute, which Cleary's stories rarely are. But the more I think about it the more apt the story-hour analogy seems. The plainspoken directness of a thoughtful librarian telling a story to a dozen or so six-year-olds and the command but also the sympathy for their concerns and tastes she'd need to keep them paying attention, and not poking at one another or squabbling, are keys to Cleary's voice as a writer, to her books' effects. Knowing her audience's disdain for flowery prose, she doesn't waste words or paragraphs. "Children told me they liked my books," she once noted, "'because there isn't any description in them.'"

In *My Own Two Feet*, Cleary offers a quote from James Thurber, a favorite writer of hers, as a touchstone for her own work: "Humor is best that lies closest to the familiar." The opening of *Henry Huggins*, published in 1950 and an instant hit with kids, critics, librarians, and teachers, can be read as a manifesto by example for the kinds of books she herself wanted to write:

> Henry Huggins was in the third grade. His hair looked like a scrubbing brush and most of his front teeth were in. He lived with his mother and father in a square white house on Klickitat Street. Except for having his tonsils out when he was six and breaking his arm falling out of a cherry tree when he was seven, nothing much happened to Henry.
>
> I wish something exciting would happen, Henry often thought.
>
> But nothing very interesting ever happened to Henry, at least not until one Wednesday afternoon in March.

So much of what is great about Cleary is packed in there. There is "description" but it counts for something. The fact that Henry's hair looks like a scrubbing brush instantly gives us a sense of what kind of boy he is—not overly fussy or sivilized, as Huck Finn, a distant literary forebear, would say—and also hints that he probably gets his hair cut at home. (Tight family budgets are a frequent theme for Cleary.) The observation about most of his front teeth being in further situates him by indicating his age, and is exactly the kind of physical detail a boy himself would be aware of and take pride in. Getting his tonsils out and breaking his arm would loom even larger in any kid's mind—signal events that shape the narrative of a young life the way successions of jobs and serial romances do for adults.

But tonsillectomies and broken bones are outliers. What I prize most about this opening is Cleary's acknowledgment that "nothing much happened to Henry," and his own wish that "something exciting would happen." Here Cleary violates one of the great taboos regarding American childhood: children are not supposed to get bored, and if they do get bored it is a near-moral failing. This is because adults tend to romanticize childhood as a time of boundless adventure and enchantment, or we so envy kids their lives free of mortgages and oil changes and Xanax that we dismiss them as delusional or ungrateful, and find their protests laughable, when they complain of boredom. *Go play outside. Go call a friend. Go play with all those toys you got for Christmas.* I heard that from my parents and my kids have heard it from me. But childhood is full of longueurs, and growing up can be tedious. By acknowledging this, and on the very first page of her very first book, Cleary establishes instant credibility with her audience. Kids know: this is an adult who's been there. Or, maybe more to the point, since everyone's been there: this is an adult who *remembers.*

Cleary nearly always hews to a kid's-eye view of the adult world as a foreign country with odd and occasionally irritating or even appalling customs. For instance, when Henry first finds Ribsy and tries to bring him home in a box on the city bus—Henry having been warned that animals have to be confined on public transportation—Ribsy escapes and eventually causes such a ruckus that a policeman is forced to intervene. He asks if Henry thinks he should be arrested.

"No sir," said Henry politely. He thought the policeman was joking, but he wasn't sure. It was hard to tell about grown-ups sometimes.

Later, Henry is amazed to hear that his friend Scooter's grandmother has given him a football for his birthday because, as Henry laments in a common but no less poignant complaint, "My grandmother sends me sweaters and socks." In the chapter that Cleary recycled from her old high school story, a teacher forces Henry to take the objectionable lead part in a Christmas pageant: a little boy named Timmy who has a dream about going to the North Pole. Most humiliatingly, the role requires that Henry wear pajamas onstage and, at one point, stand alone and sing a song with the lyrics: "Hurrah for Santa! Hurrah for Saint Nick! / He comes from the north with reindeer and sleigh, / Riding on clouds up high in the sky / With a pack full of toys so children can play." Cleary adds, "It was the dumbest song Henry had ever heard. Hurrah for Santa! It was just plain stupid. He felt a little better when he learned that Robert [a friend] had to sing an even dumber song called 'Woof, Woof, I'm a Big Brown Dog.'" Is this a veiled dig, I wonder, at the picture book whose dumbness goaded Cleary to write *Henry Huggins* in the first place? (Henry is saved from having to play Timmy when Ribsy knocks a can of green paint on his head, dyeing his skin for the duration and forcing the teacher to recast him as an unobjectionable elf.)

So in her first book Cleary has portrayed adults as alternately cryptic, clueless, and, in the case of the pageant organizers, capable of inadvertent cruelty—not quite the flagrant buffoonery that passes for grown-up behavior in contemporary Nickelodeon and Disney Channel sitcoms, but you have to remember that Cleary was writing in 1950; what today seems quaintly mordant (if that's not a contradiction in terms) might have felt like a breath of fresh air to her first readers. I don't want to exaggerate this point, because Cleary's world is at bottom a benign one, with parents and teachers who are for the most part loving and well-meaning (though Cleary portrays her own parents as difficult and distant); I just want to point it out as a sign of her gift for meeting children on their terms, without pandering.

Some of Cleary's more prominent predecessors, authors whose heroes are boys of varying degrees of unruliness, took an almost opposite approach, treating their characters the way you might treat a socially awkward friend or relative whom you're fond of but also embarrassed by. While children might have once read Booth Tarkington's Penrod books, the author keeps his small-town twelve-year-old hero at an amused, ironic distance; these are stories less about what it's like to be a child than what it's like to remember being a child, a blend of understanding and condescension. This is true as well of *The Adventures of Tom Sawyer*, as Mark Twain makes plain in his introduction:

> Although my book is intended mainly for the entertainment of boys and girls, I hope it will not be shunned by men and women on that account, for part of my plan has been to try pleasantly to remind adults of what they once were themselves, and of how they felt and thought and talked and what queer enterprises they sometimes engaged in.

Twain means "queer enterprises" affectionately, I think, but Tom himself would be horrified by the description. Henry too. Twain clearly loves Tom but can't help making fun of him; the book is knowing about childhood, but wears that knowingness on its sleeve. Here, for example, is the scene where Tom first encounters Becky Thatcher, the new girl in town, "a lovely little blue-eyed creature with yellow hair plaited into two long tails, white summer frock, and embroidered pantalettes." Tom, coming home flush with victory after a mock battle with a group of friends, spots Becky playing in her front yard:

The fresh-crowned hero fell without firing a shot. A certain Amy Lawrence vanished out of his heart, and left not even a memory of herself behind. He had thought he had loved her to distraction; he had regarded his passion as adoration; and behold it was only a poor little evanescent partiality. . . .

He worshipped this new angel with furtive eye, till he saw that she had discovered him; then he pretended he did not know she was present, and began to "show off" in all sorts of boyish ways to win her admiration. He kept up this grotesque foolishness for some little time; but by-and-by, while he was in the midst of some dangerous gymnastics performances, he glanced aside, and saw that the little girl was wending towards the house. Tom came up to the fence and leaned on it, grieving.

By way of contrast, this is how Cleary treats a parallel Cupid's-arrow moment in *Ramona the Pest*, her first book centering on Ramona Quimby, the kindergarten-age sister of Henry's friend Beezus (real name Beatrice; nickname acquired because Ramona couldn't say "Beatrice" when she was little):

The more Ramona saw of Davy, the better she liked him. He was such a nice shy boy with blue eyes and soft brown hair. Ramona always tried to choose Davy for her partner in folk dancing, and when the class played Gray Duck Ramona always tagged Davy unless he was already in the mush pot.

Then, one morning on the playground, Ramona spots Davy with "a black cape pinned to his shoulders with two big safety pins."

Ramona marched up to him, and asked, "Are you Batman?"

"No," said Davy.

"Are you Superman?" asked Ramona.

"No," said Davy.

Who else could Davy be in a black cape? Ramona stopped and thought but was unable to think of anyone else who wore a cape. "Well, who are you?" she asked at last.

"Mighty Mouse!" crowed Davy, delighted that he had baffled Ramona.

"I'm going to kiss you Mighty Mouse!" shrieked Ramona.

Davy began to run and Ramona ran after him. Round and round the playground they ran with Davy's cape flying out behind him. . . .

Every morning afterward when Ramona reached the playground she tried to catch Davy so she could kiss him. "Here comes Ramona!" the other boys and girls shouted, when they saw Ramona walking down the street. "Run, Davy! Run!"

Tom Sawyer is fun,[1] but rereading it in adulthood makes me feel old; as Twain suggested, his point of view is fundamentally nostalgic. *Ramona the Pest* was published in 1968, when Cleary was fifty-two (making her eleven years older than Twain was when he published *Tom Sawyer*), and yet, thanks to some alchemy of memory, observation, and imagination, the book plunges us back into kindergarten in a way that is immediate and recognizable whether you yourself were in kindergarten just a few years or several decades ago. Reading *Ramona the Pest* makes me feel five again—not a 100 percent pleasant sensation, but a powerful one. Ramona's vividness on the page and her headstrong joie de vivre are big reasons why. So too is Cleary's recognition of the way

---

[1]What isn't fun is Twain's treatment of the book's villain, Injun Joe, who is repeatedly referred to in racist terms, but without the satiric or moral purpose that underlies the far more infamous treatment of Jim in *The Adventures of Huckleberry Finn*.

seemingly minor details can loom so large for a young child trying to make sense of the world. There is a wonderful and telling passage early in the book, detailing Ramona's first day of school, when Miss Binney, the pretty young kindergarten teacher (and isn't Miss Binney a perfect name for a pretty young kindergarten teacher, sounding crisp and efficient yet only a single vowel sound away from "bunny"?), reads the class *Mike Mulligan and His Steam Shovel*—which, Cleary notes, "was a favorite of Ramona's because, unlike so many books for her age, it was neither quiet and sleepy nor sweet and pretty." There is Cleary the gimlet-eyed children's librarian again. But then:

> As Ramona listened, a question came into her mind, a question that had often puzzled her about the books that were read to her. Somehow books always left out the most important things anyone would want to know. Now that Ramona was in school, and school was a place for learning, perhaps Miss Binney would answer the question. Ramona waited quietly until her teacher had finished the story, and then she raised her hand the way Miss Binney had told the class they should raise their hands when they wanted to speak in school.
>
> Joey, who did not remember to raise his hand, spoke out. "That's a good book."
>
> Miss Binney smiled at Ramona and said, "I like the way Ramona remembers to raise her hand when she has something to say. Yes, Ramona?" Ramona's hopes soared. Her teacher had smiled at her. "Miss Binney, I want to know—how did Mike Mulligan go to the bathroom when he was digging the basement of the town hall?"

The teacher, "in her clear and distinct way," tells the class that going to the bathroom is "not an important part of the story."

Miss Binney spoke as if this explanation ended the matter, but
the kindergarten was not convinced. Ramona knew and the rest
of the class knew that knowing how to go to the bathroom *was*
important. They were surprised Miss Binney did not understand,
because she had shown them the bathroom the very first thing.
Ramona could see that there were some things she was not going
to learn in school, and along with the rest of the class she stared
reproachfully at Miss Binney.

Authors often say their characters take on a life of their own; you can
read Cleary's books leading up to *Ramona the Pest* as a kind of meta-
narrative describing that exact process, with Ramona, a minor figure
in *Henry Huggins*, asserting herself into more and more of Cleary's
stories, the smallest kid in the neighborhood acting up to get attention and then holding her audience—and creator—once she gets it.
"Ramona did take on a life of her own," Cleary told me. She said
Ramona had begun that life as a literal afterthought: "When I wrote
Henry Huggins, it occurred to me that all the children appeared to be
only children"—like Cleary herself—"so I threw in a little sister, and
I think she has one paragraph, maybe two in *Henry Huggins*." Indeed,
to the extent that Ramona appears at all in that first book it's as passing comic relief, a nursery school version of the town drunk in a John
Ford movie. At one point Henry and his friend Robert encounter Ramona with curlers in her hair scratching the bark of a tree. "I'm a cat
with curly hair," Ramona explains, prompting this reaction: "Henry
and Robert exchanged disgusted looks. Girls certainly started to be
dumb when they were awfully young."

By the third Henry Huggins book, *Henry and Ribsy* (1954), Ramona has blossomed into something of an antagonist: the neighborhood "pest," blessed with moxie, tenaciousness, and an intuitive grasp

of how to leverage temper tantrums for personal gain. Ramona complicates Henry's life and occasionally gets him into trouble, as when she hides one of Ribsy's bones in a lunch box as revenge because Ribsy has eaten her ice cream cone, and subsequently draws a crowd of PTA ladies who think Ribsy has treed her in a schoolyard jungle gym when he's really just waiting patiently for her to give him his bone back. "I have a samwidge in my lunch box," Ramona insists—whether from a surfeit of imagination or cunning is not clear—and the ladies, to Henry's dismay, are ready to have "vicious" Ribsy impounded, although at least one woman is on Ribsy's side: "I know that little Ramona Quimby. She's a perfect terror."

Cleary circled closer to giving Ramona the spotlight and a fuller characterization in *Beezus and Ramona* (1955), but that book is written from Beezus's point of view. It's the tale of a "sensible," conventional girl coping with a little sister who is anything but. "Sometimes I think Ramona has too much imagination," their father says, upsetting Beezus:

> Nobody, reflected Beezus, ever says anything about my imagination. Nobody at all. And she wished, more than anything, that she had imagination. How pleased Miss Robins, the art teacher, would be with her if she had an imagination like Ramona's! Unfortunately, Beezus was not very good at painting—at least not the way Miss Robins wanted boys and girls to paint. She wanted them to use their imagination and to feel free. Beezus still squirmed with embarrassment when she thought of her first painting, a picture of a dog with *bowwow* coming out of his mouth in a balloon. Miss Robins pointed out that only in the funny papers did dogs have bowwow coming out of their mouths in balloons. Bowwow in a balloon was not art.

Beezus's self-doubt is painful—the drama of the allegedly ungifted child. (I suspect that on this count, more of us identify with Beezus than with Ramona.) After Ramona ruins Beezus's tenth birthday, Beezus's conflicted feelings toward her sister are honest and genuinely moving—the love-hate fuel that most families run on. But Beezus's dilemma is not where the author's heart ultimately lies. Cleary has often insisted that she herself was a well-mannered child, more Beezus than Ramona, but then again, as she once told an interviewer, "I had Ramona-like thoughts!" While Beezus and Henry are fine as far as they go, Ramona clearly strikes a chord in Cleary, who can't help delighting in her. Nor, at times, can Beezus, and even Henry comes to have a grudging respect for Ramona's fearlessness. Is Ramona the girl Cleary wishes she had been, or some idealized version of herself? If so, it is a tribute to Cleary that the idealized self is such a handful.[2]

Still, it would be another thirteen years and some sixteen books (not just novels about the children of Klickitat Street but also picture books, young adult romances, and, believe it or not, three *Leave It to Beaver* tie-in books, which are models of their kind) until, as Cleary told me in her succinct, plain-spoken way, "I felt, well, maybe Ramona needs a book of her own. And at the time my editor said, 'Why not write a book about Ramona?' So I wrote *Ramona the Pest.*"

To my mind, the book is Cleary's absolute masterpiece—her *Adventures of Huckleberry Finn*, another masterpiece in which shifting the spotlight to a sidekick somehow allowed the writer to mine a richer vein of material than he or she previously had access to. *Ramona the Pest* is funny, of course, and memorably so, as when Ramona names a doll

---

[2]In this, she may have much in common with the creators of many imps and brats, human and animal, in children's literature, from Tom Sawyer, Penrod, and Eloise to Brer Rabbit, Mr. Toad, Squirrel Nutkin, Lily, and Olivia.

Chevrolet, to her ear "the most beautiful name in the world," and thinks the new song she's learned in kindergarten, "The Star-Spangled Banner," is about a kind of lamp, a "dawnzer," that gives off a "lee light." (For me that remains the go-to example of a "mondegreen," a neologism for a misheard lyric.) What truly distinguishes *Ramona the Pest*, though, is the way Cleary gets inside Ramona's head, illuminating her shifting moods and conflicting impulses, her vulnerabilities as well as her brashness—all in hothouse flower. This is a girl who likes action, a girl who likes to stir the pot, a girl who is frustrated by her friend Howie because he's so phlegmatic. Better yet, in Cleary's words, "Ramona was a girl who could not wait. Life was so interesting she had to find out what happened next." One of my favorite lines in the book, small but resonant, concerns Howie's drooling, zwieback-encrusted little sister, Willa Jean, who, Cleary writes, "was interesting to Ramona because she was so sloppy." *Interesting*, again. It's such a telling word here. Cleary might have written that Ramona found Willa Jean *funny* or *gross* or *babyish* or *boring*, but Ramona is a girl who can always see possibility, and even sloppiness sparks her imagination—a toddler's sloppiness that a kindergartner might well view as a window onto herself not so long ago. So *interesting* it is.

But there is a downside to Ramona's exuberance. She suffers a training-wheels version of an existential panic during her school's Halloween parade when, hidden behind a rubber witch mask amid a crowd full of similarly costumed witches, she realizes she has made herself anonymous. For an extrovert like Ramona, what could be worse?

> Nobody knew who Ramona was, and if nobody knew who she was, she wasn't anybody.
>
> "Get out of the way, old witch!" Eric B. yelled at Ramona. He did not say, Get out of the way, Ramona.
>
> Ramona could not remember a time when there was not someone near her who knew who she was. . . . The feeling was the

scariest one Ramona had ever experienced. She felt lost inside her costume. She wondered if her mother would know which witch was which, and the thought that her own mother might not know her frightened Ramona even more. What if her mother forgot her? What if everyone in the whole world forgot her?

The novel's narrative turns on a day that begins wonderfully for Ramona and ends with her becoming a kindergarten pariah thanks to a mix of abandon, ego, and stubborness—an emotional recipe many a tragic hero or heroine might ruefully recognize. Ramona loses her first tooth at school, the bloody gap in her mouth making her an instant celebrity. Miss Binney even calls her "a brave girl." Heaven. But at recess, "filled with the glory of losing her first tooth and love for her teacher," Ramona can't help pulling one of the long reddish-brown curls of bossy tattletale Susan while shouting "boin-n-n-ng!" Miss Binney asks her to stop, but Ramona can't resist another yank after Susan calls her a "pest," a word that gets under Ramona's skin like no other. (The book's very first sentence: "'I am *not* a pest,' Ramona Quimby told her big sister Beezus.") Suddenly, the temperature on the playground changes. Miss Binney tells Ramona she will have to go home until she can learn to stop pulling Susan's hair—a crossroads for Ramona:

> Ramona thought. Could she really stop pulling Susan's curls? She thought about those thick, springy locks that were so tempting. She thought about Susan who always acted so big. In kindergarten, there was no worse crime than acting big. In the eyes of the children acting big was worse than being a pest. Ramona finally looked up at Miss Binney and gave an honest answer. "No," she said. "I can't."

Ramona is then sent home, convinced that Miss Binney doesn't love her anymore. Almost worse, that evening Ramona tells Beezus to turn on "the dawnzer" and Beezus, dissolving into a fit of laughter, realizes that Ramona has garbled the lyrics to "The Star-Spangled Banner." For Ramona, this is the last straw. An epic tantrum results, the long dark night of a five-year-old soul:

> Ramona looked at her mother and father who had the straight mouths and laughing eyes of grown ups who were trying not to laugh out loud. Beezus was right and she was wrong. She was nothing but a girl who used to go to kindergarten and who got everything wrong and made everyone laugh. She was a stupid little sister. A dumb little sister, who never did anything right.

She runs to her room and throws herself on her bed.

> Ramona wanted to be wicked, really wicked, so she swung around and banged her heels on the wall. Bang! Bang! Bang! That noise ought to make everyone good and mad. . . . Ramona drummed harder to show everyone how bad she was. She would not take off her shoes. She was a terrible, wicked girl! Being such a bad, terrible, horrible, wicked girl made her feel *good*! She brought both heels against the wall at the same time. Thump! Thump! Thump! She was not the least bit sorry for what she was doing. She would *never* be sorry. Never! Never! Never!

Ramona eventually exhausts herself and collapses on her bed thinking "wild fierce thoughts." This reminds me of Max stewing supperless in his room in *Where the Wild Things Are*. (Perhaps someday the two could have a play date. . . .) Ramona doesn't embark on a strange, emotionally-resonant adventure, but thanks to a very believable combustion of stubbornness and shame, she does end up staying home from kindergarten for what seems to be a week or so—Cleary doesn't give the exact time span, but it lasts long enough to earn Ramona the sobriquet "kindergarten dropout" from Beezus—until she and Miss Binney finally reach détente. It is a happy ending, but hard-won, and arrived at following more harrowing turns than Cleary had previously allowed herself.

"So I wrote *Ramona the Pest.*"

Just like that. No fuss.

If those words had come from anyone but Cleary, I would think she was being disingenuously modest. In discussing *Ramona the Pest* I don't want to overstate its claim to literary greatness but I do believe that Ramona is as complex, vivid, and singular a character as has ever been put to paper, and that her first headlong collision with the civilizing forces of kindergarten is in its smaller way as quintessentially American a story as Huck Finn's escape down the Mississippi or Jay Gatsby's reinvention or Daisy Miller's and Isabel Archer's headlong collisions with decadent old Europe. (They too were girls who had to find out what happened next.) I can also well imagine Cleary wrinkling her nose at the very idea.

Tribute must also be paid to Louis Darling, who illustrated the majority of Cleary's books until his death in 1970, at the age of fifty-three. If *Ramona the Pest* is Cleary's masterpiece, I think it is also Darling's (though some, I'm sure, would argue for his work on Rachel Carson's *Silent Spring*, in collaboration with his wife, Lois Darling). All his line drawings for Cleary's novels strike a perfect balance between precision and fluidity, realism and esprit, capturing the inner lives of her characters while grounding them in time, place, and a consistent physicality. When author and illustrator arrived at *Ramona the Pest*, he seemed to know the children of Klickitat Street as well as she did. His rendering of Ramona, with her round face, shock of black hair, and uninhibited smiles and grimaces, had become bold, even iconographic, like a more

finely etched (and better natured) version of Charles Schulz's Lucy. Take
Louis's drawing of Ramona not lining up at the door before school: she
has both a dancer's grace and a kindergartner's happy abandon as she
skips across the asphalt, her limbs as loose as noodles but still seemingly
made of flesh, bone, and sinew. By contrast in his sketch of her epic
tantrum, Darling draws Ramona as a compact bundle of anger wedged
into a corner of her bedroom as if by the gravity of her own dark mood,
her fury all the more startling for being visually constrained. And that
tattoo of heel scuffs on the wall! It is a crime that Cleary's current publisher, HarperCollins, has cashiered Darling's illustrations and reissued
her novels with "updated" illustrations bereft of flair and charm.

I wish for my purposes, for the juiciness of this book, that Cleary
had lived a more knotty or dramatic life, a life more in the style of
Margaret Wise Brown's or even Beatrix Potter's. Cleary's two memoirs,
which take her up to the publication of *Henry Huggins*, reveal the usual
bumps and bruises earned in growing up and finding one's place in the
world, but there is nothing particularly remarkable in them. That they
are wonderful reads is due to Cleary's sympathetic but incisive eye and
ear, her honesty, her open mind, and her generous spirit—not so different from her novels' best qualities. She got married in 1940, at the
age of twenty-four, to Clarence Cleary, an accountant she had met at a
dance when she was an undergraduate at Berkeley. (Her family name
was Bunn.) The couple had twins, a boy and a girl, and stayed married
for sixty-four years, until Clarence's death in 2004. Whatever issues
there may have been in her family and marriage, she has kept them to
herself. Meanwhile, she hit the bulls-eye with her first book, has won
all the honors she could want, and has been as productive as anyone.

So nothing much to sensationalize there, and oh well. Cleary
wrote six more Ramona books after *Ramona the Pest*, all excellent,
though none quite match it. The sequels take Ramona through fourth
grade. She endures and thrives despite further dustups with Susan,

school years spent with teachers less compassionate than Miss Binney, stresses in her parents' marriage, her father's unemployment, the death of a pet cat, the birth of a baby sister, Beezus's adolescence, and the earliest, faintest glimmers of her own adulthood. *Ramona and Her Father* (1978) and *Ramona Quimby, Age 8* (1982) were both Newbery Honors books—the equivalent of being a National Book Award finalist—and Cleary won her first actual Newbery Award in 1984 for *Dear Mr. Henshaw*, a fine epistolary novel about a boy coping with his parents' divorce, but this belated benediction felt to me like giving Martin Scorsese an Oscar as best director for *The Departed* when he should have won decades earlier for *Taxi Driver, Raging Bull,* or *GoodFellas*.[3]

When Cleary and I spoke I wanted to know if she was working on anything new, which is a horrible thing to ask a writer (trust me), let alone one who is turning ninety. But as a fan I couldn't help myself, and it wasn't a totally unfair question: she had published her most recent book, *Ramona's World*, only seven years earlier, at the age of eighty-three. As for new works? "Not at the moment," she said. "I do have some notes on a new book, but I doubt very much I'll write it. I think it's important to know when to retire."

Ramona's World ends with Ramona celebrating her tenth birthday—the same milestone she ruined for her older sister in *Beezus and Ramona*, written more than four decades earlier. Here is the last line of the book, and if we never have another one from Beverly Cleary (who marked her one hundredth birthday with more interviews), I think this is a fitting farewell, equally generous and sensible, warm but unsentimental, like the author herself:

"The day was perfect—well not really, but close enough."

---

[3]Speaking of film, there was a Cleary adaptation made in 2010, entitled *Ramona and Beezus*. It looked awful and avoidable, an impression I chose to believe. But if you're curious . . . it exists.

7

God and Man in Narnia

"There was a boy called Eustace Clarence Scrubb, and he almost deserved it."

That is the opening line from C. S. Lewis's *The Voyage of the Dawn Treader*, the third book in his Narnia series, and it is so wonderful and evocative I thought I might as well open this chapter with it too. There, studding a single sentence, is so much of what is great about Lewis:

- It's funny.
- It displays a sure-handed grasp of craft. For as any novelist who has ever tried to come up with an evocative, euphonious, credible name for a character will tell you, this is not an easy task. (The Charles Dickenses and J. K. Rowlings, who nail name after memorable name with a sniper's unfailing

marksmanship—*Snape! Smike! Cratchit!*—are rare.) Take a closer look. *Eustace Clarence*: formal, homely, yet also strangely melodic. And then *Scrubb*: a single-syllable brick wall stopping the name in its tracks, the extra "b" a little stroke of genius, making the thing look as ugly on the page as it sounds coming off the tongue. We have learned something about this boy.

- It is generous. He *almost* deserved it. So on-point, that word. Redemption, the key theme for Lewis, is possible even if you are named Eustace Clarence Scrubb, and even if, as we learn about Eustace a couple of sentences later, you come from a family that is "very up-to-date and advanced."

That last dig—it's sarcasm—is very Lewis, too. As a man who, when he wasn't writing for children, juggled parallel careers as a medievalist and a Christian apologist, he was no friend to modernism.

I should mention here that I don't believe in God, any kind of God, not even a 99 percent secular one who holds the universe together like glue or netting but doesn't much care what kind of sex you have or whether the shooting guard who prayed in the locker room sinks a game-winning basket. I will spare you the details of how I came to this conclusion because they're not very interesting—not even to me, sadly. I just don't . . . believe.

I bring this up only because I don't otherwise know how to discuss what I have come to love about Lewis. Like a lot of irreligious readers, I have had a thorny relationship with Narnia, one that has evolved, across decades, from passionate love to feelings of betrayal and scorn to, at long last, respect and admiration—like the best possible divorce, I suppose. But any work that can whipsaw readers like that must be a signal achievement.

In his 1939 essay "On Fairy Stories," J. R. R. Tolkien wrote that at some point what had been part of a vital folk tradition was "relegated to the 'nursery,' as shabby or old-fashioned furniture is relegated to the play-room, primarily because the adults do not want it, and do not mind if it is misused." This is where Aesop's fables were stashed as well. But the adults who bothered to stick around in the playroom, like Lewis and Tolkien, did some amazing things with what they found, stretching and pulling the fairy-tale form, bending it through the prism of their own personalities and agendas, and using it to create entirely new, often lavishly detailed worlds—Wonderland, Neverland, Oz, Narnia, Middle Earth, Hogwarts. This was not magic or faith, but art; and while others may have been more gifted at it than Lewis, none were more, let us say, idiosyncratic.

I encountered the first book in the Narnia series,[1] *The Lion, the Witch and the Wardrobe*, when it was read to my second-grade class by our teacher, Mrs. Anastasia. (That was her real name, and there's the germ of a great story: a second-grade teacher turns out to be the long-lost princess of Russia.) The title alone was mysterious and intriguing—what lion? which witch? and no one growing up in suburban California in the 1960s had any idea what a wardrobe was. The story itself was even better, doled out a chapter a day after lunch while we listened, as in quiet time, with our heads down on our smooth, cool Formica desktops, Mrs. Anastasia at the front of the classroom, turning the pages with her cat glasses on, the early afternoon air heavy with the perfume of workbooks, paste, and the residue of lunchtime corn chips.

---

[1] Lewis's publisher, HarperCollins, now argues that the books should be read not in the order in which they were first published but in the chronologic order in which the stories take place in the Narnian universe. I think of this as the "George Lucas fallacy." Anyone not already invested in Narnia who comes cold to the new "Book One," *The Magician's Nephew*, the sixth Narnia book Lewis published and one of the weakest, will never go on with the rest.

I doubt any of us had previously encountered a fantasy that seemed so real and palpable and gripping: the sheer, transporting delight of the book's heroes, the four Pevensie family children, passing through the wardrobe and finding themselves in a strange but charming winter world populated by fauns, dwarves and talking beavers; the delicious fright of the White Witch and her castle full of people and animals turned to stone; the shock of younger brother Edmund's betraying his siblings and all that is good for a mere dessert, Turkish delight (no one in California knew what that was, either); and, most vividly of all, the even greater shock, and horror, of Aslan's murder at the hands of the White Witch, which must have been the first time most of my classmates and I had been exposed to a major character's death in fiction. (I wouldn't see *Bambi*, the usual icebreaker, until it was rereleased in theaters several years later.)

Aslan, you may know, is the true king of Narnia, a talking lion who is presented as a figure of unfathomable power and righteousness—"the son of the great emperor from across the sea." He arrives three quarters of the way through the book to free Narnia and put an end to the White Witch's rule, but surrenders himself to her in exchange for Edmund's life. To this day I remember Mrs. Anastasia explaining the mechanics of how the Witch could kill Aslan simply by slitting his neck with a single stroke, that his severed arteries would quickly bleed out; it was as if she were conducting a class on "wetwork" for very young CIA agents. Funny, though, that Lewis himself declines to describe the actual blow—perhaps Mrs. Anastasia was just showing off, adding her own little grisly touch; or perhaps she was venting a little pent-up hostility toward her pupils. At any rate, Lewis otherwise spares his young audience no details of the humiliation and pain of Aslan's ritual murder atop the Stone Table.

The horror of listening to this passage, our heads no longer dreamily on our desks—we were bolt upright now—remains one of my most vivid memories of grade school. First the great lion is bound, the cords cutting into his flesh, and muzzled. His mane is shaved and he is mocked, beaten, kicked, and spat on—there was something second-graders could relate to—by a nasty mob that Lewis describes with imaginative relish:

> A great crowd of people were standing all around the Stone Table and though the moon was shining many of them carried torches which burned with evil-looking red flames and black smoke. But such people! Ogres with monstrous teeth, and wolves, and bull-headed men; spirits of evil trees and poisonous plants; and other creatures whom I won't even describe because if I did the grown-ups would probably not let you read this book—Cruels and Hags and Incubuses, Wraiths, Horrors, Efreets, Sprites, Orknies, Wooses, and Ettins.

Lewis the writer was having himself a fine time here, as was the illustrator of the series, Pauline Bynes, who contributed a full-page portrait of this ghoulish assemblage. (Lewis crafted a fairly multicultural cast of evildoers, by the way, drawing on Norse, Celtic, and Arab mythologies. Pagan diversity!) The scene is witnessed by the two Pevensie sisters, Lucy and Susan, hiding in some bushes, and after the deed is done and the Witch and her rabble move on, Lewis takes the girls' point of view to drive home the monstrousness of what has happened:

> At any other time they would have trembled with fear; but now the sadness and shame and horror of Aslan's death so filled their minds that they hardly thought of it. . . . The moon was getting low and thin clouds were passing across her, but still they could see the shape of the Lion lying dead in his bonds. And down they both knelt in the wet grass and kissed his cold face and stroked his beautiful fur—what was left of it—and cried until they could

cry no more. And then they looked at each other and held each other's hands for mere loneliness and cried again; and then they were silent. . . . I hope no one who reads this book has been quite as miserable as Susan and Lucy were that night; but if you have been—if you've been up all night and cried until you have no more tears left in you—you will know that there comes in the end a sort of quietness. You feel as if nothing was ever going to happen again. At any rate, that is how it felt to these two.

Having lost his mother to cancer when he was only nine, Lewis presumably knew something about crying all night; and this passage, in the way it blends beauty, empathy, and sorrow with formality and even stiffness ("At any rate, that is how it felt to these two"), could be the work of no other writer. But what struck me in second grade, though I wouldn't have been able to articulate it, and what strikes me again now, particularly in Lewis's use of the word "shame," is the vivid sense he gives of Aslan's humiliation. That, and the pathos of his dead, cold, muzzled body, is what made this whole passage so excruciating and so memorable, beyond just the shock of a hero's murder. Am I wrong in divining a hint of relish in Lewis's descriptions of Aslan's being bound up and submitting passively to the Witch's will? Lewis, having made his way through the English public school system in the early years of the twentieth century, presumably also knew something about taking one's punishment manfully. But shame and brutality just make Aslan's resurrection all the more exhilarating, captured in another lovely passage where Lewis has the revived Aslan daring Lucy and Susan to try to catch him, leading them on a merry chase before they all tumble into "a happy laughing heap of fur and arms and legs. . . . [W]hether it was more like playing with a thunderstorm or playing with a kitten Lucy could never make up her mind."

Nowadays, by which I mean at least since the 1982 premiere

of *E. T.: The Extra-Terrestrial*, the conceit of dead or seemingly dead heroes coughing and sputtering back to life has become a staple, if not a cliché, of children's literature and film, on through and including *Harry Potter and the Deathly Hallows*. But back in the mid-1960s when Mrs. Anastasia was reading us *The Lion, the Witch and the Wardrobe*, dead characters in children's stories typically stayed dead—Old Yeller being a prominent example, along with fairy-tale birth mothers. Indeed for the most part, with the exception of giants, wolves, ogres, and the like, plus pets, characters in the gentle children's stories of the day didn't die in the first place, and certainly not from ritualized throat slitting. Aslan's death was dark, dark stuff for second-graders, making his resurrection—its power increased for us by the twenty-four-hour wait between chapter readings—all the more joyous. A true miracle: at least that's how it felt to me. Which of course was the point.

The only place I would have previously encountered such a resurrection was in Sunday school, where every springtime we were duly taught the story of *the* Resurrection and how Christ redeemed mankind by dying on the cross, which, as it was explained to us, never made much sense to me—I thought the story was unforgivably mean on everyone's account, especially God's. It adds up better when considered under the full weight and complexity of Christian theology, but we were spared all that in my Sunday school. We must have learned some homilies, but mostly what I remember are three things: being shown pictures of people in antique robes, always accompanied by sheep, sitting at the feet of a beatific, blue-eyed Jesus who loved everyone (I don't recall learning much about the severe, exacting, sometimes frightening Jesus you encounter in the actual gospels); being forced to sing "Michael Row the Boat Ashore," "He's Got the Whole World in His Hands," and, yes, "Kumbaya"; and, as I got a little older, sitting in the back of the class and making fart sounds with a friend

who suffered from severe cerebral palsy and could speak only with
great effort but who had an easy, openhearted laugh.

That last bit is as close as I ever came, in church, to a state of
grace.[2] But in fairness to Christianity, believers and nonbelievers alike
would agree that the strain I was exposed to was pretty thin stuff,
the sort of bloodless, namby-pamby theology Lewis himself once dismissed as "vague slush." Perhaps surprisingly for someone who became internationally famous first as a Christian apologist and then as
a writer of Christian-inflected fantasies, he had intimate acquaintance
with being turned off by rote, unthinking worship. Growing up as a
Protestant in Belfast in the first decade of the twentieth century, Lewis
had found churchgoing to be a chore, received no nourishment from
worship, and decided by his teens that he was an atheist. As he once
wrote, describing "a certain inhibition which had paralyzed" any religious impulse in his childhood: "Why did one find it so hard to feel
as one was told one ought to feel about God or about the suffering
of Christ? I thought the chief reason was that one was told one ought
to. An obligation to feel can freeze feelings. And reverence itself did
harm. The whole subject was associated with lowered voices; almost
as if it were something medical."

I won't go into the complex ins and outs of his change of heart,
which occurred when he was in his early thirties, after he had become a professor of medieval and Renaissance literature at Oxford,
and which was partially midwifed by his friend and colleague J. R. R.
Tolkien. If you're curious, Lewis offers an account of his two-stage
conversion—first to theism and then, two years later, to Christianity

---

[2]Feeling I owed my own children at least a nodding acquaintance with Christianity,
I sought help from picture books to explain the Easter story, but the ones I found
were hopeless: either so vague about the particulars of Christ's Passion as to be in-
comprehensible or so grisly as to be terrifying. I abandoned even this slim pretense
of religious instruction.

proper—in his memoir, *Surprised by Joy*, but it isn't a tale that would stir envy in the heart of a nonbeliever, or cause one to fear that one's atheism is constructed of flimsy materials. In Lewis's telling, he experienced no ecstatic, flash-of-light revelation; instead he presents his salvation as a slow, even grudging submission to what he comes to see as the relentless logic of God's existence. Perhaps rapture is too much to expect of a mid-century Oxford don, but still, Lewis makes his moment of coming to Jesus sound rather grim, referring to himself as "the most dejected and reluctant convert in all of England." Or, as he conceded to the *New York Times* in 1946, "I'm not the religious type," adding that he had been "philosophically converted." The point being that his brand of Christianity was no vague slush; it was rigorous and well thought out, not really a matter of faith at all, but something more like the orderly, inexorable logic of the periodic table.

Blessed with certitude, Lewis could be an intellectual bully when the mood struck him. "If the whole universe has no meaning, we should never have found out that it has no meaning; just as, if there were no light in the universe and therefore no creatures with eyes, we should never know it's dark. *Dark* would be a word without meaning," he writes in his most famous apologia, *Mere Christianity*, before concluding, "Very well then, atheism is too simple." You can imagine him slapping the dust of disbelief off his hands in the universal gesture for finishing someone off. This essay, originally delivered as a series of radio addresses begun in 1941, is essentially an if-A-then-B proof, with A being mankind's innate sense of right and wrong and B being the existence of God. I'm vastly oversimplifying, of course, and Lewis almost always writes with charm and wit as well as purpose, but still I find little magic in Lewis's purely religious books and essays.

That magic was all back in Mrs. Anastasia's class. It's not quite right to call the Narnia books straight-out allegories; they're too singular, too muddled in their symbolism, too grounded in their author's odd imagination, and they take too much delight in storytelling for its own sake (all of which could be said of the Bible as well). At any rate, the tale's Christian overtones went completely over my head and I'm sure everyone else's in the second grade. Which was intentional. "The author almost certainly did not want his readers to notice the resemblance of the Narnian theology to the Christian story," writes Lewis's friend and biographer George Sayer. "His idea, as he once explained to me, was to make it easier for children to accept Christianity when they met it later in life. He hoped that they would be vaguely reminded of the somewhat similar stories that they had read and enjoyed years before. 'I am aiming at a sort of pre-baptism of the child's imagination.'" Sayer adds, using Lewis's nickname (he needed one; his given name was Clive): "Jack's main object, of course, was to write good stories."

And he did. It was the yarn we responded to, the clash of good and evil, the destiny of an entire world set squarely on the shoulders of young people (as it always seems to be in children's fantasies as well as graduation speeches), the suits of armor and singing swords, talking beasts and witches, and, best of all, the seductive notion of being able to stumble into an extraordinary world through the most ordinary means. (Adding further allure for me was the exoticism of the book's Briticisms, the references to "looking glasses" and "the wireless," the characters who blurt out adjectives such as "beastly" and "horrid" and "jolly good." The flip side, which I didn't notice until I reencountered the books in adulthood, is an imperial tendency to describe certain human characters from lands south of Narnia as "dark," "grave and mysterious," and "smelling of garlic and onions.")

Lucy, the youngest and most openhearted character in the series, is the first of the Pevensie siblings to stumble upon Narnia. The initial story is set during World War II; the four children have been evacuated from London and are staying in the big empty house of an "old

Professor," somewhere out in the country. One day, as they explore the house, Lucy pushes her way into an old wardrobe:

> It was almost quite dark in there and she kept her arms stretched out in front of her so as not to bump her face into the back of the wardrobe. She took a step further in—then two or three steps— always expecting to feel woodwork against the tips of her fingers. But she could not feel it.
>
> "This must be simply an enormous wardrobe!" thought Lucy, going still further in. . . . Then she noticed there was something crunching under her feet. "I wonder is that more moth-balls?" she thought, stooping down to feel it with her hand. But instead of feeling the hard smooth wood of the floor of the wardrobe, she felt something soft and powdery and extremely cold. "This is very queer," she said, and went on a step or two further.
>
> Next moment she found that what was rubbing against her face and hands was no longer soft fur but something hard and rough and even prickly. "Why, it is just like the branches of trees!" exclaimed Lucy. And then she saw there was a light ahead of her; not a few inches away where the back of the wardrobe ought to have been, but a long way off. Something cold and soft was falling on her. A moment later she was standing in the middle of a wood at nighttime with snow under her feet and snowflakes falling through the air.

I feel like sighing whenever I read that. The passage (in both the literary and the physical senses of the word) is, or seems, as brilliantly effortless as good magic should be. Lewis is cribbing from Edith Nesbit, a British children's author at the turn of the twentieth century and a favorite of Lewis's childhood; she wrote a short story, "Amabel and the Aunt," about a girl also sent away to live at an old house who finds a giant crystal railway station at the back of a wardrobe. (Nesbit, the sort of narrator who informs readers she won't repeat a magic word "for fear you should say it by accident and then be sorry," may also be the source of Lewis's taste for avuncular asides.)

This tumble through the back of the wardrobe left me, as I think it leaves a lot of children, hoping into adulthood that I might somehow, sometime, stumble into a magic land of my own—knowing all the while that it would never happen but hoping nonetheless, just as I've heard kids more recently admit to the snuffing of a secret hope when they don't receive an invitation to attend Hogwarts on their eleventh birthday. Was I yearning for transcendence or merely adventure, for God or for dragons? Is transcendence only a fancier name for adventure? Lewis's friend Tolkien, who knew something about the subject, wrote in "On Fairy Stories" about "the primal 'desires' that lie near the heart" of the genre: "the glimpsing or making of Other worlds." I'm not sure why he put quotes around *desires*—maybe the word was too hot-blooded—but he continued, discussing his own childhood enthusiasms, "At no time can I remember that the enjoyment of a story was dependent on belief that such things could happen, had happened in 'real life.' Fairy stories were plainly not primarily concerned with possibility but with desirability. If they awakened desire, satisfying it while often whetting it unbearably, they succeeded."

Satisfying it while whetting it unbearably. Well, yes. I read all seven Narnia books as quickly as I could. And reread them, and re-reread them, except for the final two—*The Magician's Nephew* and *The Last Battle*—which I found weirder and harder to follow and far less transporting than the others. As it happens, the last two are the most nakedly allegorical of the bunch, less fully-realized novels than connect-the-dots puzzles. *The Magician's Nephew* is the story of Narnia's genesis while *The Last Battle*, as the name suggests, relates Narnia's end days and Armageddon, complete with a "false Aslan" subbing for the

Antichrist of Revelation. In those two books, Lewis the apologist gets the better of Lewis the storyteller. But, as I said, that all went over my head in the second grade (just like the fact that the TV series *Batman*, the other great cultural revelation of that school year, was funny). For the most part, I was simply in thrall to what remains one of the most memorable experiences with narrative I've ever had.

Thus the dismay, even anger I felt when, while rereading *The Lion, the Witch and the Wardrobe* for a children's lit class in high school, I now understood the whole enterprise as a Christian Trojan horse. What had been rich and mysterious, strange and thrilling was revealed, in the unforgiving glare of teenage enlightenment, as phony and tawdry—as kiddie propaganda, lollipops spiked with dogma. This feeling of betrayal is common to many nonreligious readers.[3]

Thirty-odd years later, I was eager to read Lewis's books to my kids and give Narnia another shot, but they would have none of it. They had seen a crummy animated version of *The Lion, the Witch and the Wardrobe* at a friend's home—had I known that this cartoon existed, I would never have let them near it—and it soured them on the idea of the books, despite my entreaties that the real things were something else altogether.[4] So I reread the books on my own.

Did I realize how funny Lewis is when I was a kid? Did I take

[3]The critic Laura Miller has written an entire book on the subject of her love of, rejection of, and renewed passion for Narnia—girl gets book, girl loses book, girl gets book back—entitled *The Magician's Book: A Skeptic's Adventures in Narnia*. I chose not to read it, because I feared it might overshadow my own thoughts about Lewis, but it came highly recommended to me by many smart readers.

[4]The kids enjoyed the live-action Narnia films that began coming out a few years later, but though they sound like perfectly reasonable adaptations, I have strenuously avoided them, not wanting to literalize such a core part of my childhood imagination. The calculations involved in deciding when and when not to see movies of books you love, and when to forgo reading books you probably wouldn't love but might enjoy on-screen starring Matt Damon or Emily Blunt, could be the subject of another volume altogether.

delight in that opening sentence from *The Voyage of the Dawn Treader*, with its droll, succinct snap? Or this passage, from *The Magician's Nephew*, sketching in the book's turn of the twentieth century setting: "In those days, if you were a boy, you had to wear a stiff Eton collar every day, and schools were usually nastier than now. But meals were nicer; and as for sweets, I won't tell you how good and cheap they were, because it would only make your mouth water in vain." At one point in *The Lion, the Witch and the Wardrobe*, there is a false sighting of the evil title character, which sends our heroes into hiding. "Come out," shouts a beaver who is protecting the children. "It's all right! It isn't *Her!*" Lewis adds, "This was bad grammar of course, but that is how beavers talk when they are excited; I mean, in Narnia—in our world they don't usually talk at all." (I'm an editor by trade, but I'll confess I had to check with a copy editor that what the beaver should have said was, "It isn't *She!*") Another detail from the first book that made me smile is the title of a volume Lewis draws attention to in the home of Lucy's friend Mr. Tumnus: *Men, Monks, and Gamekeepers: A Study in Popular Legend.* (Half man, half goat, Mr. Tumnus is identified as a faun, though most would think of him as a satyr.) Even if you didn't know of Lewis's professorial background, you'd call his sense of humor "donnish."

But the biggest surprise was finding myself charmed and persuaded by the religious undercurrents of Lewis's tales—in the sense that I am moved and persuaded not by the theology itself but rather by Lewis's ability to convey in tangible, organic terms what his religion means to him, what Christianity *feels* like for him. Not surprisingly, this is most apparent when he writes about Aslan, Christ's leonine stand-in, whose name alone in the first book, before the Pevensie children have even met him, is enough to strike deep, yearning chords. "Aslan is on the move," Mr. Beaver (his formal name; not quite as good as Eustace Clarence Scrubb) tells the children at one point in a conspiratorial whisper:

And now a very curious thing happened. None of the children knew who Aslan was any more than you do; but at the moment the Beaver had spoken these words everyone felt quite different. Perhaps it has sometimes happened to you in a dream that someone says something you don't understand but in the dream it feels as if it had some enormous meaning—either a terrifying one which turns the whole dream into a nightmare or else a lovely meaning too lovely to put into words, which makes the dream so beautiful you remember it all your life and are always wishing you could get into that dream again. It was like that now. At the name of Aslan each one of the children felt something jump in its inside.

A skeptic might insist that dream logic is an apt metaphor for religious belief, but this nonbeliever is instead moved by Lewis's earnest stab at expressing the ineffability of religious feeling, and by the grace of his prose. Fifty pages later, when Aslan finally turns up, he is a figure worthy of that fanfare:

People who have not been in Narnia sometimes think that a thing cannot be good and terrible at the same time. If the children had ever thought so they were cured of it now. For when they tried to look at Aslan's face they just caught a glimpse of the golden mane and the great, royal, solemn, overwhelming eyes; and they found they couldn't look at him and went all trembly.

Aslan goes on to evince empathy and generosity—he becomes approachable—but that line about him being terrible as well as good (terrible in the sense of being frightening rather than bad) is a key to the book's power. It's like that lovely phrase I quoted earlier when Lucy couldn't make up her mind whether she had been playing with

a thunderstorm or a kitten. Aslan is a complex, sometimes frightening character who stirs complex, sometimes frightening emotions, not
unlike the Jesus you read about in the gospels, who can be a bit of
a tough guy and a stickler—and not at all like the dumbed-down,
construction-paper Jesus I grew up with. Aslan is worthy of awe and
reverence; he feels like a full meal rather than the sugary snack or
bland heap of roughage (or vague slush) that religion so often seems
to be. I'm no expert, but Lewis's ostensible fantasy strikes me as an unusually sophisticated, not to mention graceful and humane, portrayal
of belief, no matter the age of the intended audience. Or perhaps I
should just say that the Narnia books allow me to "get it" in a way that
most religious expression, whether art or testament, does not.[5]

Lewis was going for precisely that. He himself was led to Christianity in part through his love and study of mythology, with the Christian myth having, in his view, the added benefit of being true. Fairy
stories and other children's fantasies—the good ones, anyway—were
to his mind rich with glimmers and intimations of metaphysical truth.
Indeed, one of his first experiences with what he came to call "joy"—
he personalizes the word to denote a kind of bittersweet longing for
transcendence that ultimately led him to Christ—came while he was
reading Beatrix Potter's *Squirrel Nutkin* as a boy. The book "troubled
me with what I can only describe as the Idea of Autumn," Lewis
would write. "It sounds fantastic to say that one can be enamored of a
season but that is something like what happened." And actually I get

---

[5]I should add that I was left cold by Philip Pullman's trilogy *His Dark Materials*, an
allegory about killing God, I think, but it's hard to say: though the trilogy gets off
to a crackling start with the first volume, *The Golden Compass*, it eventually collapses
under the heavy ambition of Pullman's imagination like an elaborate cavernous cathe-
dral designed by an architect who's gotten in over his or her head. Irreligious readers
looking to confirm their prejudices would be better off sticking with Christopher
Hitchens.

that too. *Squirrel Nutkin* is way down the list of my favorite Potters, but I was also enamored of autumn when I was a kid. In November's turning leaves, lengthening shadows, and rotting pumpkins, there was something to be grasped about transition and impending quietude, maybe a foretaste, not yet understood, of mortality. It inspired a kind of longing in me, too, and in that longing, in that imaginative leap, however inchoate—like that "something" the Pevensie children feel in their guts upon hearing the name Aslan—Lewis saw the hand of the divine. "I do not think the resemblance between the Christian and the merely imaginative experience is accidental," he wrote in *Surprised by Joy*. "I think that all things, in their way, reflect heavenly truth, the imagination not least."

That Lewis would write for children was perhaps inevitable, though he came to it relatively late in life. (*The Lion, the Witch and the Wardrobe* was published in 1950, when he was fifty-one; the other six books were published over the next six years.) For one thing, he seems never to have gotten over his own childhood. Not that any of us really do, but Lewis held on to his more tightly than most, even the unhappy parts: the mother who died, prematurely; the father he couldn't respect; the grim English boarding school he was eventually shunted off to, run by a sadistic headmaster out of *Nicholas Nickleby*. But the happier parts of his childhood maintained an almost talismanic hold on him. One of his biographers, A. N. Wilson, notes a time, during Lewis's undergraduate years at Oxford, when a fellow student remarked that Mozart had stayed a six-year-old his entire life: "Lewis's disarmingly revealing response was that he thought nothing could be more delightful." Wilson also links this impulse to the fact that in later years, as a critic and scholar, Lewis turned a "blind eye" to modernist authors: "No doubt this rooted conservatism had something to do with his uncontrollable nostalgia for childhood. . . . In latter days, he made rather a 'thing' of preferring children's books to grown-up literature." A "longing at some unconscious level" may have also explained why, as an adult, Lewis set up housekeeping with Janie Moore, a woman twenty-six years his senior—the mother, in fact, of a dead friend—whom he supported and with whom he may or may not have had a romantic relationship. (Some of Lewis's Christian partisans accept as a matter of faith that the relationship was chaste.) This arrangement lasted some three and a half decades, until Mrs. Moore's death. The household also included his older brother, Warnie (Warren), who never married and whom Lewis also supported, though Warnie did manage to write a couple of notable military histories between bouts of alcoholism.

As a child, Lewis himself had exhibited an extraordinary imagination, writing and illustrating a series of stories about an invented world full of talking animals and with an elaborate history, mythology, and geography—"already the mood of the systematizer was strong in me"—which he called Animal-Land. (Beatrix Potter was strong in him too.) Animal-Land was an obvious but apparently impoverished antecedent to Narnia, as Lewis himself was quick to admit: "For readers of my children's books, the best way of putting this would be to say that Animal-Land had nothing whatever in common with Narnia except the anthropomorphic beasts. Animal-Land, by its whole quality, excluded the least hint of wonder."

Lewis began work on the Narnia books in earnest in the late 1940s, a period when Britain was struggling to recover from the war and he himself was coping with disappointments both personal and professional: he had failed to win a chair he coveted at Oxford; Mrs. Moore was sinking into dementia; a theological debate he had taken part in had shaken his certitude in the logic of his belief. The time was right for retreat, and while it would probably be too poetic, and psychologically neat, to say that Lucy's wardrobe also served as a portal back to his childhood, I think there is truth in it. The Narnia books at their best are suffused with a sense of play and a seemingly effortless affinity—and respect—for children's feelings and concerns. Maybe even more important, they often teeter toward incoherence but in a good way, a way that suggests the author has cast aside polemic strata- gems and is striking deeper, older chords, from both traditional fairy tales and myths as well the resonances in his own psyche—and that's why, too, the Christianity goes down easily in most of the books, be- cause it emerges naturally. As he put it, "Some people seem to think that I began by asking myself how I could say something about Chris- tianity to children; then fixed on the fairy tale as an instrument; then collected information about child-psychology and decided what age group I'd write for; then drew up a list of basic Christian truths and hammered out 'allegories' to embody them. This is all pure moon- shine. I couldn't write that way at all." Instead, the first book initially came to him in a series of images, some of which had been lingering since his teenage years: a faun carrying parcels through a snowy for- est, a witch riding a sleigh, a lion who came "bounding into it," as Lewis told Sayer. "Once he was there," Lewis continued, "he pulled the whole story together, and soon he pulled the other six stories in after him."

Lewis had been part of an informal group at Oxford called the In- klings who met regularly and shared their writings. Tolkien was another member. He had taken twelve years to write *The Lord of the Rings* and was the type of creator who worked out elaborate multigenerational histories and languages with complete grammars and lexicons for his stories; he was a fantasy wonk. Allegories as a general matter weren't to his taste, and when Lewis showed him the manuscript for *The Lion, the Witch and the Wardrobe*, Tolkien was appalled at its inconsistencies. Not only had Lewis tossed together creatures from different mytho- logical traditions, he had even dragged Santa Claus into the story; as many critics have pointed out, a secularized Christmas figure (even if derived from a saint) has no logical business butting into a Christian allegory, especially one where, if it is to have internal consistency, the characters should be celebrating Aslanmas. It "just won't do," Tolkien said of Narnia. "The effect was incongruous and, for him, painful," writes Sayer. Lewis, for his part, was "hurt and astonished" by the criticisms, which further damaged an already faltering friendship.

You want somehow to reach out to both men and say: systematic or intuitive, it's not a contest! (And also: internal consistency? The Bible? Hello?) At any rate, Tolkien's preferences notwithstanding, the Narnia books were written, in A. N. Wilson's phrase, "white hot," and they show it in their purity of feeling. Lewis would later maintain he didn't even know what order the stories were written in, though this seems unlikely. They all came quickly, Sayer reports, except for *The Magician's Nephew* and *The Last Battle*—which makes sense, since those are the volumes where Lewis seems to be ignoring his own best instincts and indeed hammering out allegories.

As the series goes on, Aslan himself, so moving and mysterious in *The Lion, the Witch and the Wardrobe*, becomes a more predictable deus ex machina, as it were, intervening when the plot requires some juice or Lewis has painted himself into a corner. As a character, Aslan presents storytelling hurdles similar to those raised by Superman: both are indomitable heroes who are forever showing up in the nick of time, and this tends to stifle conflict and suspense. (Lewis's lesser efforts make me wonder if this is my real issue with God: that he is interesting as a character but lazy as a narrative device.) Worse, as Lewis's intent turns more didactic in the last two books—*The Magician's Nephew* shoehorns a not entirely metaphoric warning about nuclear weapons into its creation myth—Aslan becomes a scold. "Oh Adam's sons," he laments (using the Narnian form of address for non-magical male humans), "how cleverly you defend yourselves against all that might do you good!"

The Last Battle is the weirdest and worst of the Narnia books, but it too has its moments. In its way, *The Last Battle* is a signal achievement: the only children's story I know of fashioned from the roiling, apocalyptic stew that is the Book of Revelation. There is a Beast (in this case, a cunning, malevolent ape), a false prophet (an easily manipulated donkey in an Aslan suit), a clash of civilizations, the end of the world, and the birth of a new, perfected Narnia. The climax might be a little much even for Christians: most of the human characters who have magically visited Narnia over the course of the series—the Pevensie family and various relatives, friends, and mentors—are drawn back once again, after having assembled at an English rail station. There is some sort of mishap with an arriving train at the moment they transport to Narnia, and everyone is confused about just what has happened, until Aslan, as usual, sorts things out:

> "Have you not guessed?"
>
> Their hearts leaped and a wild hope rose within them.
>
> "There *was* a real railway accident," said Aslan softly. "All of you are—as you used to call it in the Shadowlands [i.e., the "real" world]—dead. The term is over: the holidays have begun. The dream is ended: this is the morning." And as He spoke He no longer looked to them like a lion; but the things that began to happen after that were so great and beautiful that I cannot write them.

This is the first time Lewis capitalizes "He" in reference to Aslan; the jig is now up, even for the witless. I suppose this is a proper ending for a Christian allegory, and if it strikes me, for one, as morbid and a bit willed in its "joy," maybe my beef is less with Lewis than with his church. On the other hand, even believers—those who aren't former British schoolboys—may find it odd that at this transcendent moment Aslan uses a school metaphor, term and holidays, to make his metaphysical point.

There is one sour note amid the rapture that I think is a key to

Lewis and to Narnia: Susan is the only Pevensie sibling who is denied the linked pleasures of dying and joining Aslan. We learn that she is no longer a "friend of Narnia," having dismissed the fairyland as little more than a pleasant childhood fantasy. "She's interested in nothing nowadays except nylons and lipstick and invitations. She was always a jolly sight too keen on being a grown-up," one character explains, and you imagine the word "grown-up" pronounced with jolly good disdain. Here, in equating faith with youth and innocence, Lewis is at loggerheads with the intellectualism of his earlier Christian writing. (It is telling that Susan, poor thing, seems to have fallen simply by donning the trappings of a sexually active woman, before she's even had a chance to sin, or sin much.) At the same time, Lewis takes a preemptive swat at those who would argue that religious belief is childish, in the pejorative sense, when another character dismisses Susan with a huffy "Grown up indeed. I wish she *would* grow up." The idea seems to be that adult concerns—lipstick and, ew, boys—are a distraction from true wisdom and that childhood itself is a higher plane of being. How patronizing, it seems to me, and sentimental.

Granted, Lewis was not as far gone in this regard as was J. M. Barrie, who made a career of fetishizing youth with Peter Pan. Lewis is guilty of the lesser charge of flattering his audience, though in his defense, as with so many children's authors, his creative powers were deeply rooted in his own childhood. Consciously or not, he is working out more than just a theological analogy here: he is speaking the truth, I think, of his own emotional experience—and he certainly wouldn't be the first or the last artist whose creations link arrested development and grace; examples range from Shakespeare's fools to Judd Apatow's heroes. Like all great authors, no matter the intended age of their audience, Lewis is ultimately telling stories to himself, and that is where Narnia's real power lies: not in God or Christ or Arthurian legend but in Lewis's own singular echo chamber.

8

One Nation: Washington's Cherry Tree, Rosa Parks's Bus, and Oz

Educators, historians, and fanatics have long used children's books to pass along national myths and values—a hallowed if not always honorable tradition. Here in the United States we have the famous example, dating to 1800, of Parson Weems's bestselling George Washington biography, published over the years in expanding editions under varying titles, my favorite of which is *The Life of George Washington: With Curious Anecdotes, Equally Honourable to Himself, and Exemplary to His Young Countrymen.* It is within the pages of this book that young George first confessed to chopping down his father's cherry tree, having done no such thing during his actual boyhood.[1]

---

[1] Here is Weems's surprisingly dramatic account of Washington's reply to his father's asking about the damaged tree: "This was a tough question; and George staggered under it for a moment; but quickly recovered himself: and looking at his father, with the sweet face of youth brightened with the inexpressible charm of all-consuming

Abraham Lincoln probably never walked miles to return a penny to a woman he overcharged when he was a young store clerk, either. Disillusioning? Perhaps. Then again, maybe it's all to the good that these anecdotes, meant to persuade American youngsters that their leaders were uniquely, even perversely honest, are apocryphal: if Washington and Lincoln had really been that rigidly scrupulous, they likely wouldn't have had the cunning and flexibility to navigate the politics of nation building (and rebuilding) and two very messy wars.

Books are still feeding children national myths, of course, but today they tend to be more truthful, complex, and inclusive. Examples include Maira Kalman's warts-and-nearly-all picture-book biography of Thomas Jefferson, subtitled *Life, Liberty, and the Pursuit of Everything* (2014), and Kadir Nelson's magnificent celebration of Negro League baseball, *We Are the Ship* (2008). A display I saw at my local independent bookstore during a recent Black History Month featured five separate books on Rosa Parks: two chapter-book biographies and three picture books, one from the point of view of a little boy riding on the bus on which Parks refused to give her seat to a white man, one from Parks's point of view, and one from the point of view of the bus itself—and that is only a small fraction of the Rosa Parks bookshelf for children. This abundance makes sense: Parks's story is important, it is easy for kids to understand, and it speaks to the cherished American belief that we are a nation of common, humble people who in a pinch do great, heroic things. Better still, it is true, even if Parks's act of resistance was more calculated than legend sometimes has it.

---

truth, he bravely cried out, 'I can't tell a lie, Pa; you know I can't tell a lie. I did cut it with my hatchet.'" Washington's father's response makes me wonder if this is truly a story with a moral about honesty or rather one about knowing how to read your parents: "Run to my arms, you dearest boy. . . . Such an act of heroism in my son is worth more than a thousand trees, though blossomed with silver, and their fruits of purest gold."

Fantasy inculcates national myths and values, too. There are many ways to interpret *The Lord of the Rings*, for instance, and I am not the first reader to see a reflection of World War II in Tolkien's saga of peaceable hobbits, lovers of home, hearth, and pipe, forced to leave their pastoral Shire in order to defeat ultimate evil. The hobbits, in this reading, would be the English, naturally, with Sauron filling in for Hitler—though Indians, Zulus, and other former subjects of the British Empire might find the reluctant and peaceable parts of the allegory inapt. America's great contribution to fantasy is the superhero, once upon a time a wholesome, square-jawed crime fighter—and typically a loner, like so many American icons. What does it say about the nation's psyche that in an age of terror, interminable war, and blue state–red state polarization, our superheroes have become so conflicted, tortured, and angry?

Like his British successors Tolkien and Lewis, L. Frank Baum was another magpie who rummaged among the discarded furniture and toys in the fairy-tale playroom and crafted something new from what he found. He had Wilhelm and Jacob Grimm very much in mind, nearly a century after they published their first collection, when he began his own prolific, even profligate career as an author of children's books, most famously *The Wonderful Wizard of Oz*. One of his first volumes, an 1899 collection of nursery rhymes titled *Father Goose, His Book* (Baum's then-topical premise: Mother Goose has run off to a suffragettes' meeting, forcing Dad to entertain the goslings), included the poem "Who's Afraid," a eulogy for the traditions preserved by the Grimms (who were well aware themselves that they had been performing literary taxidermy):

> *Ev'ry Giant now is dead. . . .*
> *Jack has cut off ev'ry head. . . .*
> *Every Goblin known of old*
> *Perished years ago, I'm told*

Ev'ry Witch on broomstick riding
Has been burned or is in hiding.

In Baum's view, which was characteristic of the turn of the twentieth century, Progress and Science, those nineteenth-century paragons, had left an imaginative void in the wake of their globe-shrinking discoveries and element-taming feats, a problem Baum diagnosed succinctly in another *Father Goose* poem, "Civilized Boy":

Pray, what can a civilized boy do now
When all the Dragons are dead?

What indeed? Baum was in many ways an emblematic man of his time and place, and he had a forward-thinking, all-American answer: what civilized boys and girls needed were "modern, up-to-date fairy tales" that would "feed the imaginative instinct of the little ones and develop the best side of child nature." Unlike the Grimms' stories, these new tales would be adventurous but healthful, "not marred by murders or cruelty, by terrifying characters, or by mawkish sentimentality, love and marriage." In this, Baum presented himself as something of a literary counterpart to John Harvey Kellogg, the nutritionist and sanatorium director, born four years before Baum, who believed that a bland vegetarian diet would temper sexual appetites—a desirable goal in his view. (That is how cornflakes began life, as an alleged libido suppressant.) Baum was far less severe than Kellogg: he didn't want to inflame unruly passions or give children nightmares, but he still wanted to throw some fun and excitement their way. Thus, in his fairy tales, witches would be melted by water, accidentally, rather than shoved into ovens and burned alive, as in "Hansel and Gretel"—not a terrific denouement either way, from the witch's point of view, but Baum's is surely the more humane and, more to his point, less scary.

His real contribution to literature, though, wasn't to drain all the blood out of fairy tales—his are still fairly gory by twenty-first-century nursery standards—but to help carve out a new imaginative space for them. If magic no longer existed in the mysterious forest next door it would take place in an altogether new world located somewhere over the rainbow, as the notion was later put: the Land of Oz.

Or make that New World, with capital letters. The geographies of all the great modern fairylands—from Wonderland to Hogwarts—are contoured by their authors' emotional needs; they are places for readers to escape to but also, inevitably, interior landscapes. Oz is that too, but it is also a funhouse-mirror reflection of the America that produced it: just as mutty and improvised, as sprawling and diverse, as vital and confused. On one hand, it can be a hard-nosed, brass-tacks fairyland. As the title character tells Dorothy in *The Wonderful Wizard of Oz*, after she asks him to assist her in returning to Kansas, "In this country everyone must pay for everything he gets. . . . Help me and I will help you." Paul Ryan couldn't have said it better. But Oz is also a utopian fairyland, a place where, Baum wrote in a later book, "It must be stated that the people . . . were generally so well-behaved that there was not a single lawyer among them."

Cynical and idealistic, Howard Hawks and Frank Capra—that certainly sounds like America. And how do you get to Oz? No genteel English rabbit holes or looking glasses or snowy wardrobes for Baum. His heroine travels in a big, hard-blowing midwestern tornado, one that can lift an entire house, like a twister out of a Paul Bunyan tall tale. *Whooosh!*

For decades children's librarians looked down their noses at Oz. It would be too strong to say the books were banned by many school and city libraries; it seems rather that they were ignored. Why isn't

clear. Perhaps it was Baum's soft spot for hokum. Perhaps it was the
fact that his books are eager to entertain and don't showcase their literary qualities the way their English cousins do, hewing to a more plain-
spun voice. In the mid-century librarian's view, as best I can tell, Oz
seems to have occupied a no-man's-land between true literature and
abject junk, maybe a notch or two above the Hardy Boys and Nancy
Drew. At any rate, the books weren't available in my school library. I
had to buy or be given all fourteen of the originals written by Baum,
from *The Wonderful Wizard of Oz*, first published in 1900, through
Glinda of Oz, published posthumously in 1919.[2]

I was drawn to Oz by the movie, of course, and by Narnia, which
had sparked in me a keen taste for alternative worlds. In junior high
school I would graduate from Baum to several years of reading nothing but science fiction, weaning myself from that passion in the last
moment or two before it would have become socially scarring. I have
to confess I was mildly embarrassed as well by my enthusiasm for Oz,
given that the books are perfumed by a sometimes precious air that
Ray Bradbury, though a fan of Baum's, referred to as "faintly old-
maidish." Baum's two most important characters are Dorothy, the
little girl from Kansas who after five visits to Oz across six volumes
becomes a permanent resident, with the title of princess; and Ozma,
introduced in the second book, *The Land of Oz*, who is the magical
country's awkwardly named but benevolent ruler and herself a girl of
fourteen or so. (If this sounds like a dubious political arrangement,
you should know that Ozma is different from most fourteen-year-old

---

[2]The series was continued by several different authors after Baum's death, perhaps
another reason librarians may have viewed it more as product than as literature. Reilly
and Lee, the original publisher, brought out its last volume, the fortieth, in 1963.
That quasi-canon has subsequently been expanded by writers both authorized and
not, and includes the 1995 novel by Gregory Maguire that was adapted for the long-
running Broadway musical *Wicked*. Maguire himself has written three more sequels.

girls in that she is never flighty or moody; no bedroom doors are slammed in the Emerald City.) But my boyhood problem with the books was not simply that they had female protagonists; it was that Baum, writing in the early twentieth century, was a product of the Victorian era and often sugarcoated his heroines the way Dickens, one of his own favorite authors, sentimentalized the likes of Little Nell and Little Dorrit. As a fairly conventional-minded ten-year-old boy, I didn't want my peers to know that I had been savoring passages such as this, from *The Tin Woodman of Oz*, the twelfth book in the series:

> In her magnificent palace in the Emerald City, the beautiful girl Ruler of all the wonderful Land of Oz sat in her dainty boudoir with her friend Princess Dorothy beside her. Ozma was studying a roll of manuscript which she had taken from the Royal Library while Dorothy worked at her embroidery. . . . Everyone in Oz loved Dorothy almost as well as they did their lovely Ruler, for the little Kansas girl's good fortune had not rendered her at all vain. She was just the same brave and true and adventurous child as before she lived in a royal palace and became the chum of the fairy Ozma.

I have a vivid memory of a friend's mother asking me, at nine or ten, what I liked so much about the Oz books. I stammered out an answer, which I can't really recall. I only remember feeling self-conscious, sensing an implicit rebuke, which I was probably projecting. Did I even know what a dainty boudoir was? I certainly wasn't going to admit that the lovely fairy Ozma, as rendered by illustrator John R. Neill in diaphanous gowns and showing the occasional graceful limb, provided an early source of erotic fascination. Oz could be a confusing place.

On that score, Baum made things even more complicated by introducing Ozma, at the beginning of *The Land of Oz*, as a scrappy, Tom Sawyerish boy named Tip; only at the end of the book, after various adventures that also introduce such Oz stalwarts as Jack Pumpkinhead and the Sawhorse, is it revealed, both to the reader and to Tip himself, that he is in fact a fairy princess who had been turned into a common boy by a witch's spell. Tip's first reaction is to sulk, but an incantation later and—poof!—he is once again the lovely Ozma, none the worse for wear or for having harbored a temporary Y chromosome. I believe this was one of my first experiences with both shock-twist endings and gender fluidity. I remember closing the book and feeling titillated as well as discombobulated—not the last time those two emotions would coincide. This was fantasy at its most mind-bending, but I wasn't going to brag on the playground about reading it.

If only I had been familiar with Gore Vidal's 1977 essay "On Rereading the Oz Books," in which he declares flat out: "Dorothy is a perfectly acceptable central character for a boy to read about. She asks the right questions. She is not sappy (as Ozma can sometimes be). She is straight to the point and a bit aggressive."

I appreciate Vidal's back up, though he gives Dorothy too much credit. (Ozma he nails.) True, Dorothy is plucky, levelheaded, and a good sport, and is at times possessed of a becoming midwestern egalitarianism, though she also adapts quite readily to life as a princess of Oz. But still, at bottom, she is a bit of a blank slate, like Lucy and Susan Pevensie or Lewis Carroll's Alice. She may grow in pluck as the books go on, but after I read *The Wonderful Wizard of Oz* to my children several years ago, my single biggest takeaway was renewed awe at Judy Garland's performance in the 1939 movie. She grounds the story and provides it with an emotional center that the book lacks, investing Dorothy with a moving sense of longing, first for escape

and then for home—a double-edged poignancy that I doubt existed
in the letter of the film script any more than it does in Baum.[3] Despite the fact that the adaptation offended many Oz fans by rendering
Dorothy's adventures as a dream—in the books, Oz remains a very
real country—the movie is an improvement over its source material in every way, shedding excess plot, strengthening what remains,
deepening the characters, focusing the themes, linking the characters
more closely to American archetypes, making the Wicked Witch of
the West so thrillingly scary (contra Baum's intent), and giving her
that amazing acid-green skin, which makes splendid use of 1930s
Technicolor. Plus, there are the wonderful songs by Harold Arlen and
Yip Harburg. ("Over the Rainbow" could just as well score the yearning that underlies Narnia.) I don't doubt that the books would have
survived into the twenty-first century without the film, but Baum's
heirs should thank MGM for having kept Oz such a central place in
American childhood.

But let's return to the "problem" of the Oz books' girlishness.
Vidal also writes that "what matters most even to an adolescent is
not the gender of the main character who experiences adventures
but the adventures themselves, and the magic, and the jokes, and
the pictures." I think this is exactly right; certainly it was true for
me. And, boudoirs aside, there was nothing traditionally "feminine"
about Dorothy's and Ozma's adventures, unlike, say, those of the
March sisters or Anne of Green Gables. Dorothy and Ozma tangle
with monsters and black magic, shape-shifters and greedy nomes (as
Baum spelled "gnomes" for some reason) who thirst for territorial

---

[3]Garland was reportedly directed by George Cukor, an uncredited hand on the film,
to "be herself," and we know how difficult *that* role was. Cukor must have sensed that
as a vulnerable girl cast adrift in a land of make-believe full of dodgy characters eager
to manipulate her, or worse—I am referring to MGM, not Oz—Garland would have
a natural affinity for Dorothy.

conquest. There is no shortage of weird characters or of spectacle in the Oz books, which are peripatetically plotted after the first two but kept aloft on the wings of Baum's compulsive creativity. Even for a fantasy writer he had an unusually fertile imagination; new characters could "strike at any time," he once told an interviewer. Couple that fecundity with his speed and facility as a writer, and the fact that he had a big family and large debts, and the upshot is a series of books of spectacular inventiveness that can also, at times, feel more typed than written, with an "and then . . . and then . . ." quality.

Baum's whole life had an "and then" quality. He was born in 1856 to a prosperous family in upstate New York, he enjoyed a mostly happy if often sickly childhood, and before finding success in his forties as a writer for children, he had, by my count, pursued at least ten different careers, among them: chicken farmer; playwright and theater troupe owner; salesman for a family industrial concern, Baum's Castorine ("A great lubricator . . . the best axle oil in use!"); fireworks salesman; newspaperman; traveling china salesman; and publisher of a trade journal for store window dressers (*The Show Window, a Journal of Practical Window Trimming for the Merchant and the Professional*). He was as peripatetic as his Oz characters: in 1888, several years after marrying, he moved his family (four children total) from New York State to Aberdeen, a frontier town in the Dakota Territory, where he tried to make a go of it as a store owner, newspaper editor-publisher, baseball team manager, and all-around civic booster; but after those businesses failed he moved to Chicago, where he tried on and discarded several more careers. From there, after his career as an author had taken off in the late 1890s, he migrated all the way west to Hollywood, where in 1914 he founded a movie studio, the Oz Film Manufacturing Company, to produce adaptations of his books. (Though their visual effects were cutting-edge, the pictures failed—in part because a market for family films hadn't yet been established and early audiences balked at movies geared for children.)

Baum's first book, published in 1886, was a guide to raising Hamburgs, a breed of chicken. In thrall to the power of positive thinking, or self-delusion, he insisted that "every season and nearly every day . . . renders [Hamburgs] more fascinating and delightful." His byline gained real notice for the first time in 1897 with the publication of *Mother Goose in Prose*, his first children's book (illustrated by Maxfield Parrish, no less). From then until his death in 1919, he wrote upward of seventy books, not just the Oz stories but also numerous one-off fantasies (some with characters that would be incorporated into subsequent Oz books); a series of adventures for girls, the Aunt Jane's Nieces books (under the tony pseudonym Edith Van Dyne); the Boy Fortune Hunters series (under the less tony pseudonym Floyd Akers); and even a spicy novel for adults, *The Last Egyptian: A Romance of the Nile* (as "Anonymous"). An unusually warm-blooded newspaper profile captured him at the age of forty-five, not long after publication of *The Wonderful Wizard of Oz*. Baum, we learn, was "a young man of splendid physique, with a handsome head, a fine, strong face, brown eyes and hair . . . exceedingly well-groomed, a brilliant conversationalist; in fact, an ideal society man. It is seldom one finds combined in one man, and especially a handsome man, all the manly virtues, but Mr. Baum is a loving husband and father, a staunch friend, an indefatigable worker and a moneymaker, in spite of the fact that he is a successful author."

I will let that final clause lie. But if Baum was neurotic or flighty, as I assume the phrase "successful author" is meant to imply, he never let it interfere with his productivity. He banged out six books in 1906 alone, another six in 1907, then slumped to a mere four in 1908. "It is hard to read the later Oz books without feeling the exploitation in progress, by a writer who only dimly understands his own masterpiece," John Updike once complained. "As a writer Baum rarely knew when to quit, unfurling marvel after marvel while the human content . . . leaked away." As Baum himself explained his methods to a friend in 1915, while working simultaneously on *The Scarecrow of Oz* and *Aunt Jane's Nieces in the Red Cross* (the ninth and tenth books in their respective series), "I am not wasting time on either story, but I want them to be as good as I can make them." That expression of détente between practicality and inspiration could have served as Baum's credo. He was an industrialist in dreamer's clothing, or vice versa: the Henry Ford of children's fantasy.

What his approach meant in practice seems to have been sitting down with a pad of paper or a typewriter and just letting his imagination rip, with theme and plot falling where they may and great ideas stumbled over as if they were happy but unexpected bumps in the road. Typically in an Oz adventure, travelers assemble as a group under some flimsy pretext; set off on a journey, often with only a vague goal in mind; and enjoy a random series of unrelated encounters with strange people and odd creatures—men and women with wheels for feet or hammers for heads or made out of root vegetables; inflatable people and invisible people; kingdoms of foxes and kingdoms of donkeys—until some magic spell is remembered and invoked and the plot, such as it is, is resolved, and everyone ends up back in the Emerald City, where Ozma often sponsors a parade and always throws a big party that, as Vidal observes, is "carefully described in a small-town newspaper style of the Social-Notes-from-all-over variety." *Padding*, a less charitable critic might call it. None of the subsequent Oz stories has the simple, fable-like drive of the original and its four-part quest: Dorothy's wish to go home, the Scarecrow's desire for a brain, the Tin Woodman's longing for a heart, and the Cowardly Lion's yen for courage. Baum knew it was the best thing he'd done even as he was writing it.

But as the awful contemporary cliché goes, it is the journey, not the destination that matters; and one of Baum's great strengths as a traveling companion is that he is often engaging and nearly always pleasant. That is the upside of his books' "and then" quality: the sense they give that they are being told, that the reader is at the knee of an excellent and generous raconteur. His clubman's bonhomie is palpable on the page.

And the jokes, yes: the humor is what really sets the Oz books apart, their secret weapon. Whereas C. S. Lewis's droll asides are icing on the cake, Baum's humor is often the only thing on the menu. His whimsy isn't as madcap or as threatening as Lewis Carroll's—Baum is sometimes corny in a way Carroll wouldn't have stomached—but Baum was an admirer of Carroll's and the two share a love of word-play, pretzel logic, and gentle satire. Baum, like Carroll, was also a master of deadpan. There's a great moment early in *The Wonderful Wizard of Oz*, for instance, when Dorothy meets the Scarecrow and explains she's on a quest to return home:

> The scarecrow listened carefully, and said, "I cannot understand why you should wish to leave this beautiful country and go back to the dry, grey place you call Kansas."
>
> "That is because you have no brains," answered the girl. . . .
>
> The scarecrow sighed.
>
> "Of course I cannot understand it," he said. "If your heads were stuffed with straw, like mine, you would probably all live in beautiful places, and then Kansas would have no people at all. It is fortunate for Kansas that you have brains."

A few pages later, Dorothy and the Scarecrow meet up with the Tin Woodman, who accidentally steps on a beetle, crushing it. Dismayed, he cries, rusting himself. Once re-oiled he vows to be more careful about where he steps:

The Tin Woodman knew very well he had no heart, and therefore he took great care never to be cruel or unkind to anything.

"You people with hearts," he said, "have something to guide you, and need never do wrong; but I have no heart, and so I must be very careful. When Oz gives me a heart of course I need not mind so much."

One frequent and peculiar source of humor comes from Baum's Edison-like preoccupation with the nuts and bolts of his fantasy.[4] It is not that his make-believe world was as rigorously worked out as Tolkien's or J. K. Rowling's or even Lewis's—slapdash Oz, from book to book, is full of inconsistencies—but rather that Baum is continually fascinated by the nitty-gritty physicality of his make-believe characters. Throughout the series, there is frequent disquisition on the superiority of the magical characters, like the Scarecrow, the Tin Woodman, Jack Pumpkinhead, and Scraps the Patchwork Girl, compared with their human and animal counterparts, such as Dorothy, Ozma, and the Cowardly Lion—superior because the magical characters don't have to eat and sleep whereas the "meat" characters, as they are frequently described, do.[5] Baum's world being fundamentally decent, the Scarecrow et al. are always willing to pause during an adventure so that their friends can take care of their biological needs, as in this passage from *The Wonderful Wizard of Oz* describing Dorothy and company's first night in the Emerald City:

---

[4]This may have come naturally to Baum. Where the "real" world was concerned, he was a Theosophist, following a quintessentially American philosophy that believed in a spirit world, but a spirit world governed by natural law, one that, like the physical world, could be studied and quantified.

[5]This was decades before the coinage of "meatspace," attributed to William Gibson, as a retronym for reality ("reality" as opposed to cyberspace).

Each one of them found himself lodged in a very pleasant part of
the Palace. Of course, this politeness was wasted on the Scarecrow
for when he found himself alone in his room he stood stupidly in
one spot, just within the doorway, to wait until morning. It would
not rest him to lie down, and he could not close his eyes [be-
cause they were painted on; Baum never explains how his painted
mouth could open and close to speak]; so he remained all night
staring at a little spider which was weaving its web in a corner of
the room, just as if it were not one of the most wonderful rooms
in the world. The Tin Woodman lay down on his bed from force
of habit, for he remembered when he was made of flesh; but not
being able to sleep he passed the night moving his joints up and
down to make sure they kept in good working order.

To my mind, that is black comedy nearly worthy of Beckett, but
Baum is not toying with metaphors for existential despair, at least
not consciously; he's just imagining what life would really be like for
a Scarecrow and a Tin Woodman, how they'd get through their days
and nights—a feat of peculiar empathy.

One of his biographers, Katharine M. Rogers, does a nice job of
summarizing both the nature and the roots of Baum's imagination:

> Baum's conventional, convivial businessman's side contributed to
> the distinctive quality of his fantasy. His respect for plain com-
> mon sense and his assumption that people naturally feel good
> fellowship with one another represent the American businessman
> at his best. His practical orientation produced the solid quasi-
> realistic foundations of his imaginative worlds.

Occasionally, Baum's muse would lead him to more perverse corners
of his imagination, as with the story of the Tin Woodman's origins: he

was once a normal "meat" man named Nick Chopper who fell in love with a Munchkin girl, Nimmie Amee, who was under the protection of a minor-league backwoods witch. To break up the courtship, the witch put a hex on Nick Chopper's ax, which caused it to cut off one of his arms. He had a new arm made by a tinsmith, but then the ax cut off his other arm, so he had a second tin arm made, and then—following further mishaps with his spellbound blade—two tin legs, a tin torso, and finally a tin head. This grisly if amusing backstory (omitted in the movie) comes to a perverse climax in *The Tin Woodman of Oz*, in which the title character decides to seek out his old flame to see if she still loves him and, along the way, runs into a Tin Soldier, Captain Fyter, who had also once been flesh and blood and was himself in love with Nimmie Amee, and who suffered a fate identical to Nick Chopper's when the same backwoods witch put a spell on his sword. (Witches in Oz can be literally emasculating, though Baum, who by all accounts was happily married, leaves the point implicit.) Chopper and Fyter eventually find their mutual ex living on a remote farm, where, in a climax out of *Andy Capp* or *The Lockhorns* by way of Mary Shelley, they discover she has married a man cobbled together from their own discarded flesh. In Baum, this is played not as tragedy, horror, or parable but as absurdist comedy. "Why he's a scoundrel—a thief! *The villain is wearing my own head!*" exclaims an outraged Captain Fyter.

"Yes, and he's wearing my right arm!" notes the equally aggrieved Tin Woodman. "I can recognize it by the two warts on the little finger."

It is left to Nimmie Amee, rather cool-headed given the circumstances, to sound a practical note regarding her pastiche of a spouse:

> "I won't say he's a husband to be proud of, because he has a mixed nature and isn't always an agreeable companion. There are times when I have to chide him gently, both with my tongue and with

my broomstick. But he is my husband and I must make the best
of him. . . . I see no reason why you should object to him. You
two gentlemen threw him away when you became tin because you
had no further use for him, so you cannot justly claim him now.
I advise you to go back to your own homes and forget me, as I
have forgotten you."

Indeed, the tin men take this to heart, departing from their former
sweetheart with a "there but for the grace of God" epiphany. "Let us
be willing to donate our cast-off members to insure the happiness of
Nimmie Amee," says the Tin Woodman, "and be happy it is not our
fate to hoe cabbages and draw water—and be chided—in the place of
this creature."

I wish I could remember what I made of this when I first read it
as a child. It strikes me now as quintessential Baum. Unlike Lewis,
he has (I think) no larger aims in mind here, but with its flecks of
anxiety, aggression, and mortification, the scene, looked at in the right
light, offers refracted glimpses of a personality more perverse than the
Babbitt-like one Baum showed the public. Lewis never led me toward
Christianity, but Baum, for me, was a gateway drug to *Mad*.

The Tin Woodman of Oz was published in 1918, and while you might
think a story turning on serial dismemberment would have played
poorly against the backdrop of World War I, the book proved to be
among Baum's bestsellers. One of his biographers believes the am-
putation fantasies—and Baum's general obsession with the follies of
"meat" bodies—may have been inspired by the disfigured Civil War
veterans that he likely encountered during his childhood. Is that a
stretch? Would it also be a stretch to suggest that Nick Chopper and
his friends the Scarecrow and the Cowardly Lion embody, or poke sly

fun at, the characteristically American drive for reinvention? In traditional fairy tales, the hero or heroine sets off on a quest for food or
money or marriage—survival stuff. *The Wonderful Wizard of Oz* reads
more like a self-help parable; its heroes risk death in pursuit of indi-
vidual virtues, of brains, heart, courage. If you cut the jokes, it could
be a fairy tale spun by Dale Carnegie or Oprah Winfrey.

As mentioned above, the toothsome all-Americanness of the Oz
books is consciously wrought. Dorothy, of course, hails from Kansas,
not the Black Forest or the Shire; she could be Jo March's Midwestern
cousin. Though technically a monarchy, Oz is a decidedly egalitarian
one. "Manners in Oz are those of rural America at its best—pleasant
and friendly to everyone one meets, but disregardful of decorum or
deference to rank," notes another of Baum's biographers, Katharine M.
Rogers, who points out that while Dorothy "speaks politely to a hen"
in one story she later "outspokenly defies" a snobby, arrogant princess (not Ozma, of course). Even geographically, Oz, with its myriad
lands, "wild" territories, and topographical diversity, and especially
its isolation—it is surrounded by a vast, mostly impassable desert—
recalls the United States of Baum's day, both in continental sprawl
and in the sense of security provided by the Atlantic and Pacific. As
Alison Lurie writes, "Oz itself can be seen as an idealized version of
America in 1900—happily isolated from the rest of the world, un-
derpopulated, and largely rural, with an expanding magic technology
and what appear to be unlimited natural resources."[6]

---

[6]I read one academic paper claiming that *The Wonderful Wizard of Oz* is an extended
parable about the fight for a silver standard, which animated William Jennings Bryan's unsuccessful presidential campaigns of 1896 and 1900. Baum was a supporter
of Bryan's, and this interpretation of his first Oz story hinges on the magic slippers
Dorothy is given by Glinda, which in the book are silver. (The movie's ruby red
slippers, which popped off the screen in Technicolor, were yet another of Hollywood's improvements.) The Yellow Brick Road thus represents the prevailing gold
standard, the Wizard Bryan, and so on. I have a hard time reading the book this

I would add that Oz, with its four separate ethnic groups—Munchkins, Winkies, Gillikens, and Quadlings—and its mix of magical and "meat" people and animals, is its own kind of melting pot, though a jostling and imperfect one, like its real-world counterpart. Oz was conjured at a time of increasing furor in the United States over immigration—1907 was the peak year for European immigration—and Baum was either satirizing or channeling the furor in the sixth Oz book, *The Emerald City of Oz*, published in 1910, in which Dorothy, her aunt Em, and her uncle Henry settle permanently in Oz, even as Ozma is forced to repel an invasion of hostile nomes. The book ends with the following discussion. Says Ozma:

> "It seems to me there are entirely too many ways for people to get to the Land of Oz. We used to think the deadly desert that surrounds us was enough protection; but that is no longer the case. The Wizard and Dorothy have both come here through the air, and I am told the earth people have invented airships that can fly anywhere they wish them to go."
>
> "Why, sometimes they do, and sometimes they don't," asserted Dorothy.
>
> "But in time the airships may cause us trouble," continued Ozma, "for if the earth folk learn how to manage them we would be overrun with visitors who would ruin our lovely, secluded fairyland. . . . So I believe something must be done to cut us off from the rest of the world entirely, so that no one in the future will ever be able to intrude on us."

---

narrowly—the last thing any Oz book is is "worked-out"—but it wouldn't surprise me if the issue was one more rumpled shirt in the overflowing laundry basket that was Baum's imagination.

The solution arrived at is to have Glinda the good witch cast a spell that turns Oz invisible to all but its current residents. (The United States settled for enacting quotas and restrictions aimed at Asians and southern and eastern Europeans.) Whatever Baum's own feelings about immigration, assuming they were even coherent,[7] his primary aim here was finding an excuse to bring the Oz stories, which he had tired of, to a conclusion: Glinda's spell precluded any communication with the outside world, so Baum declared that *The Emerald City of Oz* would be his final effort as "Royal Historian." That vow lasted three years. Compelled by shaky finances to keep the Oz series going—these were his bestselling books, to the frustration of his restless narrative gifts—he wriggled out of his straitjacket by claiming that Dorothy and Ozma were now sending him accounts of their adventures by "wireless telegraphy."

That was a bit of improvised flimflammery worthy of the Wizard himself, a consummate con artist, as Dorothy, the Scarecrow, the Tin Woodman, and the Cowardly Lion discover at the climax of *The Wonderful Wizard of Oz*, when the title character is revealed to be not Great and Terrible, as the residents of the Emerald City refer to him, but rather a small bald man with no real magic powers whatsoever, just a few circus and theatrical tricks. He is, in the Scarecrow's words, a "humbug." " 'Exactly so!' exclaimed the little man, rubbing

---

[7]Baum, though he shared most of the ethnic prejudices of his time and caste, was progressive in some ways. He supported women's rights—his mother-in-law, Matilda Gage, was a suffragette leader—though he also satirized the women's movement in his books. When he was running a newspaper in South Dakota, he editorialized against the 1890 massacre at Wounded Knee, during which three hundred Lakota Sioux men, women, and children were murdered by the U.S. Army. A "disgrace," Baum wrote. But then he inexplicably followed that up by calling for the "total extermination" of the Lakota. "Having wronged them for centuries, we had better . . . follow it up by one more wrong, and wipe these untamed and untamable creatures from the face of the earth." Which is, or so I hope, the worst sentence ever written by a writer I'm otherwise fond of.

his hands together as if it pleased him. 'I am a humbug.'" It is a typically genial stroke of Baum's that the Wizard is relieved to be giving
up his charade.

Perhaps it is not a coincidence that the Wizard, like Dorothy,
is a midwesterner, having been blown to Oz from Nebraska while
ascending in a balloon to promote a circus. (This isn't as fanciful as
it sounds: in the late nineteenth century balloonists disappeared with
some regularity.) Baum had not only the wit to make the Wizard a
phony, but also the wit to make him a humble, likable phony. He tries
to tell the Scarecrow, Tin Woodman, and Lion that they already have
what they seek—the moral you expect—but they still insist on getting what they came for; they want what they want. "Very well," the
Wizard says with a seeming shrug. "I have played Wizard for so many
years that I may as well continue the part a little longer." So the next
day he stuffs the Scarecrow's head full of bran and pins; cuts a hole in
the Tin Woodman's chest and inserts a heart of satin stuffed with saw-
dust; and gives the Lion a potion to drink that he claims will provide
valor. (A joke on liquid courage?) This is another sequence that the
movie condenses and improves upon, highlighting the implicit moral
about finding one's strengths within, but I do like Baum's point about
the stubbornness of delusion, about people's willingness to believe in
the face of all contrary evidence—a darker moral.

Perhaps that was a wink from the religious skeptic in Baum—
here he is writing as the anti-Lewis—or a practical insight he gleaned
from his labors as a salesman. It could even be a kind of shrug at his
own persistence in life and stubborn adherence to his dreams. Updike
complained that Baum "didn't quite grasp that his wizard concerns
our ability to survive disillusion; miracles are humbug." I think there
was much in his work that Baum didn't grasp, and that Updike is
right, in part, about what we might take away from the book. It occurred to me, in rereading Baum, that the wizard's exposure echoes

the shattering, inevitable moment when we realize our parents are not all-knowing and not omnipotent. (In my case, that happened when I was four or five and I asked my dad why glass was clear and he admitted he didn't know; I never saw him the same way again.) But that's my spin. Baum is more blithe, and here I think he knew exactly what he was up to: he is less interested in humankind's ability to survive disillusion than in humankind's eagerness to ignore it altogether. That is another great American trait that Oz reflects: our national susceptibility to—and gift for—con artistry. We are, after all, the country that gave birth to or nurtured P. T. Barnum, Charles Ponzi, Wilhelm Reich, Joe McCarthy, L. Ron Hubbard, Bernie Madoff, and Donald Trump.[8] Characteristically, however, Baum undercuts whatever point he was trying to make about the Wizard when in subsequent books he has the little man return to Oz and learn some actual magic under the tutelage of Glinda. But Oz, like America, is nothing if not second chances and second acts. Whatever F. Scott Fitzgerald thought, Baum knew better.

Maira Kalman writes at the end of her book on Jefferson, "If you want to understand this country and its people and what it means to be optimistic and complex and tragic and wrong and courageous, you need to go to Monticello." This is good advice, and if you can't make the trip to Jefferson's Virginia plantation, you can get a good taste of all that in Oz.

---

[8]The day after I wrote that sentence, a documentary opened in New York City about John Romulus Brinkley, a quack who made a fortune in the 1920s and 1930s claiming he could cure impotence by transplanting goat testicles into men, which doesn't seem so far removed from the surgical arts practiced in Oz.

9

Going on Seventeen (Or Not):
Little Women, Little Houses, and Peter Pans

My wife recently asked one of her oldest friends, now middle-aged, what he would be if he could be anything, anything at all. "An eleven-year-old boy" was his response. It wouldn't have been mine—my answer, at this moment, might be *asleep*—but I get the impulse. While C. S. Lewis dreamed of being six again, for many men, if I may generalize, preadolescence is a pinnacle, remembered, or romanticized, as a sweet spot between the dependence of early childhood and the rising responsibilities and hormonal tumult of teenage-dom. From this perspective, preadolescence is the best of both worlds: freedom without consequence, or without much. The Tom Sawyer years.

These thoughts were prompted by my reading of two monumental works of American children's literature I had never cracked until I embarked on this project: Louisa May Alcott's *Little Women* and its sequels; and Laura Ingalls Wilder's "Little House" cycle of novels. The reason I had never read them before is that they are quintessential "girl books," and while girls are rarely made to feel lesser for reading "boy books"—or watching "boy movies" or "boy TV shows" or playing with "boy toys"—boys, alas, rarely turn their attentions in the direction of "girl" things. Why this might be so is beyond the scope of this book, but it is a phenomenon widely observed, certainly by people who market to children, and one I remember as true from my own boyhood. By way of casual corroboration I've asked dozens of men and boys over the last several years whether they'd ever read Alcott or Ingalls Wilder and 100 percent answered "no," though I did come across one case of a man volunteering that he'd not only read *Little Women* and its sequel *Little Men*, but liked them: this was retired Supreme Court justice John Paul Stevens, who was asked about his favorite childhood books in an interview for the *New York Times Book Review*; he also mentioned the very masculine and bloodthirsty *Treasure Island*, a real boy book's boy book (if one saddled with an unfollowable plot). Perhaps those gender-blind tastes were prima facie evidence of Stevens's budding judicial temperament.[1]

---

[1] As research for this chapter, I also attempted to read *Anne of Green Gables*, L. M. Montgomery's novel of 1908, the first in a series of eight books about a sunny, cheerful, detestable orphan. Alas, I got through only thirty-some pages before I was forced to cast it aside. The deal breaker was a scene in which Anne decides to name a geranium Bonny. As Anne explains to the skeptical woman who has taken her in: "Oh, I like things to have handles even if they are only geraniums. It makes them seem more like people. How do you know but that it hurts a geranium's feelings just to be called a geranium and nothing else? You wouldn't like to be called nothing but a woman all the time. Yes, I shall call it Bonny. I named that cherry tree outside my bedroom window this morning. I called it Snow Queen because it was so white. Of course, it won't always be in blossom, but one can imagine that it is, can't one?" One can also throw the book aside. Academic note: Anne is here revealed as an early, prophetic version of the manic pixie dream girl archetype that would proliferate in the independent cinema of the early twenty-first century.

As I've mentioned, I never had a problem in childhood with female protagonists per se, being a fan of Madeline, Dorothy Gale, Ramona Quimby, and Lucy Pevensie. All the same, *Little Women* and the Little House books struck me then as fatally steeped in girlishness, their very titles signaling a dollhouse sensibility. (A boy book would announce itself more in the vein of *Big House on the Huge Prairie*.) The copy of *Little Women* I knew growing up was my mother's, treasured from her Depression childhood, which she passed along to my sisters, who read it almost as many times as they read *Gone with the Wind*. As in most editions, the cover depicted four girls in long, old-fashioned dresses sitting around doing needlepoint, I think, or maybe they were outside picking apples. Either way, the cover implied that the novel was *about* girlhood—which, it turns out, it is, so nice job, anonymous illustrator. But for me, at the age of eight or ten, this was no inducement.

As for the Little House books, since 1953, when the series was reissued in uniform editions with illustrations by Garth Williams, the cover of the first volume, *Little House in the Big Woods*, has depicted a young girl in a nightgown hugging a homemade rag doll. We can wish we lived in a different world, but many boys see that and think, *Not for me.*

And they're so wrong.

I had intended to read only the first two or three Little House books, but, delighted and transfixed—cooties be damned—I breezed through all nine in the series: *Little House in the Big Woods, Farmer Boy, Little House on the Prairie, On the Banks of Plum Creek, By the Shores of Silver Lake, The Long Winter, Little Town on the Prairie, These Happy Golden Years*, and *The First Four Years*. Even if you've never read them, or never seen the very loosely adapted 1970s TV series with Melissa

Gilbert and Michael Landon, you probably know the gist of the autobiographical arc, which traces Ingalls Wilder's peripatetic childhood
on the American frontier in the 1870s and '80s, beginning when she
is a four-year-old living in a log cabin in Wisconsin and ending when
she is an eighteen-year-old bride in South Dakota, with stops along the
way, via covered wagon, in what was then Indian Territory and Minnesota. Though Ingalls Wilder writes in the third person, the books
are essentially memoirs. The central characters are her parents, Charles
and Caroline Ingalls, or Pa and Ma; her older sister, Mary; baby Carrie;
and, eventually, another baby sister, Grace. Almanzo Wilder, the man
Laura Ingalls would wed, gets a book of his own, *Farmer Boy*, and then
shows up in the later installments as she chronicles their courtship and
marriage. Throughout she smoothes some of the harsher edges off her
childhood (a brother who died in infancy is nowhere mentioned, nor is
the episode when the family skipped town owing rent), jiggles chronol-
ogy to suit her purposes, and straightens out the family's westward-ho
itinerary (the real Ingalls family backtracked a few times). All in all,
however, she doesn't tweak her personal history more than would be
thought standard by most memoirists—and less than would be perfectly acceptable to any "based on a true story" screenwriters. She herself
once said, "All I have told is true, but it is not the whole truth." As these
things go, that is a fairly high standard.

And yet, despite whatever polishing or forgetting took place during their composition, these books still tell a hard, forbidding saga, a
chronicle of failure: crops are destroyed; houses burn; land is lost; the
family nearly starves to death during one especially harsh winter. Even
good times are haunted by toil, deprivation, and threat. Williams's
illustrations depict a generally sunny, happy, seemingly well-fed
family—appropriately enough for a children's book—but the Native
American writer John Joseph Matthews's description of exhausted,
beaten-down white settlers in covered wagons arriving on Osage land

in 1893 (the Ingalls family had lived illegally for a period in Osage territory a quarter-century earlier) bears notice here too: "Dirty-faced children peering out from the curtains, and weary, hard-faced women lolling in the seat beside evil-eyed, bearded men."

I will return to the Native American perspective on the Little House books, which has tempered my own enthusiasm, but my initial impression, to be honest, was surprise at how much "boy stuff" there is. In fact, what with all the hunting and hammering, sawing and shooting, the books often read like nineteenth-century equivalents of *This Old House* or *Guns and Ammo.* In just the first two dozen pages of *Little House in the Big Woods,* Pa kills and skins a deer, cures the meat in a hand-hewn smoker he's made out of a hollow stump, and then butchers a pig with his brother's help. Ingalls Wilder recounts this in fine, nearly instructional detail:

> As soon as the hog was dead Pa and Uncle Henry lifted it up and down in the boiling water until it was well scalded. Then they laid it on a board and scraped it with their knives, and all the bristles came off. After that they hung the hog in the tree, took out the insides, and left it hanging to cool.
>
> When it was cool they took it down and cut it up. There were hams and shoulders, side meat and spare-ribs and belly. There was the heart and the liver and the tongue, and the head to be made into headcheese, and the dish-pan full of bits to be made into sausage.

Best of all, from four-year-old Laura's perspective, Pa inflates the pig's bladder like "a little white balloon," ties it off with a string, and gives it to Laura and her older sister Mary to play with: "They could throw it in the air and spat it back and forth with their hands. Or it would bounce along the ground and they could kick it." *Gross,* but cool.

Just a few pages later, Pa, who we have learned by now is an exemplary frontiersman, provides the family with another special treat by shooting a bear:

> Laura and Mary jumped up and down and clapped their hands, they were so glad [to hear about the bear]. Mary shouted:
> "I want the drumstick! I want the drumstick!"
> Mary did not know how big a bear's drumstick is.

So attention, boys: you should know that there is more shooting and skinning, more playing with pig bladders and gnawing on bear drumsticks than you might expect from a book with a girl holding a rag doll on the cover. Maybe too much so. I have to confess that, from the denatured vantage point of twenty-first-century urban fatherhood, where bantering with the super as he fixes your toilet counts as manly self-sufficency, Pa cuts an intimidating figure: not only does he feed and shelter his family using his own two hands—in *Little House on the Prairie*, he builds the titular home, yet another log affair, from scratch, hewing and hauling the timber himself—he also makes his own bullets. He is an excellent horseman. He can plow a field, grow wheat, raise livestock. If need be, he can also move to town, work in an office, and manage a payroll. In *On the Banks of Plum Creek* he survives for three days and three nights when caught by a blizzard in the open prairie. In *By the Shores of Silver Lake* he faces down a potentially murderous mob of railroad workers. Aside from the serial crop failures and the fact that he never really makes it as a farmer, he might be the single most *competent* character in American literature; he might have come in handy on the deck of the *Pequod*, or cleaning up after Daisy and Tom Buchanan. And yet Pa isn't just a strong, silent, distant archetype. He is also a hands-on father, loving, stern when he needs to be, frequently described as having a twinkle in his eye. A fine

storyteller, of course, and a mean fiddle player. Even his oaths and ex-
clamations, though G-rated, are terrific: "Jiminy Crickets!" he shouts
during a downpour. "It's raining fish-hooks and hammer handles!"
(I'm not the only fan of that one. I searched online to see if I could
find its derivation. No luck—it seems unique to Ingalls Wilder—but
I did discover that you could buy the phrase silk-screened on a T-shirt
from American Apparel.)

Perhaps it is just as well most boys don't read the Little House
books, as they might go through life shamed by their failure to match
Pa's masculine ideal. (James Bond embodies an imposing enough fiction.) I wonder what lessons girls draw from Ma's example. She is no
slouch. For instance, there is the scene in *Little House on the Prairie*
when Ma is helping Pa with the home-building and one of his hand-
hewn logs falls on her leg. Pa hoists it off her, then feels for broken
bones:

"Does it hurt much?" he asked.

Ma's face was gray and her mouth was a tight line. "Not
much," she said.

"No bones broken," said Pa. "It's only a bad sprain."

Ma said cheerfully, "Well, a sprain's soon mended."

Cheerfully? At any rate, after soaking the sprain for a bit in hot water,
genuinely cheerful or not, Ma is back on her feet:

The puffed ankle began to turn purple. Ma took her foot out of
the water and bound strips of rag tightly around and around the
ankle. "I can manage," she said. She could not get her shoe on.
But she tied more rags around her foot, and she hobbled on it.
She got supper as usual, only a little more slowly. But Pa said she
could not help to build the house until her ankle was well.

I wonder to what extent, if any, Ma protested that edict about holding off on construction work until her ankle mended. I also wonder what it would be like to have a log fall on your foot in a time and place that had no knowledge of Percocet, or even Advil—the Little House world can feel so remote from our own as to read less like personal history than science fiction in reverse. Twenty-first-century parents may well marvel at certain passages in the series—for instance, the Christmas morning when the girls are overjoyed to get a single stick of peppermint candy each. On another Christmas, a gift of tin cups induces ecstasy: "These new tin cups were their very own. Now they each had a cup to drink out of. Laura jumped up and down and shouted and laughed." An extra half ladleful of porridge might have stopped their hearts.

I can manage. It has been claimed that our country was built by a spirit of self-sacrifice, though the Native Americans whose land the Ingalls and their fellow white settlers were taking would have had an entirely different perspective on just who was doing the sacrificing, and who is included in that "our." Native Americans do exist in Ingalls Wilder's pages, particularly in *Little House on the Prairie*, which takes place in what was then called Indian Territory. The Ingalls family had settled there illegally, on land owned by the Osage people, under the presumption that the area would soon be opened to whites. (The Indian Territory became Oklahoma, though the Ingalls homestead may have been in a small slice of Kansas.) Ingalls Wilder portrays the Osages as alien and menacing, but also with a measure of humanity—about as well as one could hope for, I think, from a popular white writer of her generation, though that is perhaps not my call to make. A number of Native American and other critics believe that the series' inaccuracies, omissions, and racism, both explicit and implicit, disqualify it altogether. One essay, written in part as historical counter to Ingalls Wilder, makes a pungent point with its title alone: "Little Squatter on the Osage Diminished Reserve." As with Mark Twain's books, Ingalls Wilder's novels demand context, at the very least. As for balance, one place you can look is Louise Erdrich's middle-grade series focusing on the Ojibwa people of the upper Midwest. The heroine of *The Birchbark House* (1999) and two sequels, set in the 1840s and '50s, is "a nimble young girl of seven winters" named Omakayas (Little Frog), who is growing up with her mother, father, older sister, two younger brothers, and extended family on an island in Lake Superior—Moningwanaykaning (Island of the Golden-Breasted Woodpecker), her people's longtime home.

Like the Little House books, Erdrich's Birchbark novels find compelling music in the day-to-day, season-to-season rhythms of lives led in far closer proximity to nature, and far more vulnerable to its vagaries, than most of us could even imagine today. Some readers (me) will enjoy learning what goes into tanning a moose hide:

> There was a saying [Omakayas] hated. Grandma said it all too often. "Each animal," she would say, "has just enough brains to tan its own hide." Mama tanned the moose hide with the very brains of the moose and Omakayas hated the oozy feel of them on her hands, not to mention the boring, endless scraping and rubbing that went into making a hide soft enough for makazins.

One significant difference between the Birchbark and Little House series: when Omakayas and her family move westward, it is not by choice. A small pox epidemic that hits the Ojibwas is as harrowing a sequence as I think exists in contemporary children's literature.

While she can't speak to the truth of Native American experience, Ingalls Wilder offers a presumably accurate account of her family's attitudes toward the men, women, and children they are displacing. She herself is both frightened of and fascinated by the Indians she encounters. Ma expresses blunt hatred: "I just don't like them." Pa takes a more accommodating view, as in one episode when he defuses a potentially violent confrontation with an Osage man over the use of a trail: "That was a darned close call! Well, it's his path. An Indian trail, long before we came." Pa's deference only goes so far, however. One evening Laura asks him whether the U.S. government will force out the Osages (whose original homeland to the east had already been seized by whites):

> "Yes," Pa said. "When white settlers come into a country, the Indians have to move on. The government is going to move these Indians farther west, any time now. That's why we're here, Laura. White people are going to settle all this country, and we get the best land because we get here first and take our pick. Now do you understand?"
>
> "Yes, Pa," Laura said. "But, Pa, I thought this was Indian Territory. Won't it make the Indians mad to have to—"
>
> "No more questions, Laura," Pa said, firmly. "Go to sleep."

Pa was correct in the long term, though in the short term, by Laura's account, the U.S. government sent soldiers to force the Ingalls family and other whites off the territory—which, if true, was a rare (and short-lived) adherence to Indian treaty obligations.

Their racial politics aside, one reason Ingalls Wilder's books have remained hugely popular since the first was published in 1932 is her skill at using quotidian detail to re-create a distant world. This is reflected in the writing itself, which often has a terse but lyrical, Hemingwayesque flair and on other occasions displays an artless, even clumsy quality that can feel as hand-hewn as one of Pa's houses. Sometimes the prose has all of that at once, as in this short passage after Pa catches a "wagonload" of fish: "Ma cut large slices of flaky white fish, without one bone, for Laura and Mary. They all feasted on the good, fresh fish." (See what I mean by Hemingwayesque?) Or this, when Laura and Mary are playing on the prairie:

> They hunted for birds' nests in the tall grass and when they found them the mother birds squawked and scolded. Sometimes they touched a nest gently, and all in an instant a nest full of downiness became a nest full of wide-gaping beaks, hungrily squawking. Then the mother bird scolded like anything, and Mary and Laura quietly went away because they did not want to worry her too much.

If I put on an editor's hat, I can see infelicities here, but the prose just works—like a singer with a homely but moving voice. Would you tell Hank Williams or Bob Dylan to work on his pitch?

You might also think Ingalls Wilder's decision to write in the third person would feel weird or, at best, self-conscious. Often, in other hands, it does, and as a general rule speakers should at all costs avoid referring to themselves in the third person, especially if they are athletes or politicians or the significant other of someone I care about. Here, though, the device helps Ingalls Wilder fuse the authority of memoir with the immediacy of fiction, making the books feel more lived than remembered—a remarkable feat, really, since she was in her early sixties when she started work on what became *Little House in the Big Woods*, her first children's novel. To that point, her greatest claim to fame as writer had been a regular column, "As a Farm Woman Thinks," which she began writing for the *Missouri Ruralist* in her forties, and a handful of similarly themed stories for national magazines such as *McCall's*. Among her topics: "Keep the Saving Habit," "Thanksgiving Time," and "Life Is an Adventure: Voyages of Discovery Can Be Made in Your Rocking Chair."

Ingalls Wilder's daughter, Rose—her only child—was instrumental in her career. A journalist and a novelist herself, Rose encouraged her mother's writing, took the lead in getting it published, and had the brilliant idea of taking an unsold autobiographical manuscript Laura had written and refashioning it into a children's book. Thanks in large part to a 1993 biography of Rose, *The Ghost in the Little House*, by William Holtz, which first brought attention to her contributions to her mother's career, there is a literary urban legend floating around that Rose herself wrote the Little House books. This is not true, though Holtz, as his title suggests, makes the case that Rose essentially ghosted her mother's books—"nothing less than a line-by-line re-writing of [Laura's] labored and underdeveloped narratives." As Holtz describes the collaboration, "Her mother would deliver her own best effort in full expectation that Rose would work her magic on it." Laura herself once conceded in a letter to Rose while working on *By the Shores of Silver Lake*, "I know the music but I can't think of the words." Laura's most recent full-length biographers, Pamela Smith Hill and William Anderson, acknowledge that Rose was her mother's first and best editor, but they believe Holtz overstates his argument. My sense, without the benefit of having read through multiple Little House manuscripts or the complete mother-daughter correspondence, but with the benefit of being both an editor and a writer myself, is that while Rose was a very active and sometimes bossy editor, she doesn't seem to have contributed beyond the farther boundaries of that job.

It is indisputable that between mother and daughter, whatever the intricacies of their creative relationship, there was an alchemy not evident in their work apart. You can see for yourself by reading both the final, posthumous Little House book, *The First Four Years*—taken from a manuscript by Laura, which was discovered among Rose's papers in 1968, after both women's deaths—and *Let the Hurricane Roar*, Rose's short novel that was a bestseller when it was published in 1933. In fairness, *The First Four Years* may not have been a finished manuscript, even on Laura's terms; it is sketchy, not always dramatic, needs fleshing out. But it doesn't seem so far removed from passages in the first drafts of the earlier books that Rose had coaxed into richer, fuller form. As for her own fiction, *Let the Hurricane Roar*, now in print as *Young Pioneers*, is based on stories from Laura's childhood that she herself would later recount in *The Long Winter*. Rose's prose is moister and heavier than her mother's, her narrative is full of portent, her themes of frontier in-dependence and resilience are hammered on with ideological muscle. (Rose was a budding libertarian who had previously written admiring biographies of Henry Ford and Herbert Hoover.) I am fairly certain that if not for Laura's books, *Let the Hurricane Roar* would no longer be read, except by specialists, Little House completists, and the stray va-cationer browsing a dusty summer-home library on a rainy afternoon.

However the Little House novels were crafted and shaped, and whatever the proper apportioning of credit (Ursula Nordstrom at Harper surely played a role as well, though she asserted several times over the years that Wilder's manuscripts were among the few she never laid a hand on; and ultimately who cares who did what?), the books' not very secret weapon is Laura herself, the Laura we meet on the page. Not only is she a keen observer of a vivid and complex world; she herself is a vivid and complex girl. Throughout, she ping-pongs between her native impulsiveness and the caution Ma and Pa have drilled into her and her sisters, often for reasons of sheer survival in a hostile landscape where wolves and panthers could be sunning themselves just beyond the front door and the weather could turn ugly in a snap. But Laura's curiosity and zest for experience often win out over obedience. For instance, after she runs out in the same storm that had Pa exclaiming about hammer handles, Ma scolds her and warns that she'll catch her "death" of cold. "But Laura was glowing warm," Ingalls Wilder writes. "She had never felt so fine and frisky." You have to love a girl who feels fine and frisky after running through a biblical deluge (though in a subsequent chapter she nearly drowns in a swollen creek), or who, in a later book, has this response after Pa warns her and her younger sister Carrie to steer clear of some "rough" railroad men who might be using "rough language":

Carrie's eyes were large and frightened. She did not want to hear rough language, whatever rough language might be. Laura would have liked to hear some, just once, but of course she must obey Pa.

Laura is a doer, a trier, a risker; she is another girl who can't wait to see what happens next. To the extent the Ingalls family harbors a rebel, she is it, which of course endears her to us even more. Her rivalry with prim, well-behaved Mary is a theme in the early books. Laura, whose hair is "ugly and brown" resents her older sister's "lovely golden curls" as well as Mary's preternatural ability to sit still and mind her manners. "Mary was a very good little girl who always did exactly as she was told," Ingalls Wilder notes at one point—still channeling sibling resentment six decades after the fact. When Mary performs a flagrantly selfless good deed, showing up her younger sister, Laura seethes: "Perhaps Mary felt sweet and good inside, but Laura didn't. When she looked at Mary she wanted to slap her."

In *On the Banks of Plum Creek*, Laura and Mary for the first time go to school, where they encounter Nellie Oleson, a stereotypical mean girl—the pretty blond daughter of a comparatively prosperous shopkeeper, a composite drawn from real girls Ingalls Wilder had gone to school with—who will become something of an antagonist for Laura in subsequent volumes (and even more so in the freely adapted television series). Mary is appalled by Nellie's cruel snobbery: "My goodness!" the older sister exclaims. "I couldn't be as mean as that Nellie Oleson." But Laura thinks to herself, "I could. I could be meaner to her than she is to us, if Ma and Pa would let me." Indeed, by the end of the series, Laura has revenged herself on Nellie several times over and is probably as much tormenter as tormentee; she is capable of spite to a degree that is unusual for a children's heroine. But Ingalls Wilder makes no bones about her struggles with her better and lesser angels—which is another way of saying that, blizzards and bear meat aside, the books' ultimate subject is the messy, two steps forward, one step back process of growing up.

That not altogether profound revelation was what got me thinking about my wife's friend and the allure of being eleven. To return to my role here as a conventionally gendered latecomer to these authors, I was fascinated that both Ingalls Wilder and Louisa May Alcott were willing and perhaps even felt obligated to follow their heroines all the way through to not only adulthood but marriage—which, in boy books, might well be the love that dare not speak its name. Mark Twain, for instance, declined to inflict such a fate on Tom and Huck, who remain forever embedded in preadolescent amber—and defiantly so, Huck in particular rejecting even the possibility of wearing long pants, bathing regularly, or, in some god-awful future, holding down a job. In fact, I can't think of any significant books or series with boy heroes that see them through to pairing off and parenthood, except for the Harry Potter books, which were written by a woman, perhaps not incidentally.[2]

It took Judy Blume herself to write a male counterpart to her justly beloved breakout novel, *Are You There God? It's Me, Margaret*, which was published in 1970 and famously explores female puberty in all its physical as well as emotional tumult. *Then Again, Maybe I Won't* came out a year later and tackles equivalently humid boy topics such as wet dreams, unwanted erections, and the ethics of using binoculars when a friend's older sister decides to undress in front of an open window. There is more to both books than just hormones and defiant bodies—notably conflicts involving class and friendship, not to mention the author's signature wit

---

[2] As mentioned in Chapter Four, Beatrix Potter's tales jump-cut, as it were, to Peter Rabbit and Benjamin Bunny in the role of husband and father. But she doesn't bother grappling with their maturation into adulthood—and regardless, they're vermin.

and compassion—but Blume's frankness is an important reason why reading *Are You There God? It's Me, Margaret* is close to a rite of passage for modern American girls, and why, for boys, *Then Again, Maybe I Won't* isn't. Perhaps the latter don't like asking directions any more than grown men allegedly don't, if folklore is to be believed. Perhaps, echoing my wife's friend, they wish they could avoid the how-and-why of puberty altogether. Personally, as I remember that age, it was a case of wanting to know, but not wanting to be *seen* as wanting to know, if that makes sense. Coolness seemed to demand an innate mastery of the subject.

But when it comes to sticking one's head in the sand, J. M. Barrie offers the definitive statement in the opening paragraph of *Peter Pan*:

> All children, except one, grow up. They soon know that they will grow up, and the way Wendy knew was this. One day when she was two years old she was playing in a garden, and she plucked another flower and ran with it to her mother. I suppose she must have looked rather delightful, for Mrs. Darling put her hand to her heart and cried, "Oh, why can't you remain like this for ever!" This was all that passed between them on the subject, but henceforth Wendy knew that she must grow up. You always know after you are two. Two is the beginning of the end.

There is an element of self-aware irony here, I think—I hope—yet Peter himself, as the one child who never grows up, is a recognizable enough type to have lent his name to a bestselling 1983 pop psychology text aimed at exasperated single women, *The Peter Pan Syndrome: Men Who Have Never Grown Up*. It just as easily could have been called *The Huck Finn Syndrome* or *The Holden Caulfield Syndrome* or *The Rabbit Angstrom Syndrome* or *The Any Movie Starring Will Ferrell or Seth Rogen or Jonah Hill Syndrome*. Recall as well that in two other series with girl protagonists, the Narnia and Oz books, both written by men, growing up is frowned upon in the former, leading to banishment from Narnia, and in the latter is done away with altogether: thanks to the magic of Oz, where no one ages, Dorothy and Ozma will remain girls forever, L. Frank Baum's paternalistic wish for them, if not necessarily their own.

But just as it is outside the scope of this book to address why girls will read boy books but rarely vice versa, so is it beyond me to explain why so many of our most popular and resonant stories for girls and young women, from "Snow White" to *Pride and Prejudice* to *Sex and the City*, are wedding-quest narratives. You probably have some hunches about that. The Little House books get a pass: they end with marriage and motherhood because that was the course of Laura Ingalls Wilder's life. *Little Women* is a different matter. With the endgame embedded in the title itself, Louisa May Alcott's novel is more prescriptive; perhaps in keeping with its having been written in the 1860s, when children's literature was still shedding the starchy didacticism of the *New England Primer* days, *Little Women* has a moralizing, instructional air, a whiff of *The Pilgrim's Progress*, a book that Alcott has her heroine Jo read in an early chapter. *Little Women* is too unruly, too full of elbows and stray ringlets to serve as any kind of parable itself, but periodically, as if it were a PBS cartoon or an after-school special, the book pauses for a life lesson, usually imparted by the gentle but firm Marmee, as the girls call their mother, from her platitudinous corner of the parlor. As Marmee notes at one point in what Alcott describes as "her serious yet cheerful way":

"I want my daughters to be beautiful, accomplished and good; to be admired, loved, and respected, to have a happy youth, to be well and wisely married, and to lead useful, pleasant lives, with as little care and sorrow to try them as God sees fit to send. To be loved and chosen by a good man is the best and sweetest thing which can happen to a woman; and I sincerely hope my girls may know this beautiful experience."

You can't fault a book for being a product of its era, though you are free not to like it, and try as I might, I didn't. But one thing I found compelling about *Little Women*—even as I struggled to get through it; and I will confess that I gave its sequels, *Little Men* and *Jo's Boys*, only the most cursory of skims—is the extent to which you can sense both author and heroine struggling against nineteenth-century social strictures, even if both ultimately knuckle under. There is an undercurrent of ambivalence that allows you, if you are so inclined, to shrug off the book's smoothly ironed and crisply folded life lessons. Probably that is one key to *Little Women*'s success then (it was an instant bestseller) and now: it was both of and ahead of its time. As one of its first reviewers observed: "The majority of children's books consist of puling, do-me-good copy-book morality, calculated to turn the stomach of any sensible child. . . . Miss Allcott [*sic*] is too appreciative of the truly beautiful in childhood to attempt to preach them into stiff-backed, spiritless propriety."

Alcott didn't come to writing late in life like Ingalls Wilder, but it took her a while to hit on her most enduring subject matter: in the spring of 1868, when she sat down to write *Little Women* at the age of thirty-five (Laura Ingalls had just celebrated her first birthday), Alcott already had a successful decade under her belt as a journalist, essayist, and pseudonymous writer of gothic thrillers. One of her biographers, Harriet Reisen, describes the flawed heroine of Alcott's 1863 story "Pauline's Passion and Punishment" as "a dark, amoral Cuban" caught up in "a melodramatic plot that raced to a cliff-hanging, poetically just conclusion that left Pauline with nothing to cling to but remorse." While that might not sound to your or my taste, the story won Alcott a handsome hundred-dollar prize from *Frank Leslie's Illustrated Newspaper*, a precursor to the pulp magazines of the twentieth century. *Little Women*, her first book for young people, was commissioned by a publisher during a postwar growth spurt in children's book publishing triggered by the bestselling likes of Horatio Alger Jr.'s *Ragged Dick* and Mary Mapes

Dodge's *Hans Brinker, or the Silver Skates*. Alcott took the assignment reluctantly and plumbed her own childhood for whatever inspiration she could find. "I plod away," she wrote in her journal, "though I don't enjoy this sort of thing. Never liked girls or knew many, except my sisters, but our queer plays and experiences may prove interesting, though I doubt it." Ten years later, she was still looking down her nose at *Little Women*, even after the book had spawned an even better-selling sequel (now typically published as the second half of *Little Women*, though originally a separate novel entitled *Good Wives*). As she wrote to a young admirer who had asked for advice:

> "Little Women" was written while I was ill, & to prove that I could *not* write books for girls. The publisher thought it *flat*, so did I, & neither hoped much for or from it. We found out our mistake, & since then, though I do not enjoy writing "moral tales" for the young, I do it because it pays well.

While it may be hard to square that cynical voice with the author who ghosted Marmee's needlepoint samplerisms, Alcott's letters and other personal writings are full of snarky and shrewd observations, rarely clotted by the pieties and forced cheer that adulterate her children's fiction. But as I said, the tension between *should* and *want* is strong in *Little Women*, and far less internalized than in the Little House books. In mining her own childhood for money or literature, or both, Alcott was more free-wheeling than Ingalls Wilder, inventing much and setting her story during the Civil War and its aftermath, rather than during the time of of her own adolescence, the 1840s, when she was growing up in Concord, Massachusetts, with figures such as Emerson and Thoreau for neighbors. The March sisters are prettier than their Alcott counterparts, and the March family's poverty is more genteel than dire, which wasn't always the case for the Alcotts, though they never had to build their own home or smoke their own venison.[3] But the spirited sisterly dynamics were mostly true to Alcott's childhood with three sisters, as she acknowledged when she had just finished the book and, perhaps flush with writer's endorphins, was in a better frame of mind about it than she would be later on, noting in a letter that the novel was "not a bit sensational, but simple and true, for we really lived most of it; and if it succeeds that will be the reason."

Jo, of course, is Alcott's stand-in: an aspiring writer with energy to burn; her enthusiasm, sincerity, and playfulness more than compensate for her temper, her quick tongue, her general lack of social graces. As Alcott once wrote, "I am 'Jo' in the principal characteristics, not the good ones." Like Laura Ingalls, Jo is impulsive and independent but without the countervailing prairie reticence. Jo is forever breaking things, running to and fro, "romping" outdoors, inventing games, writing and putting on plays, crying over silly novels, getting into "scrapes," running off at the mouth, letting her quick temper and "fiery spirit" get the better of her. Even when she sits down to the work of writing, she doesn't just dip her pen in ink and compose sentences demurely; she "falls into a vortex."

There is a passage early on that encapsulates what makes Jo such a terrific character, and what makes the novel, at times, so irritating in its insistence on diluting her ungainly verve with canned sentiment. The passage begins on a sloppy winter morning, just after the holidays, that always depressing slough in the calendar. All the March girls have been cross with each other, even Marmee is grumpy, but as Jo and Meg make their way out the door to walk to the jobs they hold down to help support the family (tending, respectively, a rich old aunt and a family of spoiled children), Jo calls out, "Good-by, Marmee; we

---

[3]After shivering and nearly starving through *The Long Winter*, which recounts a series of particularly brutal blizzards that left the Ingalls family snowbound for months, Laura and her sisters would probably laugh at the famous opening of *Little Women*, where Jo grumbles, "Christmas won't be Christmas without any presents," and older sister Meg sighs, "It's so dreadful to be poor!"

are a set of rascals this morning, but we'll come home regular angels."
The two sisters depart into the cold:

> They always looked back before turning the corner, for their mother
> was always at the window, to nod, and smile, and wave her hand
> to them. Somehow it seemed as if they couldn't have got through
> the day without that, for whatever their mood might be, the last
> glimpse of that motherly face was sure to affect them like sunshine.
>
> "If Marmee shook her fist instead of kissing her hand to us,
> it would serve us right, for more ungrateful minxes than we are
> were never seen," cried Jo, taking a remorseful satisfaction in the
> slushy walk and bitter wind.
>
> "Don't use such dreadful expressions," said Meg, from the
> depths of the veil in which she had shrouded herself like a nun
> sick of the world.
>
> "I like good, strong words, that mean something," replied
> Jo, catching her hat as it took a leap off her head, preparatory to
> flying away altogether.

Jo is like a good, strong word herself; it's no wonder so many girls
across so many generations have fallen in love with her, especially girls
of literary bent. Reisen, Alcott's biographer, quotes Cynthia Ozick
as emblematic of all "Jo-worshippers" (Alcott's own amused-irritated
epithet for her most passionate fans): "I read *Little Women* a thousand
times. Ten thousand! I am Jo in her vortex; not Jo, exactly, but some
Jo-of-the-future. I am under an enchantment."

Have readers ever sworn allegiance to any of the other March sisters? Meg is the likable oldest sister, but a bit wishy-washy and recessive
on the page. Beth, as you probably know, is the timid, wan, selfless
middle sister fated to die in the second half of the book from one
of those unnamed, ennobling nineteenth-century diseases that inspire

writing such as this: "There was a strange, transparent look about [Beth's face], as if the mortal was slowly being refined away, and the immortal shining through the frail flesh with an indescribably pathetic beauty." (Try looking up those symptoms on WebMD.) Aside from pathos, Beth doesn't have much to offer readers, and if there are any Beth-worshippers out there, they must be a morbid, masochistic sect. "Hers was a nineteenth-century personality type that has not worn well," Reisen notes, putting it nicely. (The character was based on Alcott's sister Elizabeth, or Lizzie, who died in 1858, aged twenty-two, of complications following scarlet fever.) I, however, would like to speak up for the undersung Amy, the youngest March, an aspiring artist, who is silly, pretentious, narcissistic, and spirited when we first meet her but who eventually achieves wisdom and grace without sacrificing ambition. The novel doesn't ask her to be selfless or to do any moral heavy lifting, and thus, at least to this twenty-first-century reader, she is recognizable as a human being who might be interesting to know.

In case you're wondering, there is indeed a Mr. Marmee, a minister who is off fighting the Civil War during the first half of the book. He returns to tears and huzzahs, but as a character remains an afterthought, a Rosenkrantz or Guildenstern in his own home. The anti-Pa.

No, Jo is the main event here, and another thing that put me off *Little Women* is the way, by the end, Alcott leaches so much of the exuberance out of her. Jo doesn't just grow up; she is practically neutered, as generations of otherwise delighted readers have discovered to their dismay and/or irritation. Jo herself initially wants nothing to do with adulthood: "I wish wearing flat-irons on our heads would keep us from growing up. But buds will be roses, and kittens, cats—more's the pity!" This outburst is prompted by the prospect of Meg's engagement. That teenage Jo doesn't want her family to change, doesn't want to lose her older sister to marriage, and all that marriage implies (sex, babies, distance), is understandable. That Alcott then has Jo address these anxieties in overtly masculine terms is . . . interesting. "I just wish I could marry Meg myself, and keep her safe in the family," Jo wails. And then: "Oh, dear me! why weren't we all boys? then there wouldn't be any bother!" (Note to Jo: There is always bother. Boys may try to pretend there isn't, but there is.)

Jo may be setting an example here for later literary arrivals Huck Finn and Peter Pan, but she is not permitted to remain in her own equiv- alent of Neverland or to "light out for the Territory"—as Huck vows he will at the end of his eponymous *Adventures*, rather than submit to the "sivilizing" ministrations of Aunt Sally. First, there is the famous matter of Alcott marrying Jo off to the wrong husband: the book sets up an expectation that she will pair off with her best friend, Laurie, the impish rich boy who lives next door, but when he finally declares his love, Jo spurns him. "I wish you wouldn't take it so hard," she says, sounding a bit too crisp. "I can't help it; you know it's impossible for people to make themselves love other people if they don't." Laurie: "They do sometimes." Jo: "I don't believe it's the right sort of love, and I'd rather not try it." A novelist's job is to subvert expectations, of course, but Jo's rejection of Laurie struck me as potted and arbitrary when I first read it. (On second and third read, I wonder: is Alcott implying Jo is not sexually attracted to Laurie?) Alcott has an ostensibly more ennobling husband in mind for Jo, though he's about as unexciting a lover as any novelist could dream up: a kindhearted, middle-aged, stout, rather tedious German professor and widower named Friedrich Bhaer—"old Fritz," as he refers to himself.

I wasn't surprised to learn that these plot developments *were* in fact potted and arbitrary, to a degree. As Alcott wrote to a friend shortly after finishing *Good Wives* (she noted that a "jocose friend" had suggested she title it *Wedding Marches*), "I won't marry Jo to Lau- rie to please anyone." She went on in equally defiant fashion:

A sequel will be out in early April, & like all sequels will prob- ably disappoint or disgust most readers, for publishers won't let authors finish off as they like but insist on having people married off in a wholesale manner which much afflicts me. "Jo" should have remained a literary spinster but so many enthusiastic young ladies wrote to me clamorously demanding that she should marry Laurie, *or* somebody, that I didn't dare to refuse, & out of perversity went & made a funny match for her. I expect vials of wrath to be poured upon my head but rather enjoy the prospect.

Alcott herself was and would remain a "literary spinster," a role she seemed to take pride in. "Girls write to ask who the little women marry . . . as if that was the only end and aim of a woman's life," she complained in the prepublication letter quoted above, perhaps forgetting she had had Marmee mouth more or less that same sentiment. She may have been something of a double agent in this regard. "I was born with a boy's nature," she once wrote to a friend, and near the end of her life she said much the same thing to an interviewer: "I am more than half-persuaded that I am a man's soul put by some freak of nature into a woman's body." (Like every other notably independent woman in history, Alcott has been the subject of speculation by critics, academics, and fans that she was gay.)

But "a funny match" is the least of Alcott's sins against her alter ego. Worse, I feel, is the way she treats Jo's aspirations as a writer. Earlier in the book, Jo has temporarily moved to New York and, like Alcott herself, taken a somewhat remunerative plunge "into the froth sea of sensational literature":

She thought it would do her no harm, for she sincerely meant to write nothing of which she should be ashamed. . . . But [her editor] rejected any but thrilling tales; and as thrills could not be produced except by harrowing up the souls of the readers, history and romance, land and sea, science and art, police records and lunatic asylums, had to be ransacked for the purpose. . . . [She] introduced herself to folly, sin, and misery, as well as her limited opportunities allowed. She thought she was prospering finely; but, unconsciously, she was beginning to desecrate some of the womanliest attributes of a woman's character.

Alcott, as a product of high-minded circles, had been conflicted enough about her own "blood and thunder" tales to publish most of them under pseudonyms, but I think you can detect her prostrating herself before convention in that line about desecrating a woman's womanliest attributes. Did Alcott honestly believe that?

But the worst is to come when Beth, as she finally succumbs to whatever disease it is that has been afflicting her for hundreds of pages, extracts a deathbed promise from her sister:

> "You must take my place, Jo, and be everything to father and mother when I'm gone. They will turn to you—don't fail them. . . . You'll be happier in doing that, than writing splendid books, or seeing all the world; for love is the only thing we can carry with us when we go, and it makes the end so easy."
>
> "I'll try Beth"; and then and there Jo renounced her old ambition, pledged herself to a new and better one, acknowledging the poverty of other desires.

Maybe I am doubly biased because I'm a writer *and* I grew up during the so-called Me Decade, but I find this passage punitive. *The poverty of other desires?* Not that Jo shouldn't face her familial responsibilities squarely, but in real life Alcott wrote semi-splendid books and traveled to some of the world while also managing to take care of her increasingly hapless parents. She frequently grumbled about it, but that's no sin, and when Alcott points a finger at the "old Jo" for not maintaining saintly levels of self-abnegation, she's writing down to her audience—and she seems to have known it.

Little Women ends with Jo and her husband ensconced as master and mistress of Plumfield, a school for boys they have founded thanks to an inheritance from Jo's aunt: "Three times a day, Jo smiled at her Fritz from the head of a long table lined on either side with happy young faces, which all turned to her with affectionate eyes, confiding words, and grateful hearts, full of love for 'Mother Bhaer.'" I don't mean to devalue dedicated educators, especially in the current political environment, but romping, headstrong, flyaway Jo is not meant to be Mother Bhaer any more than Tom Sawyer and Huck Finn are meant to be bookkeepers. Alcott would never have stood for such a fate for herself but she and her editors apparently didn't think her readers would accept an equally unfettered heroine, or as unfettered a heroine as Alcott herself was.

Vials of wrath? I'm surprised girls didn't descend upon Alcott's Concord home with torches and pitchforks.

In the Little House books there is a family tragedy parallel to the Marches' loss of Beth, and it similarly bends the trajectory of Laura's life. The weather-beaten reticence with which Ingalls Wilder describes this event is true to time and place (as I've said, I know something about this: my grandfather, not the most emotionally available of men but a champion whittler, was born in the 1890s in the silver-mining town of Cripple Creek, Colorado); at the same time, as prose, as narrative, it couldn't feel more modern, like something out of Raymond Carver or Ann Beattie, which is perhaps another reason why I respond to Ingalls Wilder's novels so much more strongly than I do to Alcott's.

The Ingallses' loss is set in motion on the very first page of *By the Shores of Silver Lake*, the fifth book (and fourth chronicling Laura's childhood), which opens with the family living in Minnesota. Laura, now thirteen, spots a strange woman approaching the house in a buggy:

> Ma sighed. She was ashamed of the untidy house, and so was Laura. But Ma was too weak and Laura was too tired and they were too sad to care very much.
>
> Mary and Carrie and baby Grace and Ma had all had scarlet fever. The Nelsons across the creek had it too, so there had been no one to help Pa and Laura. The doctor had come every day; Pa did not know how he could pay the bill. Far worst of all, the fever had settled in Mary's eyes, and Mary was blind.

I am willing to consider that, taken out of context, this might not be as moving to you as it was to me when I first read it with the imprint of the previous four books fresh in my mind, but the way Ingalls Wilder finally gets to Mary's blindness, at the end of the paragraph and with such plainspoken bluntness, is like a sucker punch hidden in afterthought. The next paragraph could kill you:

> [Mary] was able to sit up now, wrapped in quilts in Ma's old hickory rocking chair. All that long time, week after week, when she could still see a little, but less every day, she had never cried. Now she could not see even the brightest light anymore. She was still patient and brave.

It turns out the woman visitor is Pa's sister Docia, whom the family hasn't seen in years. She invites Pa to move out to the Dakota Territory, where her husband can get him a well-paying job in one of the towns that are growing up alongside the railroad. He accepts the offer, but has to leave his family behind until Ma, Mary, Carrie, and Grace have recovered and are well enough to follow him. Laura is left in charge. Pa's leave-taking is all the more painful because Jack, the family bulldog, has just died. Laura's predicament is starkly drawn, even frightening. Hers is a cruel coming-of-age:

> That morning Pa drove away in the rattling old wagon behind Aunt Docia's buggy. Jack was not standing beside Laura to watch Pa go. There was only emptiness to turn to instead of Jack's eyes looking up to say he was there to take care of her.
>
> Laura knew then that she was not a little girl anymore. Now she was alone; she must take care of herself. When you must do that, then you do it and you are grown up. Laura was not very big, but she was almost thirteen years old, and no one was there to depend on.

I'm quoting this at length not only because I find the writing astonishing but because to me this feels like the true climax of the series, though we are only beginning the fifth book of nine: that moment of watching Pa's wagon recede into the emptiness is for Laura the beginning of the end, as Barrie would say. I can even imagine an argument for leaving Laura here, just as I would have been happy to skip *The Godfather, Part III* and leave Al Pacino brooding on his Lake Tahoe lawn at the end of *Part II*, though I admit that, for a children's book, this would be a hard, awful ending. (Kids should be asked only so much to "buck up.")

Happily, and contra Barrie, Laura retains her fine and frisky qualities through four more books, even as adulthood bears down on her ever more heavily. This is true even of her courtship, which takes up much of *These Happy Golden Years*, the penultimate book. Almanzo, nearly a decade older than she, romances her over the course of a year's worth of chaste Sunday afternoon and evening buggy rides, but it is Laura, more often than not, who holds the reins, metaphorically and literally. She accepts his proposal under the condition that she will not have to vow to "obey" him during the wedding ceremony, a point he readily accedes to.

The book ends with the married couple moving into the sweet, snug farmhouse that Almanzo—a worthy successor to Pa—has built for them himself. It was the last novel Ingalls Wilder published in her lifetime; but as I mentioned, the couple's story continues in *The First Four Years*, which came out in 1971, fourteen years after Laura's death. Possibly intended for an adult audience, it strikes a grimmer, more conflicted tone than its predecessors. As the title implies, the novel details the first four years of Laura and Almanzo's marriage, and in some ways it is a microcosm of everything that has come before: a story of work, hardship, successive crop failures, and tragedy, including the death of the couple's second child, an unnamed infant son who is "taken with spasms." Tellingly, the death and its aftermath are handled with even more dispatch than Mary's blindness: "[Laura's] feelings were numbed and she only wanted to rest—to rest and not to think. But the work must go on. Haying had begun."

That last sentence: *Haying had begun.* As she said, Ingalls Wilder may not have told the whole truth, but even her not telling tells plenty.

I mentioned that the Little House series is in some ways a chronicle of failure, but it is also a saga of endurance. I had that in mind when, fresh off Ingalls Wilder's books, I read *Roll of Thunder, Hear My Cry*, Mildred D. Taylor's 1976 Newbery-winning novel, which takes place in the 1930s. It is the first in a series about a family of African American farmers in Mississippi, and it offers some parallels to the Little House books, including a heroine of grade-school age, Cassie Logan, who is every bit as free-spirited, sharp, and impatient as Laura Ingalls—one more girl eager to see what happens next. Taylor herself grew up in Ohio in the 1940s and '50s, and while her novels are more fictionalized than Ingalls Wilder's, she based them on stories her father had told her about his Mississippi childhood, and modeled the Logan family on her father, his siblings, and their parents; both series feel historically grounded and authentically lived, full of homespun detail, vital with joys as well as sorrows. The Logans own their land, unlike their sharecropper neighbors, and are more successful farmers than the Ingalls family. But the racism with which they have to contend—the small and large slights; the insults; the constant state of self-awareness they are forced to maintain in public; the tightrope they have to walk to avoid beatings, arrests, or worse—is as pervasive and destructive as the elements are on the prairie. I hope it doesn't seem glib or insensitive to compare a man-made system of economic and political subjugation to bad weather, bad luck, and unforgiving terrain, and to compare a white family that took on its lot voluntarily (and at the expense of Native families) to a black one that had no say in the rules it was forced to live by; I realize these are very different moral universes. But I was struck as I read *Roll of Thunder, Hear My Cry* both by a distant kinship between the Ingallses and the Logans and by the profound iniquity of their struggles, the former's putting the latter's into even greater relief—a reminder, at least for this white Californian born in 1958, that Jim Crow was intended to be as inescapable, implacable, and enduring as nature itself. The grinding, quotidian evil of institutionalized racism shouldn't come as a revelation, but Taylor's novel makes it immediate and newly horrible. Somewhere in that distinction is the difference between knowledge and art.

Cassie's loss of childhood innocence is even more frightening than Laura's. It occurs on the final pages of *Roll of Thunder, Hear My Cry*, after a long, horrible night of violence, and of worse violence narrowly averted. A troubled family friend, T. J., has been saved from a lynching but is now in jail, accused of killing a white store owner during a robbery. Cassie, who narrates the novel, and her older brother, Stacey, ask their father—a man every bit as capable and commanding as Charles

Ingalls—what will happen to T. J., who is only a teenager. Their father allows that he might well end up on a chain gang. Stacey isn't satisfied with that answer. "Papa, could he . . . could he die?" Stacey asks.

> Papa put a strong hand on each of us and watched us closely. "I ain't never lied to y'all, y'all know that."
>
> "Yessir."
>
> He waited, his eyes on us. "Well, I . . . I wish I could lie to y'all now."
>
> "No! Oh, Papa, no!" I cried. . . . Stacey, shaking his head, backed away, silent, not wanting to believe, but believing still. His eyes filled with heavy tears and then he turned and fled down the lawn and across the road into the shelter of the forest.
>
> Papa stared after him, holding me tightly to him. "Oh P-Papa, d-does it have to be?"
>
> Papa tilted my chin and gazed softly down at me. "All I can say, Cassie girl . . . is that it shouldn't be."

That frank acknowledgment of injustice is as honest and devastating a passage as exists in children's literature. Like Laura, Cassie is the child in the family left shouldering the burden of an unbidden knowledge, and like Ingalls Wilder, Taylor doesn't look away: the novel ends with Cassie crying tears of bitterness, sorrow, and mourning.

The First Four Years ends on an optimistic note, but one that feels forced, a concession to market forces perhaps not all that different from Alcott's compromises. In truth, though, life treated Laura and Almanzo about as well as it treats anyone. They eventually established a successful farm in the Missouri Ozarks and were married for sixty-four years, until he died in 1949, at the age of ninety-two. Her children's books were successful and beloved from the get-go, and she lived long enough to enjoy a nearly fifteen-year victory lap following the publication of *These Happy Golden Years*, in 1943, until her death, at ninety, in 1957. Fans of the books' Laura may recognize the girl as mother to the woman in the exasperated letter her daughter Rose wrote to her in 1924, when Laura was in her late fifties: "In some ways you're like a frolicsome dog that won't stand still to listen; you are always grabbing and jumping and in a hurry."[4] I prefer the more measured way Garth Williams described Ingalls Wilder, upon first meeting her in 1947, when he drove up to her farm and found her weeding her garden:

> I sat and watched her. I found her to be frisky, a person who seemed to be willing to try anything and go anywhere. She was a very cheerful character, very sprightly, very much alive with a very good sense of humor.

Life was a bit rougher on Alcott, who suffered from chronic health problems, possibly related to the typhoid fever she contracted serving as a Union nurse during the Civil War. She died at the age of fifty-five, in 1888, following a stroke. She had remained ambivalent about her children's books to the end, even as she appreciated the financial security they gave her. In *Jo's Boys*, her final novel about the March family,

---

[4]The particulars of their literary collaborations aside, Laura and Rose had a strained mother-daughter relationship, a least from Rose's point of view. She saw Laura as oblivious to her needs. "It's amazing how my mother can make me suffer," she wrote in her journal in 1933, a year after *Little House in the Big Woods* was published. "She made me so miserable when I was a child that I've never got over it. I'm morbid. I'm all raw nerves. I know I should be more robust." Despairing, Rose accused her mother of manipulating her by means of "implications that she hardly knows she's using." It is an unsettling perspective on a woman who in the popular imagination now occupies a no-man's-land between beloved character and actual person.

published two years before her death, Plumfield is briefly in financial
straits and Jo makes some quick money for the school by writing a
book very much like *Little Women*, which becomes a surprise bestseller and, very much against her will, turns Jo into a celebrity (a word
already in use in the nineteenth century, I learned to my surprise).
A very funny chapter, "Jo's Last Scrape," details her misadventures
in dealing with the strange demands of letter writers and autograph
hounds who show up unannounced at her house—intrusions Alcott
endured in real life. But in a wink at Alcott's readers, and at the author herself, Jo shrugs off her success, dismissing herself as "a literary
nursemaid who provides moral pap for the young." It's all very meta,
though at least Jo retains some of her old spark.

Alcott herself had spark to the end of her life, traveling and enjoying her fame, if not the "affliction" of her more aggressive fans. The
characteristic tone of dyspeptic amusement on display in her letters
and journals bubbles up in her sign-off at the end of *Jo's Boys*:

> It is a strong temptation to the weary historian to close the pres-
> ent tale with an earthquake which should engulf Plumfield and
> its environs so deeply in the bowels of the earth that no youthful
> Schliemann [i.e., Heinrich Schliemann, the German archaeolo-
> gist who discovered Troy] could ever find a vestige of it. But as
> that somewhat melodramatic conclusion might shock my gentle
> readers, I will refrain and forestall the usual question, "How did
> they end?" by briefly stating that all the marriages turned out well.

And that's how the March family saga ends, not with a bang or a
whimper, but rather with more of a grumble and a wink. And with another round of weddings, this time of a second generation of Marches
and various Plumfield pupils. More bother, as young Jo would say.

How much cleaner is the way Mark Twain finished off *Tom Sawyer*:

So endeth this chronicle. It being strictly a history of a boy, it must stop here; the story could not go much further without becoming the history of a man. When one writes a novel of grown people he knows exactly where to stop—that is, with a marriage; but when he writes of juveniles he must stop where he best can.

Twain did allow that he might pick up his pen one day to see what sort of men Tom and Huck turned out to be, and he would indeed write sequels—not just *The Adventures of Huckleberry Finn* but also *Tom Sawyer Abroad* and *Tom Sawyer, Detective*, spoofs of Jules Verne and Arthur Conan Doyle, respectively—but he kept his heroes forever young, pinned like butterflies. He does make mention in his *Autobiography* of what became of the childhood friend he had based Huck on: "I heard, four years ago, that he was a justice of the peace in a remote village in Montana, and was a good citizen and greatly respected." But that denouement—*shudder*—was manhood in real life, presumably nothing a boy would want to read about.

10

The End: Dead Pets, Dead Grandparents, and the Glory of Everything

Do you remember when you first understood, first really *knew*, that someday you were going to die? I don't, but I can recall the next worst thing: walking the half mile home from my kindergarten class one sunny noontime (by myself; that's how it was done in the 1960s) and being struck by the awful, chest-tightening realization—abruptly, perhaps between one footfall and the next—that on some future, horrible day my *mother would die*. I wish I could remember the prompt, if any. Did I see a dead robin or mouse on the pavement? Did I hear a sad song playing on the radio of a passing car? This would have been around the time of John F. Kennedy's assassination, so maybe stray morbid thoughts were simply in the air. Whatever the reason, or for no reason at all, this terrifying knowledge descended on me unbidden and in full, sickening bloom: my mother was going to die. My mother was going to *stop*. Corollary: *I* would be alone. My memory in general has never been particularly acute, but I do recall exactly where I was when I had this revelation: walking on the path that ran through an open field behind the houses on our suburban cul-de-sac; I could show you the spot today, half a century later.

I ran the rest of the way home. (Not far.) I must have blurted out something about my new feel for life's bottom line, because I recall being relieved by my mother's response that, yes, she would die, but that day was far, far away and nothing for me to worry about. I probably ought to have wondered: *How does she know?* But the answer soothed me well enough—putting difficult things off always has an appeal—and decades later I fobbed the same bit of obvious parental boilerplate off on my children when they raised the question of my own mortality. I did feel a twinge of guilt over making a possibly false promise, though so far, so good. Knock on wood.

It is hard enough to be honest with ourselves about death, and exponentially more so with kids. We don't want to die, of course, and we don't want them to worry about us dying—and what we *really* don't want to think about is them dying. But death happens and, notwithstanding euphemisms about sending missing pets to farms upstate, kids are well aware of it, just as they are of sex; they have their own ways of making sense of it, their own myths and rituals. This is captured beautifully in one of Margaret Wise Brown's less well-known works, *The Dead Bird*, a picture book first published in 1958—posthumously, as it happened—and recently returned to print. Brown's story, initially a piece of unadorned prose collected in *The Fish with the Deep Sea Smile*, is deceptively simple: a group of kids find a bird on the ground, still warm but unmoving. They feel for its nonexistent heartbeat (so much for generations of parental prohibitions against touching dead animals) and hold it as it grows cold and stiffens.

The children were very sorry the bird was dead and could never fly again. But they were glad they had found it, because now they could dig a grave in the woods and bury it. They could have a funeral and sing to it the way grown-up people did when someone died.

The unnamed kids line the grave with ferns, wrap the bird in leaves, cover the grave with more ferns and flowers, and sing a song that begins "Oh bird you're dead / You'll never fly again."

Then they cried because their singing was so beautiful and the ferns smelled so sweetly and the bird was dead.

As in *Goodnight Moon*, Brown's prose is spare; her rhythms are almost liturgical; her details are simultaneously specific and allusive. *The Dead Bird* was originally illustrated by Remy Charlip, a choreographer and theater director as well as a writer and illustrator for children. His art for Brown's text was simple, modern, and, for its time, progressive—you can feel Chagall's influence. Charlip reinforces the quietly spiritual, universal quality of Brown's text; to my eye and cultural memory, the illustrations look like what you might have seen circa 1960 in a children's Haggadah or on a UNICEF greeting card. The rendering of the forest where the bird is buried, dense with thick, towering trees, has an especially churchly quality, a sense of majestic hush. *The Dead Bird* was reissued in 2016 with new illustrations by Christian Robinson, who won a Caldecott Honor that same year for *Last Stop on Market Street*, written by Matt de la Peña (who himself won a Newbery Award for the book). While I remain partial to Charlip's mid-century sobriety, Robinson's paintings are more cheerful and literally sunnier; they may make the book more accessible. Robinson's children are also racially diverse, and one boy wears a fox costume while a girl sports what look like butterfly or fairy wings on her back—a subtle suggestion, as I take it, of the interrelatedness of all living things. A nice addition, that.

But what truly elevates *The Dead Bird* in whatever edition you choose is Brown's understanding of children's needs. The self-awareness of the kids as they improvise their rituals, the way they're moved by their own singing, the way they find excitement and pleasure in their mourning, rings especially true; this is still play, after all, that sometimes strange and mysterious process by which children make sense of the world, and Brown's wisdom or intuition is to give her young readers that same space to explore a potentially scary event. Her last line is blunt yet reassuring:

> And every day, until they forgot, they went and sang to their little dead bird and put fresh flowers on his grave.

Until they forgot. For an adult, that phrase is a heartbreaker. (I think again of Christopher Robin's disposal of Pooh.) But from a kid's perspective . . . well, of course the children in the book eventually forgot. They weren't going to spend the rest of their lives, or even the rest of second grade, leaving flowers on an anonymous bird's grave. Thus, while avoiding both corny platitudes and Kübler-Ross's grief-by-numbers determinism, Brown introduces the possibility of what we now like to call closure.

That's how you talk to children about death. But alas, most of us, parents and authors alike, aren't geniuses like Brown, and children's books on this gloomiest of subjects have rarely been as deft, before or since. It is true that fairy tales, arising organically from a primordial soup of terror and superstition, are chockablock with death and weird, spooky, half-glimpsed wisdom. But when children's authors have tried to address dying more consciously and directly, the results have tended to sink under the weight of their own good intentions, artistry (if any) drowning in agenda.

In the seventeenth and eighteenth centuries, as the very notion of children's books came into being, a bent for Christian moral instruction partnered with high infant and child mortality rates to produce works such as *A Token for Children*, which was first printed in England in 1671 and adapted for young American readers by Cotton Mather in 1700. The book's subtitle: *An Exact Account of the Conversion, Holy and Exemplary Lives and Joyful Deaths of Several Young Children*. At the time, English boys and girls had, depending on the study or estimate, about one chance in three of dying before their fifth birthdays, a rate that also held true in the American colonies, so in their authors' minds, books such as *A Token for Children* served the urgent and literal purpose of steering young readers away from an eternity of torment in hell.

As you might imagine, this was not a particularly fun genre. The Morgan Library's collection of rare children's books includes the similarly themed pamphlet *An Authentic Account of the Conversion, Experience, and Happy Deaths of Ten Boys*, which was published in Philadelphia in 1820 and intended for Sunday school use. (The Morgan also has a copy of *Triumphant Deaths of Pious Children*, but, alas, it is an 1835 edition that was translated into Choctaw for missionary work. "As if the poor American Indian children had not suffered enough," Francelia Butler, a pioneering children's lit scholar, once observed.)

This excerpt from a chapter in *An Authentic Account*, profiling one William Quayle, "who spent a life (short as it was) to the glory of God," will give you the general flavor:

William Quayle was born on October 21st, 1778. He seemed to have the fear of God from his infancy, which produced in him a holy zeal. . . . This he manifested by frequently reproving sinners, especially his mother; telling her, that she ought not to say such bad words as she sometimes did. . . . He also reproved wicked children that were playing in the streets. . . .

In September, 1787, he was seized with his last sickness, which continued about a fortnight. . . . When his father used to express his hope that he would recover, he replied, "I would rather die than stay here." Though a child he never complained of pain or sickness, but was patient and resigned to the will of God.

A few minutes before he died, he cried out, "Father! Father! Mother! Mother! O my heaven! My heaven!" He then sang a hymn and desired his mother to turn him in bed and instantly fell asleep in the arms of his dear Redeemer, September 24th, in the ninth year of his age.

Lest young readers miss the point (perhaps finding William Quayle more insufferable than inspirational, or losing the story's thread while speculating about precisely which bad words William's mother used), once all ten happy deaths have been recounted, with each boy more eager to expire than the last, a concluding chapter asks, "Do you not think they were very good children? And do you not wish to be like them, and die as they did? . . . Remember that you are sinners, and that if you die in your sins, you cannot go to heaven: but must be driven into hell, to be tormented there for ever, amongst devils and miserable creatures." Modern sensibilities may recoil from the thought of a child reading something so threatening if not terrifying. But as Kathryn Gin Lum, a religious studies professor at Stanford, writes in her social history *Damned Nation: Hell in America from the*

Revolution to Reconstruction, the authors of such works saw their scare tactics "not as a cruelty but as an act of mercy that could save the sinner from much worse to come." All the same, you can see what a great advance C. S. Lewis represented in the field.

For nineteenth-century readers raised on the likes of William Quayle or Robert Hill, a colleague of William's in blissful, premature death ("From his infancy he had on his mind a deep sense of eternal things"), encountering Jo March or Tom Sawyer must have been both astonishing and refreshing. *Little Women*, of course, features one of the most famous deaths in children's literature, and though the doomed Beth March exhibits barely more personality on the page than does William Quayle, her passing, unlike his, has left readers weeping from 1869 up to the present day—an accomplishment signaling the growing artistry of children's literature.

In 1870, six years before Tom Sawyer had the pleasure of attending his own funeral, Mark Twain poked fun at the "pious dead child" genre in a wonderful sketch, "The Story of the Good Little Boy Who Did Not Prosper." This hero is possessed of a "noble ambition to be put in a Sunday-school book":

> It felt a little uncomfortable sometimes when he reflected that the good little boys always died. . . . This was the most unpleasant feature about being a Sunday-school-book boy. He knew it was not healthy to be good. He knew it was more fatal than consumption to be so supernaturally good as the boys in the books were; he knew that none of them had ever been able to stand it long, and it pained him to think that if they put him in a book he wouldn't ever see it, or even if they did get the book out before he died, it wouldn't be popular without any picture of his funeral in the back part of it. . . . So at last, of course he had to make up his mind

to do the best he could under the circumstances—to live right, and hang on as long as he could, and have his dying speech ready when his time came.

Another antidote to the black-crepe piousness of *A Token for Children* and its ilk was *Shock-Headed Peter*. First published in Germany in 1845, and soon translated into English and numerous other languages, the book is a raucous collection of faux cautionary tales in which young reprobates suffer grotesque punishments or deaths. One troublesome lad, Conrad, is an inveterate thumb-sucker. In vain, his mother tries to wean him off his habit, until one day, when she is out running errands, a demented-looking tailor bursts into the house like a bogeyman, and cuts off both of Conrad's thumbs with a huge pair of shears. The blasé parental response to this odd home invasion: "'Ah,' said Mama, 'I knew he'd come / To naughty little Suck-a-Thumb.'" (She is lucky there were no mommy blogs in nineteenth-century Germany.) Another story is devoted to Augustus, a "chubby lad" who refuses to eat his soup and soon withers away and dies. "Foolish Harriet" plays with matches, and this leads inevitably to self-immolation:[1]

> *So she was burnt, with all her clothes,*
> *And arms, and hands, and eyes, and nose,*
> *Till she had nothing more to lose*
> *Except her little scarlet shoes;*
> *And nothing else but these were found*
> *Among her ashes on the ground.*

---

[1]Illustrations of girls and boys catching fire become for a time what we now call a meme. As Maria Tatar notes, "The number of children who go up in flames in nineteenth century storybooks is nothing short of extraordinary."

Because of its violence (which, in fairness, seems well within the standards set by fairy tales), *Shock-Headed Peter* was considered somewhat disreputable in its day, and probably because of that children found it uproariously funny, or so historians tell us. Alas, the passage of time has neutered most if not all of the book's lighthearted German wit, though you can spot a debt to *Shock-Headed Peter* in the amusingly morbid rhymes of Hilaire Belloc (*Cautionary Tales for Children*) and Edward Gorey (*The Gashlycrumb Tinies*), not to mention the gruesome fates of the loathsome Augustus Gloop, Violet Beauregarde, Veruca Salt, and Mike Teavee in Roald Dahl's *Charlie and the Chocolate Factory.*

In the first decades of the twentieth century, with child mortality rates happily decreasing, death seems also to have absented itself from nursery bookshelves. According to the scholars Louis Rauch Gibson and Laura M. Zaidman, writing in a special 1991 issue of the *Children's Literature Association Quarterly* devoted to the topic, "As death moved out of the home and into the hospital, it also nearly disappeared from children's books. Perhaps it became more comfortable to keep death sanitary if not invisible." No doubt the absence of messy mortality suited the no-fuss, pre–Dr. Spock philosophies of parents in the early to middle twentieth century. Gibson and Zaidman credit *The Dead Bird* with helping to make mortality once again "an acceptable topic for young children" and cite a survey from 1977, which found that 90 percent of all children's books dealing with death had been published since 1970—a lopsided proportion that, logic insists, can only have increased over the last four decades. Gibson and Zaidman concluded, "Today, most parents and educators would agree that youngsters need to learn not only about where babies come from, but also about this other very basic 'fact of life.'"

That is undoubtedly true, but it also suggests a nagging problem: where death is concerned, children's literature over the last fifty-some years has often returned to the old hortatory approach, although the aims are now therapeutic instead of moral; rather than warn children away from eternal damnation, contemporary books about death strive to usher them through the "grieving process"—a different sort of medicine, and more to present-day tastes, but medicine all the same. Titles in what has been called the "crisis literature" vein include *My Grandpa Died Friday*; *My Grandpa Died Today*; *Saying Good-Bye to Grandma*; *So Long, Grandpa*; *Why Did Grandpa Die?* and *Why Did Grandma Die?*

It is not just the elderly who draw last breaths in these mourning primers; pets also do yeomen's work. One prominent example is *The Tenth Good Thing About Barney*, written by Judith Viorst (also known for *Alexander and the Terrible, Horrible, No Good, Very Bad Day*) and illustrated by Erik Blegvad. The text begins, "My cat Barney died last Friday. I was very sad. I cried, and I didn't watch television. I cried, and I didn't eat my chicken or even the chocolate pudding." Asked by his mother to say ten good things about Barney at the cat's backyard funeral, the nameless young narrator can think of only nine—until the next day, when he's gardening with his father and has a revelation. The tenth good thing: "Barney is in the ground and he's helping grow flowers."

Personally, I am of two minds about Barney and his book, which has remained popular since it was published in 1971. While I wholeheartedly endorse its sentiment about the circle of life, I find the book's tone cloying and its denouement pat. I keep getting stuck on that bit about not eating the chocolate pudding—a telling and off note to my ear. It's the kind of thing an adult might think a child would find relatable, but my inner six-year-old feels condescended to. Anyway, dead pet or no, I've rarely known a kid not to be jollied up, at least a little, by a decent dessert.

The picture book *Missing Mommy*, written and illustrated by Rebecca Cobb and first published in Britain in 2011, is as good as this sort of thing gets. In it, a little boy whose mother has recently died works through a series of sometimes conflicted feelings: "I feel so scared because I don't think she is coming back. . . . And then I feel angry because I really want her to come back. . . . I am worried that she left because I was naughty sometimes. . . . The other children have THEIR moms. It's not fair." Subtitled *A Book About Bereavement*, this is less a story than a catalog of troubling but normal emotions—more a therapeutic tool than a story per se. The last spread shows the little boy watering some tulips (the circle of life again, though one hopes not quite as literally as in Barney's case) while the text concludes, "I will always remember her. I know how special I was to my mommy and she will always be special to me." *Missing Mommy* is sensitive. It's heartbreaking. It's validating. It does the trick. I hope you never have cause to read it to anyone.

It is as easy to poke fun at *An Authentic Account of the Conversion, Experience, and Happy Deaths of Ten Boys* as it is churlish to pick at *The Tenth Good Thing About Barney*. Really, my point here is twofold. One: in kids' books as in life, death is so often a flummoxing subject. And two: this has all been backstory for a discussion of the singular work that is *Charlotte's Web*.

Do wiser, funnier, more pleasurable books exist? If so, they're few and far between, no matter how old or young their intended audience. I realize that it is a bit of an apples-and-oranges comparison to put E. B. White's middle-grade novel up against old religious tracts and modern, "message" picture books (and on the subject of death I'm ignoring altogether the YA lists, where series such as the Hunger Games boast body counts that rival Shakespeare's or Thomas Harris's); but, like *The Dead Bird*, *Charlotte's Web*, which was published in 1952, is fearless, organic, and beautifully crafted—which is to say it is a work of truly first-rank literature. It is about death, but it is also about life and what makes life worth living, and about friendship, and about both nature and Nature. In its own quiet way, it is a novel of ideas.

I am going to borrow a bit here from my wife, Helen Schulman, a novelist who has taught *Charlotte's Web* in craft classes for MFA writing students and who opened my eyes to how carefully and skillfully the book is constructed. Look, for instance, at White's very first sentence, which introduces his story's theme and conveys the stakes rather dramatically:

> "Where's Papa going with that ax?" said Fern to her mother as they were setting the table for breakfast.

I suppose Papa could be planning to chop some firewood, but Fern's mother explains that her father is going out to the hog house because a litter of pigs has just been born. Fern, who we are told is "only eight," doesn't quite get the implication:

> "Well," said her mother, "one of the pigs is a runt. It's very small and weak, and it will never amount to anything. So your father has decided to do away with it."
>
> "Do *away* with it? You mean *kill* it? Just because it's smaller than the others?"

Like many children, Fern refuses to deal in euphemism. And really, you have to admire a book for children that is willing to raise the prospect of a newborn piglet being ax-murdered: though *Charlotte's Web* is a delightful book with a barnyard full of talking animals, it is also about real and even harsh things.

Fern is having none of this. She runs after her father:

The grass was wet and the earth smelled of springtime. Fern's sneakers were sopping by the time she caught up with her father.

How evocative are those two short sentences! Maybe wet grass and earthy, springtime smells are familiar to the point of bordering on pastoral cliché, but the sopping sneakers are such a specific, grounding detail, especially for those of us old enough to remember when sneakers were made only of canvas. *Squelch.* White, who spent much of his life on a farm in Maine and had one of his first big successes writing essays on rural themes, is here introducing another of the book's concerns: the rhythms and glories of rural life—of springtime, birth, axes, death. By the way, we are still on the book's very first page.

The sopping sneakers also tell us a bit more about what kind of girl Fern is: the passionate kind of girl who ignores clammy feet to fight injustice. She confronts her father, grabbing the ax and trying to wrest it away. He explains that the "weakling" will make trouble for the rest of the litter, and orders Fern to "run along."

"But it's unfair," cried Fern. "The pig couldn't help being born small, could it? If *I* had been born very small at birth, would you have killed *me*?"

Mr. Arable smiled. "Certainly not," he said, looking down at his daughter with love. "But this is different. A little girl is one thing, and a runty little pig is another."

"I see no difference," replied Fern, still hanging onto the ax. "This is the most terrible case of injustice I ever heard of."

A queer look came over John Arable's face. He seemed almost ready to cry himself.

To me, this is one of the most remarkable passages in the book. (By the way, we are only on page 3 now, and page 2 is mostly just Garth Williams's drawing of Fern tugging on her father's ax.) Fern has a child's moral clarity and conviction, and she makes her case in terms any child can relate to. But White then shifts the focus to her father and the "queer look" that comes over his face. White leaves this open to interpretation: I like to think Fern's father is moved by her youthful passion, which he realizes is as fleeting as everything else about childhood; he's mourning the loss of his daughter before she's even left. Of course, White may have had something entirely different in mind here; I may well be reading into it, projecting a constitutional melancholy vis-à-vis rapidly growing offspring. But how many books for middle-graders give one that opportunity?

As you may know, Fern's dad lets her take care of the runt, whom she names Wilbur and feeds with a baby bottle. He is eventually sold to Fern's uncle, but Fern continues to watch over him as he is raised in the cellar of a barn where, as the novel gradually and gracefully shifts from Fern's point of view to Wilbur's, he becomes friends with a crew of gabby, sometimes querulous geese and sheep, plus a rat named Templeton and, most important of all, Charlotte, a not-so-ordinary gray spider. The barn is magical in the sense that the livestock speak with the ironic erudition of *New Yorker* writers (White was a staff writer there), but at the same time, and more so than even Beatrix Potter does, White insists that his animals stay mostly true to their actual animal nature. Templeton, a sour-tempered creature of solitary vices, readily concedes that he is a "glutton, but not a merry-maker." When a sheep tells him he would live longer if he ate less and lost some weight, he responds, "Who wants to live forever? I am naturally a heavy eater and get untold satisfaction from the pleasures of the feast." In other words, he refuses to apologize for being a rat. Charlotte is similarly frank when Wilbur, expressing revulsion toward her diet of flies and other insects, timidly asks if they taste good. "Delicious" is her response.

> "Of course I don't really eat them. I drink them—drink their
> blood," said Charlotte, and her pleasant, thin voice grew even
> thinner and more pleasant.
>   "Don't say that!" groaned Wilbur. "Please don't say things
> like that!"
>   "Why not? It's true, and I have to say what is true. I'm not
> entirely happy about my diet of flies and bugs, but it's the way
> I'm made. . . . Way back for thousands and thousands of years we
> spiders have been laying for flies and bugs."
>   "It's a miserable inheritance," said Wilbur, gloomily. He was
> sad because his new friend was so bloodthirsty.

According to Michael Sims's *The Story of Charlotte's Web*, a splendid account of how White came to write the novel, he drew a line at having Charlotte make reference to having eaten her late husband; I am impressed he even considered it.

Food is naturally a big topic of conversation in the barn, never more so than when Wilbur—now well into his first summer and several months old, settled into a fine daily rhythm of eating slops, sleeping in a manure pile, and growing steadily bigger—is informed in rather cavalier and cruel fashion by an old sheep, who has seen a few things in his day, that he, Wilbur, is being fattened up for slaughter and eventual consumption as "smoked bacon and ham." Wilbur, unaware of his first brush with the ax, now experiences a full-blown panic:

> "I don't want to die! Save me, somebody! Save me. . . . I don't
> want to die. I want to stay alive, right here in my comfortable

manure pile with all my friends. I want to breathe beautiful air
and lie in the beautiful sun."

This is pretty stark, all things considered, for a children's book, even
one named for a bloodsucking spider. But that is one of White's great
attributes as a writer, both for children and for adults: like Charlotte
he is compelled to say what is true.

He picked up that habit as a solitary, introspective boy who decided
early on he wanted to be a writer. Elwyn Brooks White was born in
1899. (He was given the much preferable nickname Andy in college, at
Cornell, and happily kept it in adulthood.) He grew up in a big house
in Mount Vernon, New York, just north of the Bronx, when Westches-
ter County was still largely rural. He would spend much of his childhood haunting his family's stable, where he tended the horses and raised
pigeons, chickens, geese, and rabbits. As Michael Sims writes, "From
early childhood, Elwyn found the dark and pungent stable intoxicat-
ingly rich in romantic associations of life and death and adventure. But
it was also a refuge where a thoughtful young boy could spend time by
himself." As White himself would write decades later in some publicity
material for *Charlotte's Web*, "Animals are a weakness with me." They
also provided him with literary fodder throughout his career. At the age
of ten he submitted a poem, "To a Mouse," to *Woman's Home Companion* and won a prize for it. The following year, he published his first
essay, about taking a walk on a snowy winter morning with his dog,
in the children's magazine *St. Nicholas*, to which he would contribute
several more nature studies and animal stories. (The magazine's young
contributors included other future pros, among them Edna St. Vincent
Millay, William Faulkner, and F. Scott Fitzgerald.)

White started his adult career as a reporter and an advertising
copywriter, but caught on with *The New Yorker* shortly after it began
publishing in 1925; he became a staff writer two years later, and two

years after that he married the magazine's first fiction editor, Katharine Angell. The couple would spend much of their lives shuttling between New York City and Maine, where in 1933 they bought a farm that would serve as the model for Wilbur's home. Even before *Charlotte's Web*, the farm and its livestock provided frequent subject matter for the essays that first made White's name as a writer, at *The New Yorker* and also at *Harper's*, where in the 1930s and early 1940s he had a monthly column called "One Man's Meat"—which, come to think of it, could have been an alternative title for *Charlotte's Web* if White's sense of humor had been blacker.

His first children's book, *Stuart Little*, published in 1945, came to him in a dream, he said—in Sims's words, "a direct shipment from his subconscious." But maybe not too direct, since what began as a series of stories White told to his nieces and nephews took years to craft into a finished novel. (A biographical note on the back of the book's original edition—evidently written by White or at least very much under his influence—explained that he "began *Stuart Little* in the hope of amusing a six-year-old niece of his, but before he finished it she had grown up and was reading Hemingway.") The titular hero is a mouse born to a human family in New York City. After winning a toy sailboat race and evading the culinary designs of the family cat, he decides he must leave home on a noble, romantic quest to find his lost love: Margalo, a "perfectly pretty" little bird of an indeterminate species, who Stuart notes, by way of identifying her to anyone who may have seen her, "comes from a place with thistles" and "loves to whistle." ("I'll keep my eyes open," promises one of Stuart's interlocutors.)

Stuart Little was an instant success, but not without detractors. Before publication, Anne Carroll Moore, the children's librarian at the New York City Public Library (I previously mentioned her spats with Margaret Wise Brown and Lucy Sprague Mitchell), read galleys of the book and wrote both to Ursula Nordstrom, White's editor, and to White's wife, Katharine, who aside from her editing duties reviewed children's books for *The New Yorker*. Moore demanded that *Stuart Little* be withdrawn. Her objection: the biological implication, whatever that might be, of a mouse born to a human mother. Moore was taking fantasy far too literally (perhaps she had more in common with her Here and Now antagonists than she realized), though in fairness to her, the complaint wasn't limited to imperious children's librarians. As White remembered the episode years later, Harold Ross, *The New Yorker*'s urbane but sometimes squeamish founding editor, accosted him in the magazine's office shortly after the book came out, objecting just as adamantly as Moore to the circumstances of Stuart's birth: "God damn it, White, you should have had him adopted." White himself seems to have been sensitive on this point, always insisting that Stuart wasn't technically a mouse: "He is a small guy who *looks* very much like a mouse, but obviously he is not a mouse. He is a second son."

Charlotte's Web, rooted more firmly in reality, required no such taxonomical sleight of hand. One clear source of inspiration was an actual pig on White's farm that had become ill with some sort of gastrointestinal ailment. In "Death of a Pig," an essay he published in the *Atlantic* in 1947, White recounted his unsuccessful efforts to nurse it back to health and how that struggle raised his consciousness—as later generations would say—where pigs are concerned:

> The scheme of buying a spring pig in blossomtime, feeding it through summer and fall, and butchering it when the solid cold weather arrives, is a familiar scheme to me and follows an antique pattern. It is a tragedy enacted on most farms with perfect fidelity to the original script. The murder, being premeditated, is in the first degree but quick and skillful, and the smoked bacon and ham provide a ceremonial ending whose fitness is seldom questioned.

Once in a while something slips—one of the actors goes up in his lines and the whole performance stumbles and halts. My pig simply failed to show up for a meal. The alarm spread rapidly. The classic outline of the tragedy was lost. I found myself cast suddenly in the role of the pig's friend and physician—a farcical character with an enema bag for a prop. I had a presentiment, the very first afternoon, that the play would never regain its balance and that my sympathies were now wholly with the pig.

His presentiment proved correct, in spades. White didn't begin work in earnest on *Charlotte's Web* until two years after "Death of a Pig" was published, but the essay's empathic if unflinching voice is very much of a piece with White's great novel. He spent two years researching and writing *Charlotte's Web*, set it aside for a year to let it "ripen," then reworked it, adding Fern as a character only on the homestretch—"a lucky move on my part, a narrow squeak," he later wrote. He was serious enough about his spider studies to complain that the haphazard, haunted-house-style cobwebbing that Garth Williams (who had earlier illustrated *Stuart Little*) drew for the book's cover wasn't true to the tidier, symmetrical snares woven by Charlotte's species, *Aranea cavatica*.[2]

---

[2]Williams and White also struggled over how Charlotte herself should be depicted. The author arranged for several illustrated scholarly books about spiders to be sent to Williams in the hope that Charlotte would be drawn with absolute realism. But the illustrator was stymied by the fact that spider faces are "all gruesome." He later wrote, "I struggled to invent a loveable spider-face. They all have 8 eyes. Mouths like pincers." He eventually took a more anthropomorphic approach, creating what he called a "Mona Lisa face" for Charlotte, wanting her to look somewhat attractive—"as she is, after all, the heroine of the story." White was dismayed.

The problem was eventually solved by a compromise: Charlotte is shown only from a distance, aside from two medium shots (to borrow from film terminology) in which her face is visible and she has, at White's suggestion, only two eyes and no nose or mouth. Years later, White was still rankled about this struggle with Williams. As

It is Charlotte, Wilbur's dearest and truest friend, as well as, though she wouldn't acknowledge it, his surrogate mother, who saves his life, turning him into a local celebrity by writing SOME PIG in her web above his sty, then TERRIFIC, then RADIANT, and finally, when summer has turned to fall and Wilbur is in competition at the county fair, HUMBLE—her masterstroke. (White was an inconsistent stickler for biological accuracy but always a champion of words.) One of the novel's great jokes is that nearly all the human characters think it is Wilbur who is remarkable, not Charlotte; as Fern's uncle explains to his wife when she raises the possibility that maybe they have a miraculous spider on their hands, "Oh no. . . . It's the pig that's unusual. It says so, right there in the middle of the web." Adam Gopnik has observed that this is also a nice little jab at the dark art of advertising.

Wilbur wins a prize at the fair and his future—*not* being turned into smoked bacon and ham—is ensured. Charlotte offers him a benediction:

> "You will live, safe and secure, Wilbur. Nothing can harm you
> now. These autumn days will shorten and grow cold. The leaves
> will shake loose from the trees and fall. Christmas will come,
> then the snows of winter. You will live to enjoy the beauty of the
> frozen world. . . . The days will lengthen, the ice will melt in the
> pasture pond. The song sparrow will sing, the frogs will awake,
> the warm winds will blow again. All these sights and sounds and
> smells will be yours to enjoy, Wilbur—this lovely world, these
> precious days. . . ."

---

he wrote in a letter to Nordstrom: "His Charlotte (until we abandoned everything and just drew a spider) was horrible and would have wrecked the book." Although the reasons are not clear, Williams was not asked to illustrate White's third and final children's book, *The Trumpet of the Swan* (1970), and was rankled in turn.

As that last ellipsis (White's) suggests, this is a bittersweet triumph. For one thing, Fern has moved on, less interested in Wilbur's survival than in riding the Ferris wheel with a boy by the wonderful name of Henry Fussy. White doesn't condemn her for it. Fern's maturing, her interest in boys is as natural and inevitable as the change of seasons. (White's attitude here is quite unlike C. S. Lewis's and L. Frank Baum's bent for stunting their heroines' growth.)

But far more important than Fern's life cycle is Charlotte's. She is now, as she tells Wilbur, "done for . . . in a day or two I'll be dead." Her final energies have been spent weaving the HUMBLE web and creating an egg sac filled with, as White notes with characteristic specificity, "five hundred and fourteen unborn children." Charlotte has thus killed herself to give life to her biological progeny and spare the life of her surrogate son, but if White is suggesting this is a mother's lot, along the lines of *The Giving Tree*, his Charlotte won't bludgeon anyone over the head about it. (She is more Stella Dallas than Sophie Portnoy.) At any rate, with only minutes to spare before he is to be loaded onto a truck and driven back to the farm, Wilbur enlists Templeton to snare the egg sac and bring it back with them. Charlotte must be left behind, and in one of the most crushing paragraphs ever written, White bids her farewell:

> Next day, as the Ferris wheel was being taken apart and the race horses were being loaded into vans and the entertainers were packing up their belongings and driving away in their vans, Charlotte died. The Fair Grounds were soon deserted. The sheds and buildings were empty and forlorn. The infield was littered with bottles and trash. Nobody, of the hundreds of people that had visited the Fair, knew that a gray spider had played the most important role of all. No one was with her when she died.

Perhaps White is piling it on a bit with the forlorn fairgrounds, but it doesn't take much imagination to conjure far more maudlin, drawn-out, less tactful versions of Charlotte's death. Instead, White steps back, granting Charlotte some privacy, as it were, and also giving us maybe not a cosmic perspective but at least one in keeping with the view from the top of the Ferris wheel before it was dismantled: Charlotte dies alone; that's what spiders do.

White does provide a happy ending: the following spring, Charlotte's babies are born, and while most of them sail away to parts and adventures unknown on little balloons made of webbing, three stay behind and spin their webs in Wilbur's barn. We are told that Wilbur befriends generation after generation of Charlotte's descendants and that he spends "all the rest of his days" in comfort and happiness in his sty:

> It was the place to be, thought Wilbur, this warm delicious cellar, with the garrulous geese, the changing seasons, the heat of the sun, the passage of swallows, the nearness of rats, the sameness of sheep, the love of spiders, the smell of manure, and the glory of everything.

Those last four words, from the book's penultimate paragraph, are as perfect a distillation of White's worldview as the entire novel is an exploration of it: *the glory of everything*. As Michael Sims writes, "He hadn't planned the book as a summary of what it felt like to be E. B. White, but by the last page he had preserved in amber his response to the world." P. L. Travers, reviewing *Charlotte's Web* for the *New York Herald Tribune*, divined something similar in it, catching echoes of White's boyhood afternoons haunting his family's stable, when she wrote that the book had "an absorbed and dreamlike air such as one sometimes [observes] in a child playing alone." (Travers was an inspired choice as a reviewer: her magical but severe Mary Poppins is very much a spiritual sister to Charlotte.)

Like *Stuart Little*, *Charlotte's Web* was an instant success when it was published, in 1952, selling out its first printing of fifty thousand copies and winning a Newbery Honor. "As a piece of work it is just about perfect, and just about magical in the way it is done," Eudora Welty wrote in the *New York Times Book Review*. There were a few dissenters. Anne Carroll Moore panned *Charlotte's Web* in the *Horn Book*, offering the criticism that "Fern, the real center of the book, is never developed." (Sure. And why didn't White also devote space to Templeton's thoughts on the Marshall Plan?) A more understandable concern, though still wrongheaded, had been raised during editing by the usually unimpeachable Ursula Nordstrom. Several years later White wrote that in killing off Charlotte he had violated a kid lit "taboo," and that Nordstrom was "not very enthusiastic about this development. Apparently children are not supposed to be exposed to death, but I did not pay any attention to this." Certainly, a *Charlotte's Web* where Charlotte makes it to the final page would be a very different book, because death is an inescapable part of White's "everything." That is the book's point, or one of its points, if I may use as crass a word as "point" in relation to a work so rich and complex. It is maybe not an original point—it is perhaps the same point made in different ways by both *A Token for Children* and *The Tenth Good Thing About Barney*—but it is a point that has never been better put.[3]

---

[3]If it's true that Nordstrom objected to Charlotte's death—I find it hard to believe of such a sympathetic reader—she ultimately repented. As she wrote two decades later to a child whose letter expressing sorrow about the book's ending had crossed her desk: "When I read the manuscript I felt exactly the way you now feel. I didn't want Charlotte to die, and I too cried over her death. What I think you and I both should keep in mind is that Charlotte had a good and worthwhile life. . . . This may not be of much comfort to you now, but perhaps as time goes by you will understand why E. B. White had to tell Charlotte's story the way he told it."

White himself died on October 1, 1985, at the age of eighty-six. He had remained physically and mentally active to nearly the end of his life, but suffered a rapid onset of dementia following an accident in August 1984. He had been canoeing by himself on a lake near his farm in Maine. Back home, while he was taking the canoe down from his car's roof rack, it slipped and hit his head. Unfortunate, but White would have agreed, I think, that there are worse ways to go; and as Templeton said, "Who wants to live forever?"

White, who wasn't shy about what he accomplished in *Charlotte's Web*, always denied that it was any kind of allegory or fable, and I think he deserves the penultimate word on the subject. As he wrote in 1971 to an animator who was working (fruitlessly, as it turned out) on a film adaptation:

> I do hope . . . that you are not planning to turn "Charlotte's Web" into a moral tale. It is not that at all. It is, I think, an *appreciative* story, and there is quite a difference. It celebrates life, the seasons, the goodness of the barn. . . . But it is essentially amoral, because animals are essentially amoral, and I respect them, and I think this respect is implicit in the tale. . . . It is a straight report from the barn cellar, which I dearly love, having spent so many fine hours there, winter and summer, spring and fall, good times and bad times.

The final word goes to my own children. When I read *Charlotte's Web* to them I was, of course, blubbering by the end, as I had been at the end of *The House at Pooh Corner.* I was weeping for Charlotte, and more, I was weeping for the beauty of White's novel, his overall conception, that glorious everything. My kids had a different take. "What are you crying about, Dad? Wilbur has all these new friends now." At the time, I thought this was awfully utilitarian of them, maybe even hard-hearted. But I'm guessing that White would say that they had it exactly right.

Afterword

E. B. White was correct about *Charlotte's Web* being an "apprecia-tive" book—leave it to the coauthor of *The Elements of Style* to find such a lovely and perfect adjective—and I hope I have written one as well. For better or worse, *Wild Things* was a genuine labor of love.

Maurice Sendak had a great anecdote about appreciation, which he shared in his 1991 interview with Larry King: "A little boy wrote, 'I love your book, you're great,' and then he drew a little picture. . . . And I wrote back and I drew him a little picture and then I got a letter from his mother and she said, 'Edward liked your letter so much—he ate it.' It was like the ultimate compliment. He didn't preserve it. He didn't say, 'Oh, I have an autographed picture.' He ate it. I mean, that's how primal, that's how animalistic, that's how passionate we are as small people." Myself, I wouldn't eat a Sendak, but I honor the gesture.

I have to admit that when I decided to write this book, and then

signed a contract and received an advance for it, I was afraid that
the responsibility and the task ahead would leach all the fun out of
Brown, Seuss, Cleary, White, et al.—that a passion would become a
millstone. To my relief, the reality of researching and writing this was
nearly the opposite: the more I read about the authors and illustrators I've discussed here, and the more closely I read them and looked
at their drawings and paintings, the more remarkable their work became. Not to mention their lives. What to make of the fact that so
many were, for whatever reason, childless? And that so many didn't
even seem to care much for children? And yet their respect for their
readers, no matter how young, was profound. That respect, along
with imagination, craft, inspiration, genius—all *that*—is what really
distinguishes the best kids' books. This might seem a simpleminded
epiphany, but it is so easy and tempting to condescend to children.

In *Ezra Jack Keats: Artist and Picture Book Maker*, Brian Alderson describes the creation of Keats's breakthrough book, *The Snowy
Day*, and concludes, "Unquestionably the most important aspect [of
its making was] his discovery that he had found a language. He may
not even have known he was looking for one, or what he would say
with it once it was found, but the revelation with *Snowy Day* was that
there was something central to himself that he could articulate with a
picture book." I think the same could be said of nearly all the writers
and illustrators I've discussed: their books happened not because of
commercial calculation or literary ambition but because these books
were *needed*, by the creators themselves, which is true of any worthwhile art. (Though I'm sure I could think of a cynical counterexample
or two if I tried harder.)[1]

This book really begins and ends with my own kids, Zoë and

---

[1] OK, the first two *Godfather* films. Francis Ford Coppola claims he was holding his
nose during their entire production.

Isaac. Reading to them nearly every night before bed became a cherished ritual in our home, as it is for so many parents and children, though I don't want to get too precious here. As I've mentioned, there were books they adored that I couldn't bear, and I won't pretend there weren't plenty of nights when I was tired or distracted or frankly bored and rushed through a couple of picture books with my mind more focused on the bottle of wine waiting in the kitchen. Sometimes I'd skip a passage or an entire page or even several pages if I could get away with it, if the kids didn't have the books memorized, which they often did. For their part, I'm sure there were nights when they would have been happier just lying in bed and playing with their Game Boys or whatever the toy of the moment was.

But more often than not, I think—I hope—we were all held rapt by whatever I was reading aloud. For me, aside from the immediate pleasures of sharing great stories and art with my children, these nightly readings gave me a chance not only to reconnect with books I had loved as a boy but also to discover the great wealth of children's literature published in the decades since I had moved on to more "mature" works. Zoë and Isaac would move on, too, of course—yet another The End in that long sweet sorrow of watching your children grow. So for me, writing about kids' books has been a way both to stay engaged with this wonderful body of literature, to not let it go a second time, and also, frankly, to hold on to my children's younger selves. By one measure, I suppose, you are holding in your hands a work of sublimated grief.

I remember when Zoë, the older by two years, announced to me that she didn't want to be read to anymore, that she was now old enough to read herself to sleep. She was nine or so. I think I felt a bit like Pooh being left behind by Christopher Robin—parent as childish thing, perhaps, though irony didn't soften the sting. Maybe a "queer look" came over my face like the one that came over John Arable's when Fern challenged his sense of justice and stood up for Wilbur. But I didn't begrudge Zoë this stirring of independence. I'm certain I was absolutely 100 percent gracious about it and not at all sniffy. I'm certain.

At the time, the kids still shared a room and bunk beds, and one evening not long afterward I was reading aloud to Isaac. He was tucked into the lower bunk, while Zoë snuggled with her own book up top. I was sitting in the now fraying wicker-backed rocking chair we'd been given for just this purpose as a wedding gift, years earlier. I wish I could remember the specific title Isaac and I were reading; I think it was one of Beverly Cleary's. Halfway through the chapter I heard slow, deep, gentle breaths coming from the upper bunk: Zoë's eyes had shut; her book was splayed across her chest. Isaac soon fell asleep as well, his bed the usual chaotic, de Kooning–like snarl of blanket, sheet, pillow, and limbs. Me, I was disappointed. I wanted to know what happened next in the book. I could have gotten up, but is there any sound more enchanting than that of sleeping children? So I stayed put in the rocking chair.

I kept reading.

Acknowledgments

When you take six years to write a book, you have a lot of people to thank. . . .

Jennifer Joel is a fierce advocate, a perceptive but gentle critic, a lover of books, an asker of the right questions, and a great person to have a martini with—in other words, the ideal agent.

Jofie Ferrari-Adler inherited *Wild Things* at Simon & Schuster, but embraced it with such passion and care I never for a second felt orphaned. He is an editor's editor. Also, speaking of six years, as far as I can tell his patience is inexhaustible. On that score, gratitude as well to publisher Jonathan Karp, who put me in good hands not only with Jofie but also Anne Tate Pearce, Stephen Bedford, Julianna Haubner, and the rest of the smart, painstaking team at S&S. They have been a joy to work with.

I hope *Wild Things* is as fun to read as I know it is to look at.

Thomas Colligan designed the bright, apt, amazing cover—in tribute, of course, to Maurice Sendak. The "bug art" illustrations at the start of each chapter, which delight me to no end, are by Seo Kim. The graceful interior design is the work of Ruth Lee-Mui.

A special thanks to Sarah Hochman: not only the first editor of this book but a good friend who gave me the idea of writing it in the first place.

Another special thanks to Sam Tanenhaus, former editor of the *New York Times Book Review*, who gave me my first platform for writing about kids' books. I've been lucky to work with a succession of terrific children's books editors there: Julie Just, Pamela Paul (Sam's successor as editor of the *Book Review*), Sarah Harrison Smith, and Maria Russo.

I had first-rate research assistance from John Ortved, Louisine Frelinghuysen, Adrienne Gaffney, and Alex Beggs. I am also indebted to the librarians at the Morgan Library, who guided me through its collection of early children's books, and to Kristin Freda, the director of library services at the Bank Street College of Education, who let me range freely through Bank Street's collection of reading primers, old and new. I am grateful as well to the New York Society Library, with a special shout-out to the friendly children's librarians there; I made great use of their collection and reading room, one of the city's most charming.

Allie Jane Bruce, the children's librarian at Bank Street, gave *Wild Things* an early read, asked tough questions, pointed out errors and omissions, and made the book better.

I have been fortunate to work with and learn from the greatest magazine editors of our time: the incomparable Graydon Carter, a mentor for over thirty years; Kurt Andersen; Aimée Bell, my lodestar at *Vanity Fair*; Walter Isaacson; Jim Kelly; and Susan Morrison, who rescued me from the *Spy* slush pile a hundred years ago.

Bob Cornfield's openhearted but tough-minded love of literature, film, and dance has shaped my own critical sensibility more than I can say.

So many other friends and colleagues have supported and encouraged me throughout the writing of this book, and given me countless smart ideas: Lili Anolik, James Atlas, Claudia Zoe Bedrick, Ginia Bellafante, Peter Biskind, Jim Collins, David Delannet, Frank DiGiacomo, Anna Fels, David Friend, Chris Garrett, George Kalogerakis, David Kamp, Philomen Lancaster, Deborah Landau, Nina Munk, Robert Polito, Susan Reifer, Gloria Schulman, the late and much-missed Ingrid Sischy, Doug Stumpf, and Sylvia Whitman. I doubt I could have finished this book, or gotten through adulthood, without Tom Casciato, Trey Ellis, and Jay Martel. And I certainly couldn't have written a book in part about my own childhood without the love—and forbearance—of my mother, Marlene Handy; my late father, Ralph Handy Jr.; and my siblings Karen, Susan, and Todd Handy.

Once my children got too old for reading aloud, I occasionally brought in ringers for test-driving new picture books: Annabelle and Quinn Handy, Nora Schulman, and Cleo and Julian Martel. Thanks and love to all of you!

Of course, my own beloved children, Zoë and Isaac Handy, are the secret stars of this book. Or not-so-secret. Reading aloud to them so many nights over so many years was such a cherished, almost sacred pleasure, it seems unfair that I ended up getting a book out of it. I hope they don't mind my quoting them throughout. They remain great book lovers and astute readers, and one of the many pleasures of being their father is talking to them about whatever they're reading now, whether contemporary literary fiction or classic works of baseball history. S&S owes them thanks, too, since they gave me more grief about getting this book finished than anyone.

Last, but really first, is Helen Schulman, my brilliant, beautiful wife of twenty-five years and my first and best reader. But for her this book wouldn't have happened. Period. But for her my family and my life—the one I consider worth living—wouldn't have happened, either. I'll go the Beach Boys one better: even God doesn't know what I'd be without her.

Appendix
Read Any Good Picture Books Lately?

Having now written about children's books for the better part of a decade, I'm often asked for recommendations. In some sense, this whole book is my best stab at a response. If you want a less wordy, more functional answer, take a look at the "Partial List of Authors and Works Discussed" in the bibliography: it's not far from what I might come up with if forced to conjure a personal favorites or "best" list. I'm not a fan of every title there—as I've made pretty clear in a couple cases—but all of them have *aux-barricades* devotees. Even the books I've poked fun at are, of course, worth taking a look at and making up your own mind about. Even *Anne of Green Gables*. Otherwise, please forgive me my blind spots and what may strike you as inexplicable enthusiasms.

If you are looking for something more overtly definitive, *Time* magazine published a list in 2015 of what its editors consider the "100 Best Children's Books of All Time." (That meant picture books;

a separate list of the "100 Best Young Adult Books of All Time" mixed
Beverly Cleary, Mildred Taylor, and Roald Dahl with J. D. Salinger,
Anne Frank, and Stephanie Meyer.) The New York Public Library
created its own 100-best compilation in 2013, covering the previous
century, which combined picture books with middle-grade books. You
can easily find each list online, and I wouldn't quibble too much with
either, except for *Time*'s inclusion of *The Red Balloon*, the picture book
version of the 1956 French short film, which traumatized me as a child
and maybe you, too. What happens to the little schoolboy, Pascal,
after the balloons carry him away over the rooftops of Paris? The book
and film don't say, preferring to end with that poetic image—one that
struck me as lonely and scary, having something to do with death. Fifty
years older, I still find *The Red Balloon* creepy, also maudlin, though I
now covet Pascal's chic gray turtleneck and flannel slacks.

Rather than gin up a formal and surely wanting best-of list myself, I thought it would be more fun and more interesting to suggest
book pairings, matching well-known titles with less well-known but
just as wonderful (or nearly so) books by the same authors and/or illustrators. One of the great pleasures in a reading life—and this goes
too for music-listening, movie-watching, museum-going, and on and
on—is getting to know the writers you love, following their careers,
seeing how their interests and talents grow, what themes they come
back to, what evolves from book to book, what doesn't, what you can
enjoy even in their stinkers. There is no reason kids can't share that.
Here are a few examples to get them started (in roughly ascending
order of age appropriateness):

Goodnight Moon (1947), written by Margaret Wise Brown and illustrated by Clement Hurd; and *The Little Island* (1946), written by
Brown and illustrated by Leonard Weisgard.

The latter is as lyrical and suffused with feeling as Brown's most famous book, but widens its focus to the natural world and the effects of seasonal change—from the great green room to the wide blue sea. It's yet another touching example of her "brand-new eyes and brand-new ears." Brown also pulls off the tricky feat of giving her little island an implicit point of view without indulging in hokey anthropomorphism.

The Very Hungry Caterpillar (1969) and *The Nonsense Show* (2015), both written and illustrated by Eric Carle.

The former is Carle's very first book as both author and illustrator; the latter is his latest, as of this writing. *The Nonsense Show* is a hoot, but like its predecessor—and all of Carle's books—it has an underlying structure and rigor, in this case a kind of essay on illogic. Fun with a purpose, to quote *Highlights* magazine (the *People* of pediatricians' waiting rooms).

Where the Wild Things Are (1963) and *Pierre: A Cautionary Tale in Five Chapters and a Prologue* (1962), both written and illustrated by Maurice Sendak.

Like Max in the former book, Pierre is a stubborn, independent-minded young man, much to his parents' consternation, though Pierre's "issue" is an extreme, possibly terminal case of diffidence; he just doesn't care—about anything. Even a lion can't get a rise out of him. Study question for preschoolers: Why do you think so many of Sendak's books involve someone being eaten or threatened with such?

Green Eggs and Ham (1960) and "What Was I Scared Of?" (1953; from *The Sneetches and Other Stories*), both written and illustrated by Dr. Seuss.

Each story turns on false assumptions: that green eggs and ham are gross, or at least not to the taste of the furry fellow being hounded by Sam-I-Am; and that an empty but animate pair of pale green pants are intent on harming the latter story's narrator. The spooky pants, which ride a bicycle and row a boat, might be Seuss's greatest visual invention: despite being pants, and only pants, they exhibit genuine personality. You try making pants look sad.

Ramona the Pest (1968) and *Emily's Runaway Imagination* (1961), both written by Beverly Cleary.

If, as Cleary has suggested, Ramona is something of an alter ego, Emily, whose episodic story is set in a small town in Oregon in the 1920s, feels more literally autobiographical—and perhaps even a dry run for the Ramona books. A portrait of the artist as a young woman?

Here are some further pairings, though not by the same authors and illustrators. Think of these as bedtime double features—some resonant or illuminating, I hope; a few just silly (again, in roughly ascending order of age appropriateness):

The Snowy Day (1962), written and illustrated by Ezra Jack Keats; and *Wave* (2008), written and illustrated by Suzy Lee.

Keats's famous winter's tale finds a perfect complement in Lee's wordless, clever depiction of a girl's day at the beach playing in the waves. Both illustrators make graceful use of horizontal compositions, with much for the eye to explore. (*Wave*, by the way, has been my go-to baby gift for families that I suspect may already have *Goodnight Moon*, *The Very Hungry Caterpillar*, and *The Snowy Day*.)

Duck! Rabbit! (2009), written by Amy Krouse Rosenthal and illustrated by Tom Lichtenheld; and *They All Saw a Cat* (2016), written and illustrated by Brendan Wenzel.

Rosenthal (who died in 2017 at the age of fifty-one) and

Lichtenheld craft something new and very funny from a classic optical illusion (picture-book appropriationists) while Wenzel delights in multiple perspectives on a single tabby cat—a boy's, a dog's, a bird's, and so on. It's an essay in "eye of the beholder." Together, these two make up an intro-level *Doors of Perception*: trippy, but age appropriate.

Dim Sum for Everyone! (2001), written and illustrated by Grace Lin; and *Everyone Poops* (1977; English edition 1993), written and illustrated by Taro Gomi.

A digestive tract double feature! Lin's book is a sweet, simple story about a family's outing to a dim sum parlor, with paintings almost as delicious as the subject matter. I am a fan in particular of Lin's bright, flat colors—paint applied rich and thick and smooth, like good cake frosting (this book will make you hungry too)—which contrast with her subtly patterned backgrounds. For his part, Gomi treats a subject of intense interest among all children and many adults with nonchalant frankness and just the right touch of wit: everyone does poop, but not all poop is the same.

Are You My Mother? (1960), written and illustrated by P. D. Eastman; and *Have You Seen My Cat?* (1973), written and illustrated by Eric Carle.

Quest narratives for the very young. Eastman's just-hatched baby bird searches for its mother—she is not a dog, nor, it turns out, is she a steam shovel. Carle's young hero travels the globe looking for his missing cat—she is not a tiger, nor is she a panther. *Have You Seen My Cat?* has a twist ending that (possible spoiler!) reveals a second thematic link between these two.

Don't Let the Pigeon Drive the Bus! (2003), written and illustrated by Mo Willems; and *Last Stop on Market Street* (2015), written by Matt de la Peña and illustrated by Christian Robinson.

A public transportation twofer, though striking very different notes. Rev the kids up with Willems's funniest book (and I realize that is saying something), then quiet them down with de la Peña and Robinson's wise, gentle story about a woman teaching her grandson to find beauty, pleasure, and meaning in everyday surroundings and not-so-everyday generosity.

The Cat in the Hat (1957), written and illustrated by Dr. Seuss; and *Good Dog, Carl* (1985), written and illustrated by Alexandra Day.

Adventures in high-risk parenting: Seuss's mother leaves two school-age children in the care of a pet fish, while Day's mother asks a Rottweiler to mind her infant. In both cases cross-species babysitting works out okay. Bonus points to any child who asks where the fathers are in all this.

Bread and Jam for Frances (1964), written by Russell Hoban and illustrated by Lillian Hoban; and *Dragons Love Tacos* (2012), written by Adam Rubin and illustrated by Daniel Salmieri.

Picky eaters, if you happen to know any, will appreciate Frances's stubborn loyalty to bread and jam, the only breakfast, lunch, and dinner she will eat. Dragons, it turns out, are more catholic in their tastes, as long as whatever they're consuming can be called a taco. (Just hold the salsa.) Meanwhile, pizza, bagels, plain spaghetti, and chicken fingers await their picture-book champions.

Little House on the Prairie (1935), written by Laura Ingalls Wilder and illustrated by Garth Williams; and *The Birchbark House* (1999), written and illustrated (yes! and quite charmingly!) by Louise Erdrich.

While acknowledging Ingalls Wilder's books as "foundational literature," and telling the *Paris Review* she likes the sausage-making passages, Erdrich has said that *The Birchbark House* and its sequels, based on her own family's history, were written in part to tell "the other side," a refutation of Ingalls Wilder's "appalling view of how the American settlers went into an empty world." That Erdrich's heroine, a young Ojibwa girl named Omakayas, has so much in common with Laura Ingalls—both are strong-willed, curious, brave, observant, not always generous toward their siblings—underscores the older book's treatment of Native Americans as (at best) threatening, exotic others. Kids old enough to enjoy these novels are old enough to learn that "history" often depends on who's writing it.

Beezus and Ramona (1955), by Beverly Cleary; and *The Watsons Go to Birmingham—1963* (1995), by Christopher Paul Curtis.

Two funny and moving stories of sibling conflict, ending on very different notes. "Sensible" nine-year-old Beezus (née Beatrice) struggles with conflicted feelings toward her imaginative, provocative, exasperating little sister, Ramona, who sucks up most of the Quimby family's oxygen. Meanwhile, ten-year-old Kenny Watson suffers under the tyranny of By (né Byron), his thirteen-year-old "thug" brother, who is an expert at goading Kenny with a mean, well-targeted joke—when he's not simply clobbering him. ("I don't know why bullies always have such a good sense of humor, but they do," Kenny muses, one of the truest observations in all of children's literature.) Both novels let kids know that you can love someone and, from time to time—or maybe a lot of the time—hate him or her, too, which is a good lesson for anyone who plans on having adult relationships. But while Cleary's book comes to a gentle resolution at Beezus's tenth birthday party, the trajectory of Curtis's fictional family story is altered by real-life horror: the 16th Street Baptist Church bombing, which killed four young girls and injured nearly two dozen more parishioners. This act of racist terrorism occurred in September 1963, less than three weeks after Martin Luther King's "I Have a Dream" speech. The African American Watson family, visiting Birmingham from the North, aren't directly harmed, but the bombing's emotional reverberations, crosscurrents of pain, anger, fear, even guilt, lead to a new understanding between Kenny and By. The Watsons' hometown is Flint, Michigan, by the way—an inadvertent reminder for contemporary readers, should they need one, that America's struggles with injustice are ongoing.

Two final pieces of consumer advice:

Don't buy children's books written by celebrities (tell-alls for adults are okay), and don't buy books with sparkles on the covers.

Bibliography

A Partial List of Authors and Books Discussed

Aesop, *Fables*

Louisa May Alcott, *Little Women*; sequels

J. M. Barrie, *Peter Pan*

L. Frank Baum, *The Wonderful Wizard of Oz*; sequels

Judy Blume, *Are You There God? It's Me, Margaret*; *Then Again, Maybe I Won't*

Margaret Wise Brown, *The Fish with the Deep Sea Smile*; *The Runaway Bunny*; *Goodnight Moon*; *The Dead Bird*

Jean de Brunhoff, *The Story of Babar*

Eric Carle, *The Very Hungry Caterpillar*

Beverly Cleary, *Henry Huggins*; *Beezus and Ramona*; *Ramona the Pest*; sequels

Rebecca Cobb, *Missing Mommy*

Roald Dahl, *Charlie and the Chocolate Factory*; *Fantastic Mr. Fox*

Louise Erdrich, *The Birchbark House*

Ian Falconer, *Olivia*

Jacob and Wilhelm Grimm, *Children's and Household Tales*

Joel Chandler Harris, *Uncle Remus: His Songs and Sayings*; sequels

Kevin Henkes, *Lily's Purple Plastic Purse*

Russell Hoban, *Bedtime for Frances*; *A Baby Sister for Frances*

Heinrich Hoffmann, *Shock-Headed Peter*

Maira Kalman, *Thomas Jefferson: Life, Liberty, and the Pursuit of Everything*

Ezra Jack Keats, *The Snowy Day*

Munro Leaf, *The Story of Ferdinand*

C. S. Lewis, *The Lion, the Witch and the Wardrobe*; sequels

Sam McBratney, *Guess How Much I Love You*

A. A. Milne, *The House at Pooh Corner*

Lucy Maud Montgomery, *Anne of Green Gables*

Kadir Nelson, *We Are the Ship: The Story of Negro League Baseball*

Charles Perrault, *Tales of Times Past*

Beatrix Potter, *The Tale of Peter Rabbit*; *The Tale of Mr. Jeremy Fisher*;
    The Tale of Jemima Puddle-Duck; *The Tale of Pigling Bland*

Philip Pullman, *The Golden Compass*; sequels

H. A. Rey, *Curious George*

Maurice Sendak, *Where the Wild Things Are*; *In the Night Kitchen*;
    Outside Over There

Dr. Seuss, *And to Think That I Saw It on Mulberry Street*; *The Cat in
    the Hat*; *Green Eggs and Ham*; *The Lorax*

Anna Sewell, *Black Beauty*

Shel Silverstein, *The Giving Tree*

Booth Tarkington, *Penrod*

Mildred D. Taylor, *Roll of Thunder, Hear My Cry*

Mark Twain, *The Adventures of Tom Sawyer*

Unknown, *Reynard the Fox*
Judith Viorst, *The Tenth Good Thing About Barney*
E. B. White, *Stuart Little*; *Charlotte's Web*
Laura Ingalls Wilder, *Little House in the Big Woods*; sequels
Garth Williams, *The Rabbits' Wedding*

Works Consulted

Books

Louisa May Alcott, *The Selected Letters of Louisa May Alcott*, edited by
    Joel Myerson, Daniel Shealy, and Madeleine B. Stern. University
    of Georgia Press, 1987.
Brian Alderson, *Ezra Jack Keats: Artist and Picture Book Maker*. Peli-
    can, 1994.
Brian Alderson and Felix de Marez Oyens, *Be Merry and Wise: Ori-
    gins of Children's Book Publishing in England, 1650–1850*. British
    Library, in association with Pierpont Morgan Library and Biblio-
    graphic Society of America, 2006.
Celia Catlett Anderson and Marilyn Fain Apseloff, *Nonsense Litera-
    ture for Children: Aesop to Seuss*. Library Professional Publications/
    Shoe String Press, 1989.
William Anderson, *Laura Ingalls Wilder: A Biography*. Harper, 1988.
Bruno Bettelheim, *The Uses of Enchantment: The Meaning and Impor-
    tance of Fairy Tales*. Alfred A. Knopf, 1976.
Margaret Blount, *Animal Land: The Creatures of Children's Fiction*.
    William Morrow, 1975.
Walter M. Brasch, *Brer Rabbit, Uncle Remus, and the "Cornfield Journal-
    ist": The Tale of Joel Chandler Harris*. Mercer University Press, 2000.
Eric Carle, *The Art of Eric Carle*. Philomel, 1996.
Beverly Cleary, *A Girl from Yamhill: A Memoir*. William Morrow, 1988.

Beverly Cleary, *My Own Two Feet: A Memoir.* William Morrow, 1995.

Charles D. Cohen, *The Seuss, the Whole Seuss, and Nothing But the Seuss: A Visual Biography of Theodor Seuss Geisel.* Random House, 2004.

Rudolf Flesch, *Why Johnny Can't Read—And What You Can Do About It.* Harper and Row, 1955.

Selma H. Fraiberg, *The Magic Years: Understanding and Handling the Problems of Early Childhood.* Scribner, 1959.

Amy Gary, *In the Great Green Room: The Brilliant and Bold Life of Margaret Wise Brown.* Flatiron, 2017.

Alison Gopnik, *The Gardener and the Carpenter: What the New Science of Child Development Tells Us About the Relationship Between Parents and Children.* Farrar, Straus and Giroux, 2016.

———, *The Philosophical Baby: What Children's Minds Tell Us About Truth, Love, and the Meaning of Life.* Farrar, Straus and Giroux, 2009.

Gerald Gottlieb and J. H. Plumb, *Early Children's Books and Their Illustrations.* Pierpont Morgan Library/Godine, 1975.

Michael Patrick Hearn, Trinkett Clark, and H. Nichols B. Clark, *Myth, Magic, and Mystery: One Hundred Years of American Children's Book Illustration.* Roberts Rinehart in cooperation with Chrysler Museum of Art, 1996.

Pamela Smith Hill, *Laura Ingalls Wilder: A Writer's Life.* South Dakota State Historical Society Press, 2007.

William Holtz, *The Ghost in the Little House: A Life of Rose Wilder Lane.* University of Missouri Press, 1993.

Ursula K. Le Guin, *Cheek by Jowl: Talks and Essays on How and Why Fantasy Matters.* Aqueduct, 2009.

Linda Lear, *Beatrix Potter: A Life in Nature.* St. Martin's, 2007.

Seth Lerer, *Children's Literature: A Reader's History from Aesop to Harry Potter.* University of Chicago Press, 2008.

Claude Lévi-Strauss, *Totemism*, translated by Rodney Needham. Beacon, 1963.

C. S. Lewis, *The Complete C. S. Lewis Signature Classics* (includes *Mere Christianity*, 1952; and *The Screwtape Letters*, 1942). Harper One/HarperCollins, 2002.

————, *Surprised by Joy: The Shape of My Early Life*. Harcourt Brace, 1955.

Rebecca Loncraine, *The Real Wizard of Oz: The Life and Times of L. Frank Baum*. Gotham, 2009.

Kathryn Gin Lum, *Damned Nation: Hell in America from the Revolution to Reconstruction*. Oxford University Press, 2014.

Alison Lurie, *Boys and Girls Forever: Reflections on Children's Classics*. Penguin, 2003.

————, *Don't Tell the Grown-Ups: The Subversive Power of Children's Literature*. Little, Brown, 1990.

Leonard S. Marcus, *Margaret Wise Brown: Awakened by the Moon*. Beacon, 1992.

————, *Minders of Make-Believe: Idealists, Entrepreneurs, and the Shaping of American Children's Literature*. Houghton Mifflin, 2008.

————, *Show Me a Story! Why Picture Books Matter: Conversations with 21 of the World's Most Celebrated Illustrators*. Candlewick, 2012.

John E. Miller, *Becoming Laura Ingalls Wilder: The Woman Behind the Legend*. University of Missouri Press, 1998.

Richard M. Minear, *Dr. Seuss Goes to War: The World War II Editorial Cartoons of Theodor Seuss Geisel*. New Press, 1999.

Judith Morgan and Neil Morgan, *Dr. Seuss and Mr. Geisel: A Biography*. Random House, 1995.

Ursula Nordstrom, *Dear Genius: The Letters of Ursula Nordstrom*, edited by Leonard S. Marcus. HarperCollins, 1998.

Donald E. Pease, *Theodor Seuss Geisel*. Oxford University Press, 2010.

Samuel F. Pickering Jr., *John Locke and Children's Books in 18th-Century England*. University of Tennessee Press, 1981.

Beatrix Potter, *The Journal of Beatrix Potter: 1881 to 1897* (revised edition), edited by Leslie Linder. Frederick Warne, 1989.

Allison Prince, *Kenneth Grahame: An Innocent in the Wild Wood*. Allison and Busby, 1994.

Harriet Reisen, *Louisa May Alcott: The Woman Behind* Little Women. John Macrae/Henry M. Holt, 2009.

Katharine M. Rogers, *L. Frank Baum: Creator of Oz*. St. Martin's, 2002.

George Sayer, *Jack: A Life of C. S. Lewis*. Harper and Row, 1988.

Peter J. Schakel, *The Way into Narnia: A Reader's Guide*. William B. Eerdmans, 2005.

Maurice Sendak, *Caldecott and Co.: Notes on Books and Pictures*. Michael di Capua/Farrar, Straus and Giroux, 1988.

Dr. Seuss, *The Secret Art of Dr. Seuss*. Random House, 1995.

———, *The Tough Coughs as He Ploughs the Dough: Early Writings and Cartoons by Dr. Seuss*, edited by Richard Marschall. William Morrow, 1987.

Michael Sims, *The Story of Charlotte's Web: E. B. White's Eccentric Life in Nature and the Birth of an American Classic*. Walker, 2011.

Maria Tatar, *The Annotated Brothers Grimm: The Bicentennial Edition*. W. W. Norton, 2012.

———, *Off with Their Heads! Fairy Tales and the Culture of Childhood*. Princeton University Press, 1992.

J. R. R. Tolkien, *The Monsters and the Critics and Other Essays*. HarperCollins, 2007.

Alice Walker, *Living by the Word: Essays*. Harcourt Brace, 1988.

Elizabeth K. Wallace and James D. Wallace, *Garth Williams, American Illustrator: A Life*. Beaufort, 2016.

Marina Warner, *Once upon a Time: A Short History of Fairy Tale*. Oxford University Press, 2014.

E. B. White, *Essays of E. B. White*. Harper and Row, 1977.

————, *Letters of E. B. White* (revised edition), edited by Dorothy Lobrano Guth and Martha White. Harper, 2006.

————, *One Man's Meat*. Harper and Row, 1944.

————, *Writings from* The New Yorker, *1927–1976*. HarperCollins, 1990.

A. N. Wilson, *C. S. Lewis: A Biography*. W. W. Norton, 1990.

Jack Zipes, *Fairy Tales and the Art of Subversion*. Routledge, 1983.

————, *The Irresistible Fairy Tale: The Cultural and Social History of a Genre*. Princeton University Press, 2012.

Anthologies

The Horn Book's Laura Ingalls Wilder, edited by William Anderson. Horn Book, 2000.

Little Women and the Feminist Imagination: Criticism, Controversy, Personal Essays, edited by Janice M. Alberghene and Beverly Lyon Clark. Routledge, 1999.

Maurice Sendak: A Celebration of the Artist and His Work, curated by Justin G. Schiller and Dennis M. V. David, edited by Leonard S. Marcus. Harry N. Abrams, 2013.

Only Connect: Readings on Children's Literature (second edition), edited by Sheila Egoff, G. T. Stubbs, and L. F. Ashley. Oxford University Press, 1980.

Only Connect: Readings on Children's Literature (third edition), edited by Sheila Egoff, Gordon Stubbs, Ralph Ashley, and Wendy Sutton. Oxford University Press, 1996.

Selected Newspaper, Magazine, and Journal Articles; Talks;
Introductions; and Papers

Joan Acocella, "Once upon a Time: The Lure of the Fairy Tale." *The New Yorker*, July 23, 2012.

D. L. Ashliman, Introduction to *Aesop's Fables*. Barnes and Noble Classics, 2003.

Bruno Bettelheim, "The Care and Feeding of Monsters" ("Dialogue with Mothers" column). *Ladies' Home Journal*, March 1969.

Elizabeth Bird, "Surprise! It's Racist! Unwanted Children's Books Surprises." *School Library Journal*, September 25, 2014.

Bruce Bliven Jr., "Child's Best Seller" (Margaret Wise Brown profile). *Life*, December 2, 1946.

Saul Braun, "Sendak Raises the Shade on Childhood." *The New York Times*, June 7, 1970.

Emma Brockes, "Maurice Sendak" (interview). *Believer*, November/December 2012.

Francelia Butler, "Death in Children's Literature." Address given at English Institute, Columbia University, September 9, 1971.

A. S. Byatt, Introduction to *The Annotated Brothers Grimm*. W.W. Norton, 2004.

Robert Cahn, "The Wonderful World of Dr. Seuss." *Saturday Evening Post*, July 6, 1957.

Robert Cochran, "Black Father: The Subversive Achievement of Joel Chandler Harris." *African American Review*, March 22, 2004.

Louis Rauch Gibson and Laura M. Zaidman, "Death in Children's Literature: Taboo or Not Taboo?" *Children's Literature Association Quarterly*, Winter 1991.

Adam Gopnik, "Magic in a Web" (review of *Some Writer!*, a graphic biography of E. B. White). *The New York Times Book Review*, November 13, 2016.

————, "Maurice Sendak: Every Shadow Mattered." *The New Yorker* (website), May 8, 2012.

Stephen Greenblatt, Introduction to *Reynard the Fox: A New Translation*, by James Simpson. Liveright, 2015.

Lisa Halliday, "Louise Erdrich, The Art of Fiction No. 208" (interview). *The Paris Review*, Winter 2010.

Michael Haines, "Fertility and Mortality in the United States." EH.net Encyclopedia, Economic History Association, undated, circa 2005.

Dawn Heerspink, "'No Man's Land': Fairy Tales, Gender, Socialization, Satire, and Trauma During the First and Second World Wars." *Grand Valley Journal of History*, February 2012.

Nat Hentoff, "Among the Wild Things" (profile of Maurice Sendak). *The New Yorker*, January 22, 1966.

John Hersey, "Why Do Students Bog Down on the First R?" *Life*, May 24, 1954.

C. M. Hewins, "The History of Children's Books." *The Atlantic*, January 1888.

Kenneth Hill, "The Decline of Childhood Mortality." Paper, Department of Population Dynamics, School of Hygiene and Public Health, John Hopkins University, 1990.

Clement Hurd, "Remembering Margaret Wise Brown." *Horn Book*, October 1983.

E. J. Kahn Jr., "Children's Friend" (profile of Theodor Seuss Geisel). *The New Yorker*, December 17, 1960.

Frances W. Kaye, "Little Squatter on the Osage Diminished Reserve: Reading Laura Ingalls Wilder's Kansas Indians." *Great Plains Quarterly*, Spring 2000.

John Lahr, "The Playful Art of Maurice Sendak." *The New York Times Magazine*, October 12, 1980.

Dennis McAuliffe Jr., "Little House on the Osage Prairie." From *A Broken Flute: The Native Experience in Books for Children*, edited by Doris Seale and Beverly Slapin. AltaMira Press, 2005.

Louis Menand, "Cat People: What Dr. Seuss Really Taught Us." *The New Yorker*, December 23, 2002.

Wayne Mixon, "The Ultimate Irrelevance of Race: Joel Chandler Harris and Uncle Remus in Their Time." *Journal of Southern History*, August 1990.

Philip Nel, "Was the Cat in the Hat Black?: Exploring Dr. Seuss's Racial Imagination." *Children's Literature*, 2014 (annual publication).

Pamela Paul, "The Ageless Appeal of Beverly Cleary." *The New York Times Book Review*, April 8, 2011.

Martha Pichey, "Bunny Dearest" (Margaret Wise Brown appreciation). *Vanity Fair*, December 2000.

Joshua Harris Prager, "'Goodnight Moon' Couldn't Protect Its Heir from Life's Nightmares." *The Wall Street Journal*, September 8, 2000.

David Sadler, "'Grandpa Died Last Night': Children's Books About the Death of Grandparents." *Children's Literature Association Quarterly*, Winter 1991.

Carolyn See, "Dr. Seuss and the Naked Ladies." *Esquire*, June 1974.

Dr. Seuss, " . . . But for Grown-Ups Laughing Isn't Any Fun." *The New York Times Book Review*, November 16, 1952.

———, "How Orlo Got His Book." *The New York Times Book Review*, November 17, 1957.

John Updike, "Oz Is Us." *The New Yorker*, September 25, 2000.

Gore Vidal, "On Rereading the Oz Books." *The New York Review of Books*, October 13, 1977.

Eugen Weber, "Fairies and Hard Facts: The Reality of Folktales." *Journal of the History of Ideas*, January–March 1981.

Index

About the Author

BRUCE HANDY is a contributing editor at *Vanity Fair*, and a former writer and editor at *Time* and *Spy* magazines. His articles, essays, and criticism have appeared in *The New York Times Magazine*, *The New York Times Book Review*, *Vogue*, and *The New Yorker*. A native of Northern California, Handy lives in Manhattan with his wife, novelist Helen Schulman, and their two children.